Connecting Networks v6
Labs & Study Guide

Allan Johnson

Cisco Press

800 East 96th Street

Indianapolis, Indiana 46240 USA

Connecting Networks v6 Labs & Study Guide

Allan Johnson

Copyright© 2018 Cisco Systems, Inc.

Cisco Press logo is a trademark of Cisco Systems, Inc.

Published by:
Cisco Press
800 East 96th Street
Indianapolis, IN 46240 USA

Printed in the United States of America

1   17

Library of Congress Control Number: 2017945208

ISBN-13: 978-158713-429-6
ISBN-10: 1-58713-429-2

Editor-in-Chief
Mark Taub

Product Line Manager
Brett Bartow

Business Operation Manager, Cisco Press
Ronald Fligge

Executive Editor
Mary Beth Ray

Production Manager
Sandra Schroeder

Development Editor
Christopher Cleveland

Project Editor
Mandie Frank

Copy Editor
Geneil Breeze

Technical Editor
Patrick Gargano

Editorial Assistant
Vanessa Evans

Designer
Chuti Prasertsith

Composition
Tricia Bronkella

Proofreader
Debbie Williams

CISCO.

Trademark Acknowledgments

All terms mentioned in this book that are known to be trademarks or service marks have been appropriately capitalized. Cisco Press or Cisco Systems, Inc., cannot attest to the accuracy of this information. Use of a term in this book should not be regarded as affecting the validity of any trademark or service mark.

Warning and Disclaimer

This book is designed to provide information about networking. Every effort has been made to make this book as complete and as accurate as possible, but no warranty or fitness is implied.

The information is provided on an "as is" basis. The authors, Cisco Press, and Cisco Systems, Inc., shall have neither liability nor responsibility to any person or entity with respect to any loss or damages arising from the information contained in this book or from the use of the discs or programs that may accompany it.

The opinions expressed in this book belong to the author and are not necessarily those of Cisco Systems, Inc.

Special Sales

For information about buying this title in bulk quantities, or for special sales opportunities (which may include electronic versions; custom cover designs; and content particular to your business, training goals, marketing focus, or branding interests), please contact our corporate sales department at corpsales@pearsoned.com or (800) 382-3419.

For government sales inquiries, please contact governmentsales@pearsoned.com.

For questions about sales outside the U.S., please contact intlcs@pearson.com.

Feedback Information

At Cisco Press, our goal is to create in-depth technical books of the highest quality and value. Each book is crafted with care and precision, undergoing rigorous development that involves the unique expertise of members from the professional technical community.

Readers' feedback is a natural continuation of this process. If you have any comments regarding how we could improve the quality of this book, or otherwise alter it to better suit your needs, you can contact us through email at feedback@ciscopress.com. Please make sure to include the book title and ISBN in your message.

We greatly appreciate your assistance.

Americas Headquarters
Cisco Systems, Inc.
San Jose, CA

Asia Pacific Headquarters
Cisco Systems (USA) Pte. Ltd.
Singapore

Europe Headquarters
Cisco Systems International BV Amsterdam,
The Netherlands

Cisco has more than 200 offices worldwide. Addresses, phone numbers, and fax numbers are listed on the Cisco Website at **www.cisco.com/go/offices**.

Cisco and the Cisco logo are trademarks or registered trademarks of Cisco and/or its affiliates in the U.S. and other countries. To view a list of Cisco trademarks, go to this URL: www.cisco.com/go/trademarks. Third party trademarks mentioned are the property of their respective owners. The use of the word partner does not imply a partnership relationship between Cisco and any other company. (1110R)

About the Author

Allan Johnson entered the academic world in 1999 after 10 years as a business owner/operator to dedicate his efforts to his passion for teaching. He holds both an MBA and an M.Ed in occupational training and development. He taught a variety of technology courses to high school students and is an adjunct instructor at Del Mar College in Corpus Christi, Texas. Since 2006, Allan has worked full time for Cisco Networking Academy in several roles. He is currently engaged as Curriculum Lead.

About the Technical Reviewer

Patrick Gargano has been an educator since 1996 and a Cisco Networking Academy Instructor since 2000. He currently heads the Networking Academy program at Collège La Citè in Ottawa, Canada, where he teaches CCNA/CCNP-level courses. Patrick has twice led the Cisco Networking Academy Student Dream Team deploying the wired and wireless networks supporting the U.S. Cisco Live conferences. He coauthored *CCNP Routing and Switching Portable Command Guide* and authored the *31 Days Before Your CCNA Security Exam*. His certifications include CCNA (R&S), CCNA Wireless, CCNA Security, and CCNP (R&S). He holds Bachelor of Education and Bachelor of Arts degrees from the University of Ottawa. Find him on Twitter @PatrickGargano.

Dedication

For my wife, Becky. What a year! I couldn't ask for a better partner in life.

Acknowledgments

The Cisco Network Academy authors for the online curriculum and series of Companion Guides take the reader deeper, past the CCENT and CCNA exam topics, with the ultimate goal of not only preparing the student for certification, but also for more advanced college-level technology courses and degrees as well. Thank you to the entire Curriculum and Assessment Engineering team.

Patrick Gargano, technical editor, did the arduous review work necessary to make sure that you get a book that is both technically accurate and unambiguous. I am grateful for his conscientious attention to detail.

Mary Beth Ray, executive editor, you amaze me with your ability to juggle multiple projects at once, steering each from beginning to end. I can always count on you to make the tough decisions.

Development Editor Chris Cleveland's dedication to perfection pays dividends in countless, unseen ways. Thank you again, Chris, for providing me with much-needed guidance and support. This book could not be a reality without your persistence.

Contents at a Glance

Contents

Icons Used in This Book

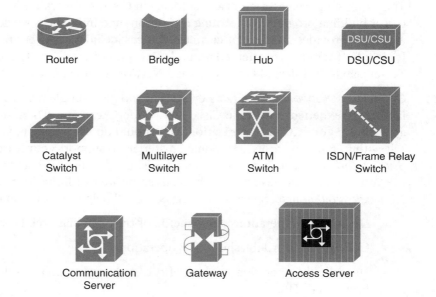

Router   Bridge   Hub   DSU/CSU

Catalyst Switch   Multilayer Switch   ATM Switch   ISDN/Frame Relay Switch

Communication Server   Gateway   Access Server

Command Syntax Conventions

The conventions used to present command syntax in this book are the same conventions used in the IOS Command Reference. The Command Reference describes these conventions as follows:

- **Boldface** indicates commands and keywords that are entered literally as shown. In actual configuration examples and output (not general command syntax), boldface indicates commands that are manually input by the user (such as a **show** command).

- *Italics* indicate arguments for which you supply actual values.

- Vertical bars (|) separate alternative, mutually exclusive elements.

- Square brackets [ ] indicate optional elements.

- Braces { } indicate a required choice.

- Braces within brackets [{ }] indicate a required choice within an optional element.

Introduction

This book supports instructors and students in Cisco Networking Academy, an IT skills and career building program for learning institutions and individuals worldwide. Cisco Networking Academy provides a variety of curricula choices including the very popular CCNA curriculum. It includes four courses oriented around the topics of the Cisco Certified Entry Networking Technician (CCENT) and Cisco Certified Network Associate (CCNA) certifications.

Connecting Networks v6.0, Labs & Study Guide is a supplement to your classroom and laboratory experience with the Cisco Networking Academy. To be successful on the exam and achieve your CCNA certification, you should do everything in your power to arm yourself with a variety of tools and training materials to support your learning efforts. This *Labs & Study Guide* is just such a collection of tools. Used to its fullest extent, it will help you gain the knowledge as well as practice the skills associated with the content area of the *Connecting Networks v6.0* course. Specifically, this book will help you work on these main areas:

- Describe the operations and benefits of the Spanning Tree Protocol (STP).

- Configure and troubleshoot STP operations.

- Describe the operations and benefits of link aggregation and the Cisco VLAN Trunk Protocol (VTP).

- Configure and troubleshoot VTP, STP, DTP, and RSTP.

- Configure and troubleshoot inter-VLAN routing.

- Configure and troubleshoot EtherChannel and HSRP.

- Configure and troubleshoot basic operations of routers in a complex routed network for IPv4 and IPv6.

- Configure and troubleshoot advanced operations of routers and implement OSPF and EIGRP routing protocols for IPv4 and IPv6.

Similar titles are also available for the other three courses: *Introduction to Networks v6 Labs & Study Guide, Routing and Switching Essentials v6 Labs & Study Guide,* and *Scaling Networks v6 Labs & Study Guide.*

Goals and Methods

The most important goal of this book is to help you pass the 200-105 Interconnecting Cisco Networking Devices Part 2 (ICND2) exam, which is the second exam for the Cisco Certified Network Associate (CCNA) certification. Passing the ICND2 exam means that you have the knowledge and skills required to manage a small enterprise network. You can view the detailed ICND2 exam topics any time at http://learningnetwork.cisco.com. They are divided into five broad categories:

- LAN Switching Technologies

- Routing Technologies

- WAN Technologies

- Infrastructure Services

- Infrastructure Maintenance

Each chapter of this book is divided into a Study Guide section followed by a Lab section.

The Study Guide section offers exercises that help you learn the concepts, configurations, and troubleshooting skills crucial to your success as a CCNA exam candidate. Each chapter is slightly different and includes some or all of the following types of exercises:

- Vocabulary Matching Exercises
- Concept Questions Exercises
- Skill-Building Activities and Scenarios
- Configuration Scenarios
- Packet Tracer Exercises
- Troubleshooting Scenarios

The Labs and Activities section includes all the online course labs and Packet Tracer activity instructions. If applicable, this section begins with a Command Reference that you will complete to highlight all the commands introduced in the chapter.

Packet Tracer and Companion Website

This book includes the instructions for all the Packet Tracer activities in the online course. You need to be enrolled in the *Connecting Networks v6.0* course to access the Packet Tracer files.

However, there are three Packet Tracer activities created exclusively for this book. You can access these unique Packet Tracer files at this book's companion website.

To get your copy of Packet Tracer software and the three unique files for this book, please go to the companion website for instructions. To access this companion website, follow these steps:

1. Go to www.ciscopress.com/register and log in or create a new account.
2. Enter the ISBN: 9781587134296.
3. Answer the challenge question as proof of purchase.
4. Click on the Access Bonus Content link in the Registered Products section of your account page to be taken to the page where your downloadable content is available.

Audience for This Book

This book's main audience is anyone taking the Connecting Networks course of the Cisco Networking Academy curriculum. Many academies use this *Labs & Study Guide* as a required tool in the course, whereas other academies recommend the *Labs & Study Guide* as an additional resource to prepare for class exams and the CCNA certification.

The secondary audiences for this book include people taking CCNA-related classes from professional training organizations. This book can also be used for college- and university-level networking courses, as well as anyone wanting to gain a detailed understanding of routing. However, the reader should know that the content of this book tightly aligns with the Cisco

Networking Academy course. It may not be possible to complete some of the Study Guide sections and Labs without access to the online course. Fortunately, you can purchase the *Connecting Networks v6 Companion Guide* (ISBN: **9781587134326**).

How This Book Is Organized

Because the content of the *Connecting Networks v6 Companion Guide* and the online curriculum is sequential, you should work through this *Labs & Study Guide* in order beginning with Chapter 1.

The book covers the major topic headings in the same sequence as the online curriculum. This book has eight chapters, with the same names as the online course chapters.

- **Chapter 1, "WAN Concepts":** This chapter reviews WAN technologies and the many WAN services available.

- **Chapter 2, "Point-to-Point Connections":** This chapter reviews the terms, technology, and protocols used in serial connections.

- **Chapter 3, "Branch Connections":** This chapter reviews DLS, cable, wireless, VPN, and the factors to consider when implementing broadband solutions. In addition, the Generic Routing Protocol (GRE) and Border Gateway Protocol (BGP) are reviewed.

- **Chapter 4, "Access Control Lists":** This chapter reviews how to use standard and extended IPv4 ACLs and IPv6 ACLs on a Cisco router as part of a security solution.

- **Chapter 5, "Network Security and Monitoring":** This chapter focuses on LAN security, Simple Network Management Protocol (SNMP), and Cisco Switch Port Analyzer (SPAN).

- **Chapter 6, "Quality of Service":** This chapter reviews QoS concepts, models, and implementation techniques.

- **Chapter 7, "Network Evolution":** This chapter reviews emerging trends in today's networks.

- **Chapter 8, "Network Troubleshooting":** This chapter reviews network documentation, general troubleshooting methods, and tools.

CHAPTER 1

WAN Concepts

Wide-area networks (WANs) are used to connect remote LANs together. Various technologies are used to achieve this connection. This chapter reviews WAN technologies and the many WAN services available.

WAN Technologies Overview

WAN access options differ in technology, speed, and price. Each has advantages and disadvantages. Selecting the best technology depends largely on the network design.

Network Types and Their Evolving WAN Needs

The WAN needs of a network depend greatly on the size of the network. These network types run the spectrum from small offices that really need only a broadband connection to the Internet, all the way up to multinational enterprises that need a variety of WAN options to satisfy local, regional, and global restrictions.

In Table 1-1, indicate the network type that fits each of the descriptions. Some descriptions may apply to more than one network type.

Table 1-1   Identify the Network Type

Network Description	Small Office Network	Campus Network	Branch Network	Distributed Network
Outsourced IT support				
Very large-sized business				
Connectivity to the Internet				
Converged network and application services				
Hundreds of employees				
Home, branch, and regional offices, teleworkers, and a central office				
Limited number of employees				
In-house IT staff and network support				
Thousands of employees				
Several remote, branch, and regional offices (one central office)				
Small-sized business				
LAN focus of operations with broadband				
Small to medium-sized business				
Multiple campus LANs				
Medium-sized business				

WAN Operations and Terminology

WANs operate at which layers of the OSI model?

Which organizations are responsible for WAN standards?

_____

_____

_____

What are some of the Layer 2 WAN technologies?

_____

Why is the Layer 2 address field not usually used in WAN services?

_____

Match the definition on the left with a term on the right. This exercise is a one-to-one matching.

Definitions

a. The boundary between customer equipment and service provider equipment

b. Devices inside the enterprise edge wiring closet that are owned or leased by the organization

c. Provider equipment that resides in the WAN backbone capable of supporting routing protocols

d. Digital modem used by DSL or cable Internet service providers

e. Dynamically establishes a dedicated circuit before communication starts

f. Provides an interface to connect subscribers to a WAN link

g. Splits traffic so that it can be routed over the shared network

h. Local service provider facility that connects the CPE to the provider network

i. Physical connection between the CPE and the CO

j. Required by digital leased lines to provide termination of the digital signal and convert into frames ready for transmission on the LAN

k. Consists of the all-digital, long-haul communications lines, switches, routers, and other equipment in the provider network

l. Customer device that provides internetworking and WAN access interface ports

m. Customer device that transmits data over the WAN link

n. Multiport device that sits at the service provider edge to switch traffic

o. Legacy technology device that converts digital signals into analog signals transmitted over telephone lines

p. Legacy technology device that can support hundreds of dial-in and dial-out users

Terms

____ Packet-switched network

____ WAN switch

____ Customer premises equipment (CPE)

____ Central office (CO)

____ Dialup modem

____ Access server

____ Data communications equipment (DCE)

____ Router

____ Data terminal equipment (DTE)

____ Local loop

____ CSU/DSU

____ Circuit-switched network

____ Demarcation point

____ Broadband modem

____ Toll network

____ Core multilayer switch

Selecting a WAN Technology

The WAN access connections your small to medium-sized business purchases could use a public or private WAN infrastructure—or a mix of both. Each type provides various WAN technologies. Understanding which WAN access connections and technologies are best suited to your situation is an important part of network design.

Varieties of WAN Link Connections

Your ISP can recommend several WAN link connection options based on your specific requirements. These options can be classified in various categories. Use the list of WAN access options to label Figure 1-1.

Figure 1-1   WAN Access Options Labels

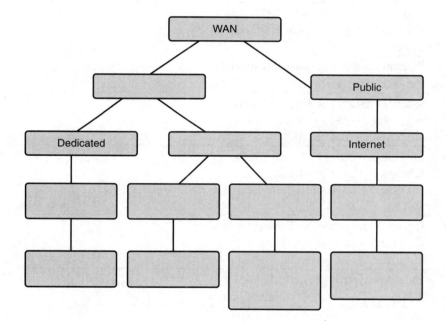

T1/E1/T3/E3	ATM	Switched
Frame Relay	Circuit switched	Packet switched
Metro Ethernet	Cable	Wireless
MPLS	PSTN	DSL
VPN	Private	Broadband
ISDN	Leased lines	

Private and Public WAN Access Options

As shown in Figure 1-1, WAN access options can first be classified as either private or public. Table 1-2 lists descriptions for various private WAN access options. Indicate which one is described. Some options are described more than once.

Table 1-2 Private WAN Access Options

Private WAN Access Options	Leased Lines	MPLS	Metro Ethernet	ATM	ISDN	VSAT	Dialup	Frame Relay
Considered the most expensive of all WAN access technologies.								
Analog telephone lines are used to provide a switched WAN connection.								
A permanent, dedicated WAN connection that uses a T- or E-carrier system.								
Satellite to router communications for WAN connections.								
Delivers data using fixed 53-byte packet cells over permanent and switched virtual circuits.								
Service providers and short-path labeling are used for leased lines, Ethernet WANs, and Frame Relay WANs.								
Connects multiple sites using virtual circuits and data link connection identifiers.								
Includes MetroE, EoMPLS, and VPLS as WAN connection options.								
Converts analog to digital signals to provide a switched WAN connection over telephone lines.								
A popular replacement for traditional Frame Relay and ATM WAN access technologies.								

Match the definition on the left with a public WAN access option on the right. This exercise is a one-to-one matching.

Definitions

a. Radio and directional-antenna modem WAN access option provided to public organizations

b. WAN access option that uses telephone lines to transport data via multiplexed links

c. High-speed long-distance wireless connections through nearby special service provider towers

d. Cellular radio waves WAN access option used with smartphones and tablets

e. Dish and modem-based WAN access option for rural users where cable and DSL are not available

f. Secure Internet-based WAN access option used by teleworkers and extranet users

g. Entire networks connected together by using VPN routers, firewalls, and security appliances

h. A shared WAN access option that transports data using television-signal networks

Public WAN Access Options

___ 3G/4G Cellular

___ VPN Remote

___ WiMax

___ Satellite Internet

___ DSL

___ Cable

___ Municipal WiFi

___ VPN site-to-site

Labs and Activities

There are no Labs or Packet Tracer Activities in this chapter.

1.0.1.2 Class Activity–Branching Out

Objective

Describe WAN access technologies available to small-to-medium-sized business networks.

Scenario

Your medium-sized company is opening a new branch office to serve a wider, client-based network. This branch will focus on regular, day-to-day network operations, but will also provide TelePresence, web conferencing, IP telephony, video on demand, and wireless services.

Although you know that an ISP can provide WAN routers and switches to accommodate the branch office connectivity for the network, you prefer to use your own customer premises equipment (CPE). To ensure interoperability, Cisco devices have been used in all other branch-office WANs.

As the branch-office network administrator, it is your responsibility to research possible network devices for purchase and use over the WAN.

Resources

- World Wide Web
- Word processing software

Step 1. Visit the Cisco Branch-WAN Business Calculator site. Accept the agreement to use the calculator.

Step 2. Select the IT Infrastructure Requirements Tab.

Step 3. Input information to help the calculator determine a preferred router or ISR option for your branch and WAN (both).

Note: There is a slider tool within the calculator window that allows the choice of more service options for your branch office and WAN.

Step 4. The calculator will suggest a possible router or ISR device solution for your branch office and WAN. Use the tabs at the top of the calculator window to view the output.

Step 5. Create a matrix with three column headings and list some information provided by the output in each category:

- Return on investment (ROI)
- Total cost of ownership (TCO)
- Energy savings

Step 6.   Discuss your research with a classmate, group, class, or your instructor. Include in your discussion:

- Specifics on the requirements of your network as used for calculator input
- Output information from your matrix
- Additional factors you would consider before purchasing a router or ISR for your new branch office

1.2.4.3 Lab–Researching WAN Technologies

Objectives

Part 1: Investigate Dedicated WAN Technologies and Providers

Part 2: Investigate a Dedicated Leased Line Service Provider in Your Area

Background/Scenario

Today's broadband Internet services are fast and affordable. With the use of VPN technology, the connection can also be secure. However, many companies still need a 24-hour dedicated connection to the Internet, or a dedicated point-to-point connection from one office location to another. In this lab, you will investigate the cost and availability of purchasing a dedicated T1 Internet connection for your home or business.

Required Resources

A device with Internet access.

Part 1: Investigate Dedicated WAN Technologies and Providers

In Step 1, you will research basic characteristics of dedicated WAN technologies, and in Step 2, you will discover providers that offer dedicated WAN services.

Step 1. Research WAN technology characteristics.

Use search engines and websites to research the following WAN technologies. Put your findings in the table below.

WAN Technology	Dedicated Connection (yes/no)	Last Mile Media			Speed/Range
		Copper (yes/no)	Fiber (yes/no)	Wireless (yes/no)	
T1/DS1					
T3/DS3					
OC3 (SONET)					
Frame Relay					
ATM					
MPLS					
EPL (Ethernet Private Line)					

Step 2. Discover dedicated WAN technology service providers.

Navigate to http://www.telarus.com/carriers.html. This web page lists the Internet service providers (also known as carriers) that partner with Telarus to provide automated real-time telecom pricing. Click the links to the various carrier partners and search for the dedicated WAN technologies that they provide. Complete the table below by identifying each service provider's dedicated WAN services, based on the information provided on the website. Use the extra lines provided in the table to record additional service providers.

Internet Service Provider	T1/DS1/PRI	T3/DS3	OC3 (SONET)	Frame Relay	ATM	MPLS	EPL Ethernet Private Line
Comcast							x
CenturyLink	x	x				x	
AT&T							
Earthlink							
Level 3 Communications							
XO Communications							
Verizon							

Part 2: Investigate a Dedicated Leased Line Service Provider in Your Area

In Part 2, you will research a local service provider that will provide a T1 dedicated leased line to the geographical area specified. This application requires a name, address, and phone number before the search can be performed. You may wish to use your current information or research an address locally where a business might be looking for a WAN connection.

Step 1.   Navigate to http://www.telarus.com/geoquote.html to try GeoQuote.

GeoQuote is a web application that automates the search for WAN technology service providers, and provides price quotes in real-time. Complete the required fields.

  a. Click the **Service Type** drop-down list and select **Data (High Speed Internet)**.

  b. Type your **First Name** and **Last Name**, your sample **Company**, and your **Email** address.

  c. Type the **Phone Number** to connect to the WAN. This number should be a landline number.

  d. Click the button marked **Step 2**.

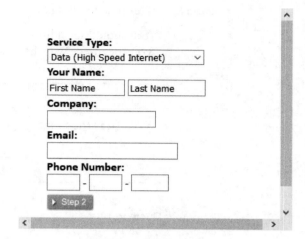

TEST DRIVE GEOQUOTE!

Not a Telarus Partner and looking to try out our patented GeoQuote Real-Time Pricing Tool?

Fill out the requested information in this form and proceed to specifying your service type you are looking to get pricing for. Then let the tool serve you up a quote that has plan combinations for bandwidth , install cost, monthly cost, and more!

See GeoQuote FAQ

Step 2.   Provide Information.

   a.   Choose **Internet T1 (1.5 MB)** in the GeoQuote Step 2 window (below).

   b.   In the GeoQuote Step 3 window, in the **Installation BTN** field, enter your sample business telephone number.

   c.   Enter your address, city, state, and zip code in the GeoQuote Step 3 window.

   d.   In the GeoQuote Step 4 window, click **I am just window shopping**.

   e.   Click **Continue** in the GeoQuote Step 4 window to display the results.

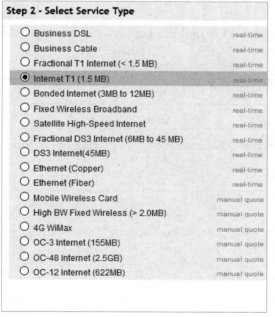

Step 3.   Examine the results.

You should see a list of quotes showing the available pricing of a T1 connection to the location you specified. Was the pricing in the area you chose comparable to those pictured below?

_____

_____

What was the range of prices from your results?

_____

_____

Your Quote Results

	Plan	Service Type	Bandwidth	Install	Rebate	Term	Router	Loop	Monthly Cost ↓	Order
🔎	1	Internet T1 (1.5 MB)	1.5M x 1.5M	$0.00	$0.00	3 Year	Yes	$161.00	**$318.00**	Order Now
🔎	2	Internet T1 (1.5 MB)	1.5M x 1.5M	$0.00	$0.00	2 Year	Yes	$161.00	**$340.00**	Order Now
🔎	3	Internet T1 (1.5 MB)	1.5M x 1.5M	$0.00	$0.00	3 Year	Yes	included	**$352.90**	Order Now
🔎	4	Internet T1 (1.5 MB)	1.5M x 1.5M	$0.00	$0.00	2 Year	Yes	included	**$372.12**	Order Now
🔎	5	Internet T1 (1.5 MB)	1.5M x 1.5M	$0.00	$0.00	1 Year	Yes	$231.00	**$433.00**	Order Now
🔎	6	Internet T1 (1.5 MB)	1.5M x 1.5M	$0.00	$0.00	3 Year	No	$310.81	**$455.81**	Order Now
🔎	7	Internet T1 (1.5 MB)	1.5M x 1.5M	$444.07	$0.00	1 Year	No	$318.83	**$463.83**	Order Now
🔎	8	Internet T1 (1.5 MB)	1.5M x 1.5M	$0.00	$0.00	2 Year	No	$327.66	**$472.66**	Order Now
🔎	9	Internet T1 (1.5 MB)	1.5M x 1.5M	$0.00	$0.00	3 Year	Yes	$310.81	**$490.81**	Order Now

Reflection

1. What are the disadvantages to using a T1 leased line for personal home use? What would be a better solution?

_____

_____

2. When might the use of a dedicated WAN connection, of any type, be a good connectivity solution for a business?

_____

_____

3. Describe other WAN technologies that provide high-speed, low-cost options that could be an alternative solution to a T1 connection.

_____

_____

1.3.1.1 Class Activity–WAN Device Modules

Objective

Select WAN access technologies to satisfy business requirements in a small-to-medium-sized business network.

Scenario

Your medium-sized company is upgrading its network. To make the most of the equipment currently in use, you decide to purchase WAN modules instead of new equipment.

All branch offices use either Cisco 1900 or 2911 series ISRs. You will be updating these routers in several locations. Each branch has its own ISP requirements to consider.

To update the devices, focus on the following WAN modules access types:

- Ethernet
- Broadband
- T1/E1 and ISDN PRI
- BRI
- Serial
- T1 and E1 Trunk Voice and WAN
- Wireless LANs and WANs

Resources

- World Wide Web
- Word processing software

Directions

Step 1.   Visit Interfaces and Modules http://www.cisco.com/c/en/us/products/interfaces-modules/index.html. On this page, you will see many ISR interface modules options—remember that you currently own and use only the Cisco 1900 and 2900 series routers.

Note: If the above link is no longer valid, search the Cisco site for "Interfaces and Modules."

Step 2.   Create a comparison matrix listing the following WAN access types for your branch networks:

- Ethernet
- Broadband
- T1/E1 and ISDN PRI
- BRI
- Serial WAN
- T1 and E1Trunk Voice and WAN
- Wireless LANs and WANs

Step 3.   In the matrix, record the interface module type you need to purchase for your ISRs for upgrade purposes.

Step 4.   Use the Internet to research pictures of the modules. Provide a screenshot of the module or a hyperlink to a picture of each module.

Step 5.   Share your matrix with a classmate, group, class, or your instructor.

CHAPTER 2

Point-to-Point Connections

Point-to-point connections are the most common type of WAN connections. These connections are also called serial or leased lines. This chapter reviews the terms, technology, and protocols used in serial connections.

Serial Point-to-Point Overview

Understanding how point-to-point serial communication across a leased line works is important to an overall understanding of how WANs function.

Serial Communications

Briefly explain the difference between serial and parallel communications.

_____

_____

What is clock skew in parallel communications?

_____

WAN Protocols

Just like LANs, data is encapsulated into frames before transmission onto a WAN link. Various encapsulation protocols can be used to achieve the framing. In Table 2-1, indicate which protocol best fits the description.

Table 2-1   WAN Encapsulation Protocols

WAN Protocol Description	HDLC	PPP	SLIP	X.25/ LAPB	Frame Relay	ATM
Provides connections over synchronous and asynchronous circuits						
International standard for cell relay						
Predecessor to Frame Relay						
Default encapsulation on a serial link between two Cisco devices						
Eliminates the need for error correction and flow control						
Forms the basis for synchronous PPP						
Built-in security with PAP and CHAP						
Transfers data 53 bytes at a time so that processing can occur in hardware						
Next-generation protocol after X.25						
Largely replaced by PPP						
An ITU-T standard that defines connections between a DTE and DCE						

HDLC Encapsulation

What is the major difference between the ISO 13239 HDLC standard and Cisco's implementation of HDLC?

_____

In Figure 2-1, label the fields of Cisco HDLC frame.

Figure 2-1   Cisco HDLC Frame Format

List the three different formats of the Control field.

_____

_____

_____

HDLC Configuration and Troubleshooting

Although High-Level Data Link Control (HDLC) is the default encapsulation on Cisco synchronous serial lines, you may need to change the encapsulation back to HDLC. Record the commands, including the router prompt, to change the first serial interface on a 1900 series router to HDLC.

_____

_____

_____

Troubleshooting Serial Interfaces

Troubleshooting the cause of a serial interface issue usually begins by entering the **show interface serial** command. This command can return one of six possible statuses for the line. In Table 2-2, indicate what status would display for each of the conditions of the serial interface. Some statuses are used more than once.

Table 2-2   Line Conditions and Status Indicators

Condition of the Serial Interface	Serial X Is Up, Line Protocol Is Up	Serial X Is Down, Line Protocol Is Down	Serial X Is Up, Line Protocol Is Down	Serial X Is Up, Line Protocol Is Up (Looped)	Serial X Is Up, Line Protocol Is Down (Disabled)	Serial X Is Administratively Down, Line Protocol Is Down
A high error rate has occurred due to a WAN service provider problem.						
Keepalives are not being sent by the remote router.						

Condition of the Serial Interface	Serial X Is Up, Line Protocol Is Up	Serial X Is Down, Line Protocol Is Down	Serial X Is Up, Line Protocol Is Down	Serial X Is Up, Line Protocol Is Up (Looped)	Serial X Is Up, Line Protocol Is Down (Disabled)	Serial X Is Administratively Down, Line Protocol Is Down
The router configuration includes the **shutdown** interface configuration command.						
Cabling is faulty or incorrect.						
The **clockrate** command is not configured on the interface.						
This is the proper status line condition.						
The router is not sensing a carrier detect (CD) signal.						
The same random sequence number in the keepalive is returned over the link.						

What command will show whether a DTE or DCE cable is attached to the interface?

PPP Operation

PPP encapsulation has been carefully designed to retain compatibility with most commonly used supporting hardware. PPP encapsulates data frames for transmission over Layer 2 physical links.

PPP Components

Briefly described the three main components of PPP.

In Figure 2-2, fill in the missing parts of the PPP layered architecture.

Figure 2-2 PPP Layered Architecture

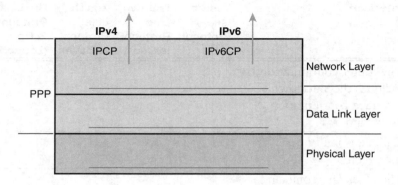

List the type of physical interfaces supported by PPP.

_____

_____

_____

What automatic configurations does the Link Control Protocol (LCP) provide at each end of the link?

_____

_____

_____

Briefly describe how PPP uses Network Control Protocol (NCP).

_____

_____

_____

In Table 2-3, indicate whether each characteristic describes LCP or NCP.

Table 2-3 LCP and NCP Characteristics

Characteristic	LCP	NCP
Can configure authentication, compression, and error detection		
Bring network layer protocols up and down		
Encapsulate and negotiate options for IPv4 and IPv6		
Negotiate and set up control options on the WAN circuit		
Handle limits on packet size		
Establish, configure, and test the data link connection		
Use standardized codes to indicate the network layer protocol		
Determine if link is functioning properly		
Terminate the link		
Manage packets from several network layer protocols		

Figure 2-3 shows the PPP frame format. Answer the following questions about the specific features and purpose of each field.

Figure 2-3   PPP Frame Format

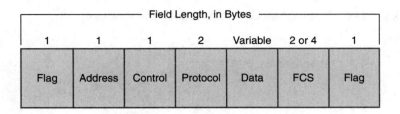

What is the bit pattern for the Flag field?

_____

Why is the Address field all 1s or 0xFF?

_____

What is the purpose of the Control field?

_____

_____

What is the purpose of the Protocol field?

_____

_____

What is the default size of the information stored in the Data field?

_____

What does FCS stand for and what is the purpose of this field?

_____

_____

_____

PPP Sessions

What are the three phases for establishing a PPP session?

_____

_____

_____

Figure 2-4 shows a partially labeled flowchart for the LCP link negotiation process. Complete the flowchart by properly labeling it with the provided steps.

- Send Configure-Reject
- Receive Configure-Ack
- Process Configure-Request

- Send Configure-Ack
- Authentication Phase
- Send Configure-Nak

Figure 2-4   Steps in the LCP Link Negotiation Process

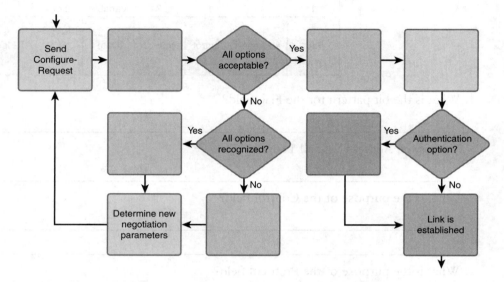

PPP can be configured to support optional functions, including the following:

- _____ using either PAP or CHAP
- _____ using either Stacker or Predictor
- _____ that combines two or more channels to increase the WAN bandwidth

After the link is established, the LCP passes control to the appropriate NCP. Figure 2-5 shows the NCP process for IPv4. Complete the figure by properly labeling it with the provided phases and steps.

Missing Labels for Figure 2-5

- IPv4 Data Transfer
- NCP Termination
- IPCP Configure-Request
- IPCP Configure-Ack
- IPCP Terminate-Request
- LCP Maintenance
- IPCP Terminate-Ack
- NCP Configuration

Figure 2-5   The NCP Process

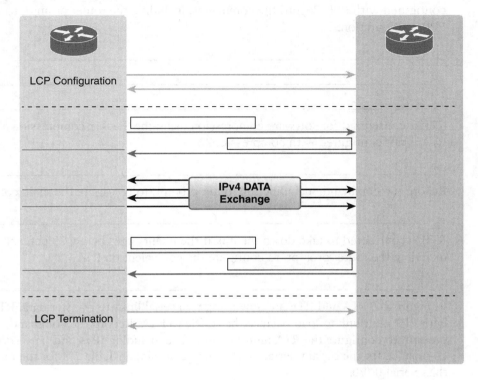

Configure PPP

PPP is a robust WAN protocol supporting multiple physical layer and network layer implementations. In addition, PPP has many optional features the network administrator can choose to implement.

Basic PPP Configuration with Options

Figure 2-6 shows the topology and Table 2-4 shows the addressing we will use for PPP configuration.

Figure 2-6   PPP Topology

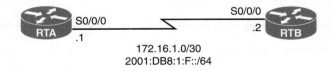

Table 2-4   Addressing Table for PPP

Device	Interface	IPv4 Address	Subnet Mask
		IPv6 Address/Prefix	
RTA	S0/0/0	172.16.1.1	255.255.255.252
		2001:DB8:1:F::1/64	
RTB	S0/0/0	172.16.1.2	255.255.255.252
		2001:DB8:1:F::2/64	

Assume that the router interfaces are already configured with IPv4 and IPv6 addressing. RTB is fully configured with PPP. Record the commands, including the router prompt, to configure RTA with a basic PPP configuration.

_____

_____

RTB is configured for software compression using the Stacker compression algorithm. What happens if RTA is not configured with compression?

_____

Record the command, including the router prompt, to configure the same compression on RTA.

_____

RTB is configured to take down the link if the quality falls below 70 percent. Record the command, including the router prompt, to configure the equivalent on RTA.

_____

In Figure 2-7, RTA and RTB are now using two serial links to transfer data. RTB is already configured with PPP multilink to load balance the traffic to RTA. Record the commands, including the router prompt, to configure the RTA multilink interface including IPv4 and IPv6 addressing and the necessary commands for the serial interfaces. Use the addressing in Table 2-4 for the multilink interface rather than Serial 0/0/0.

Figure 2-7   PPP Multilink Topology

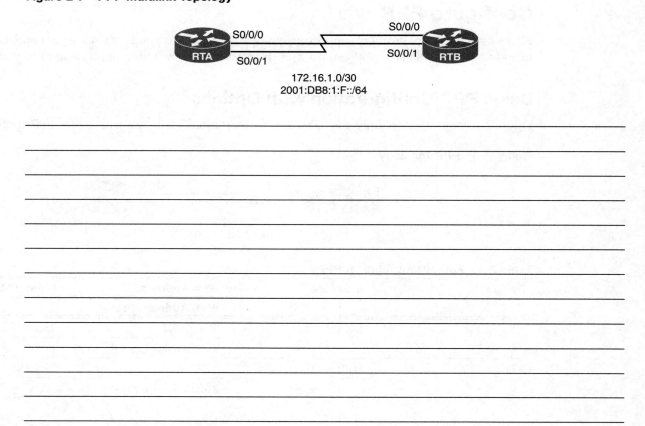

_____

_____

_____

_____

_____

_____

_____

_____

_____

_____

You can verify the operation of PPP using the following **show** commands. Record the commands used to generate the output on RTA.

```
RTA# _____

Serial0/0/0 is up, line protocol is up
   Hardware is WIC MBRD Serial
   Internet address is 172.16.1.1/30
   MTU 1500 bytes, BW 1544 Kbit/sec, DLY 20000 usec,
      reliability 255/255, txload 1/255, rxload 1/255
   Encapsulation PPP, LCP Open
   Open: IPCP, IPV6CP, CCP, CDPCP, loopback not set
   Keepalive set (10 sec)
<output omitted>

RTA# _____

Multilink1
   Bundle name: RTA
   Remote Endpoint Discriminator: [1] RTB
   Local Endpoint Discriminator: [1] RTA
   Bundle up for 00:01:20, total bandwidth 3088, load 1/255
   Receive buffer limit 24000 bytes, frag timeout 1000 ms
      0/0 fragments/bytes in reassembly list
      0 lost fragments, 0 reordered
      0/0 discarded fragments/bytes, 0 lost received
      0x2 received sequence, 0x2 sent sequence
   Member links: 2 active, 0 inactive (max 255, min not set)
      Se0/0/0, since 00:01:20
      Se0/0/1, since 00:01:06
No inactive multilink interfaces
```

PPP Authentication

Briefly explain the difference between PAP and CHAP.

_____

_____

_____

PAP is not interactive. When you configure an interface with the **ppp authentication pap** command, the username and password are sent as one LCP data package. You are not prompted for a username. The receiving node checks the username and password combination and either accepts or rejects the connection.

List three situations where PAP would be the appropriate choice for authentication.

_____

_____

_____

Once PAP authentication is established, the link is vulnerable to attack. Why?

_____

CHAP challenges periodically to make sure that the remote node still has a valid password. Complete the missing information in the following steps as RTA authenticates with RTB using CHAP.

Step 1.   RTA initially negotiates the link connection using LCP with router RTB, and the two systems agree to use CHAP authentication during the PPP LCP negotiation.

Step 2.   RTB generates an _____ and a _____ number, and sends that and its _____ as a CHAP challenge packet to RTA.

Step 3.   RTA uses the _____ of the challenger (RTB) and cross references it with its local database to find its associated _____. RTA then generates a unique _____ number using the RTB's _____, _____, _____ number, and the shared _____.

Step 4.   RTA then sends the challenge _____, the _____ value, and its _____ (RTA) to RTB.

Step 5.   RTB generates its own _____ value using the _____, the shared _____, and the _____ number it originally sent to RTA.

Step 6.   RTB compares its _____ value with the _____ value sent by RTA. If the values are the same, RTB sends a link established response to RTA.

When authentication is local (no AAA/TACACS+), what is the command syntax to configure PPP authentication on an interface?

_____

Assume that both PAP and CHAP are configured with the command **ppp authentication chap pap** on the interface. Explain how authentication will proceed.

_____

_____

PAP Configuration

In Figure 2-6, RTB is already configured with PAP authentication with the password cisco123. Record the commands to configure PAP on RTA.

_____

_____

_____

_____

CHAP Configuration

CHAP uses one less command than PAP. Now record the commands to remove PAP and configure RTA to use CHAP authentication.

_____

_____

_____

_____

Packet Tracer Exercise 2-1: PPP Implementation

Now you are ready to use Packet Tracer to configure PPP with authentication. Download and open the file LSG04-0201.pka found at the companion website for this book. Refer to the Introduction of this book for specifics on accessing files.

Note: The following instructions are also contained within the Packet Tracer Exercise.

In this Packet Tracer activity, you will configure the RTA and RTB to use PPP with CHAP. You will then verify that RTA and RTB can ping each other using IPv4 and IPv6 addresses.

Requirements

Configure RTA and RTB with the following settings:

- The hostname is the username. Use **cisco123** as the password.
- Configure and activate the connected interfaces to use dual-stack IP addressing. Refer to the topology for addressing information.
- Configure PPP with CHAP authentication.
- Verify that the interfaces are up and that RTA and RTB can ping each other's IPv4 and IPv6 addresses.

Your completion percentage should be 100%. All the connectivity tests should show a status of "successful." If not, click **Check Results** to see which required components are not yet completed.

Troubleshoot WAN Connectivity

If you cannot ping across a PPP link and you have checked the physical and data link layer issues reviewed in the "Troubleshooting Serial Interfaces" section earlier, the issue is probably the PPP configuration. You can use the **debug** command to troubleshoot PPP issues using the **debug ppp** {*parameter*} syntax. Based on the descriptions in Table 2-5, fill in the corresponding parameter you would use with the **debug ppp** command.

Table 2-5   Parameters for the debug ppp Command

Parameter	Usage
	Displays issues associated with PPP connection negotiation and operation
	Displays information specific to the exchange of PPP connections using MPPC
	Displays PPP packets transmitted during PPP startup
	Displays PPP packets being sent and received
	Displays authentication protocol messages
	Displays protocol errors and statistics associated with PPP connection negotiations using MSCB

Labs and Activities

Command Reference

In Table 2-6, record the command, including the correct router prompt that fits the description. Fill in any blanks with the appropriate missing information.

Table 2-6   Commands for Chapter 2, Point-to-Point Connections

Command	Description
	Configure HDLC encapsulation.
	Display whether serial 0/0/0 is DCE or DTE.
	Configure PPP encapsulation.
	Configure PPP to use the predictor compression algorithm.
	Configure PPP to take down the link if the quality falls below 50 percent.
	Create a multilink interface with group number 1.
	Configure an interface to multilink.
	Configure an interface to belong to multilink group 1.
	Verify serial 0/0/0 is using PPP and that LCP and NCPs are open.
	Verify that multilink is operational.
	Configure RTA to use CHAP.
	Configure RTA to use PAP.
	Configure RTA to send the PAP username RTA and password cisco123.

2.0.1.2 Class Activity–PPP Persuasion

Objectives

Describe the benefits of using PPP over HDLC in a WAN.

This activity can be completed individually or in small groups of 2-3 students per group.

Scenario

Your network engineering supervisor recently attended a networking conference where Layer 2 protocols were discussed. He knows that you have Cisco equipment on the premises, but he would also like to offer security and advanced TCP/IP options and controls on that same equipment by using the Point-to-Point Protocol (PPP).

After researching the PPP protocol, you find it offers some advantages over the HDLC protocol, currently used on your network.

Create a matrix listing the advantages and disadvantages of using the HDLC vs. PPP protocols. When comparing the two protocols, include:

- Ease of configuration
- Adaptability to non-proprietary network equipment
- Security options
- Bandwidth usage and compression
- Bandwidth consolidation

Share your chart with another student or class. Justify whether or not you would suggest sharing the matrix with the network engineering supervisor to justify a change being made from HDLC to PPP for Layer 2 network connectivity.

Resources

- Internet access to the World Wide Web
- Word processing or spreadsheet software

2.1.2.5 Packet Tracer–Troubleshooting Serial Interfaces

Topology

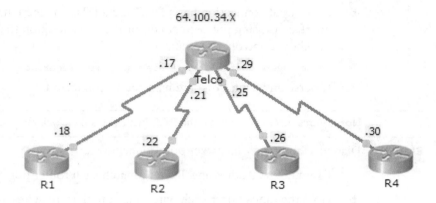

Addressing Table

Device	Interface	IP Address	Subnet Mask	Default Route
Telco	S0/0/0 (DCE)	64.100.34.17	255.255.255.252	N/A
	S0/0/1 (DCE)	64.100.34.21	255.255.255.252	N/A
	S0/1/0 (DCE)	64.100.34.25	255.255.255.252	N/A
	S0/1/1 (DCE)	64.100.34.29	255.255.255.252	N/A
R1	S0/0/0	64.100.34.18	255.255.255.252	64.100.34.17
R2	S0/0/1	64.100.34.22	255.255.255.252	64.100.34.21
R3	S0/0/0	64.100.34.26	255.255.255.252	64.100.34.25
R4	S0/0/1	64.100.34.30	255.255.255.252	64.100.34.29

Objectives

Part 1: Diagnose and Repair the Physical Layer

Part 2: Diagnose and Repair the Data Link Layer

Part 3: Diagnose and Repair the Network Layer

Scenario

You have been asked to troubleshoot WAN connections for a local telephone company (**Telco**). The Telco router should communicate with four remote sites, but none of them are working. Use your knowledge of the OSI model and a few general rules to identify and repair the errors in the network.

Part 1: Diagnose and Repair the Physical Layer

Step 1.   Diagnose and repair the cabling.

    a.   Examine the Addressing Table to determine the location of the DCE connections.

    b.   Each serial connection has a DCE and a DTE connection. To determine if each **Telco** interface is using the correct end of the cable look on the third line of output following the **show controllers** command.

```
Telco# show controllers [interface_type interface_num]
```

    c.   Reverse any cables that are incorrectly connected.

Note: In real network settings, the DCE (which sets the clock rate) is typically a CSU/DSU.

Step 2.   Diagnose and repair incorrect port connections.

    a.   Examine the Addressing Table to match each router port with the correct **Telco** port.

    b.   Hold the mouse over each wire to ensure that the wires are connected as specified. If not, correct the connections.

Step 3.   Diagnose and repair ports that are shut down.

    a.   Show a brief interface summary of each router. Ensure that all of the ports that should be working are not administratively down.

    b.   Enable the appropriate ports that are administratively down:

_____

_____

Part 2: Diagnose and Repair the Data Link Layer

Step 1.   Examine and set clock rates on DCE equipment.

    a.   All of the DCE cables should be connected to **Telco**. Show the running configuration of **Telco** to verify that a clock rate has been set on each interface.

    b.   Set the clock rate of any serial interface that requires it:

_____

_____

_____

_____

Step 2.   Examine the encapsulation on DCE equipment.

    a.   All of the serial interfaces should be using HDLC as the encapsulation type. Examine the protocol setting of the serial interfaces.

```
Telco# show interface [interface_type interface_num]
```

    b.   Change the encapsulation type to HDLC for any interface that is set otherwise:

_____

_____

Part 3: Diagnose and Repair the Network Layer

Step 1.   Verify the IP addressing.

    a.   Show a brief interface summary of each router. Check the IP addresses against the Addressing Table and ensure that they are in the correct subnet with their connecting interface.

    b.   Correct any IP addresses that overlap, or are set to the host or broadcast address:

       _____

       _____

Step 2.   Verify connectivity between all routers.

Packet Tracer
☐ **Activity**

2.3.2.6 Packet Tracer–Configuring PAP and CHAP Authentication

Topology

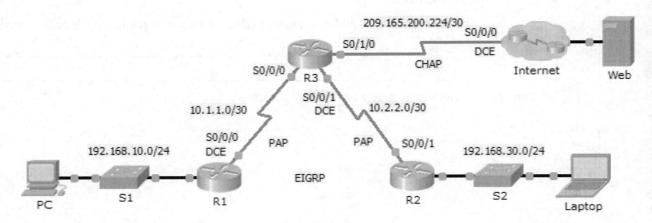

Addressing Table

Device	Interface	IP Address	Subnet Mask	Default Gateway
R1	G0/0	192.168.10.1	255.255.255.0	N/A
	S0/0/0	10.1.1.1	255.255.255.252	N/A
R2	G0/0	192.168.30.1	255.255.255.0	N/A
	S0/0/1	10.2.2.2	255.255.255.252	N/A
R3	S0/0/0	10.1.1.2	255.255.255.252	N/A
	S0/0/1	10.2.2.1	255.255.255.252	N/A
	S0/1/0	209.165.200.225	255.255.255.252	N/A
ISP	S0/0/0	209.165.200.226	255.255.255.252	N/A
	G0/0	209.165.200.1	255.255.255.252	N/A
Web	NIC	209.165.200.2	255.255.255.252	209.165.200.1
PC	NIC	192.168.10.10	255.255.255.0	192.168.10.1
Laptop	NIC	192.168.30.10	255.255.255.0	192.168.30.1

Objectives

Part 1: Review Routing Configurations

Part 2: Configure PPP as the Encapsulation Method

Part 3: Configure PPP Authentication

Background

In this activity, you will practice configuring PPP encapsulation on serial links. You will also configure PPP PAP authentication and PPP CHAP authentication.

Part 1: Review Routing Configurations

Step 1. View running configurations on all routers.

While reviewing the router configurations, note the use of both static and dynamic routes in the topology.

Step 2. Test connectivity between computers and the Web Server.

From **PC** and **Laptop**, ping the Web Server at 209.165.200.2. Both **ping** commands should be successful. Remember to give enough time for STP and EIGRP to converge.

Part 2: Configure PPP as the Encapsulation Method

Step 1. Configure **R1** to use PPP encapsulation with **R3**.

Enter the following commands on **R1**:

```
R1(config)# interface s0/0/0
R1(config-if)# encapsulation ppp
```

Step 2. Configure **R2** to use PPP encapsulation with **R3**.

Enter the appropriate commands on **R2**:

_____

_____

Step 3. Configure **R3** to use PPP encapsulation with **R1**, **R2**, and **ISP**.

Enter the appropriate commands on **R3**:

_____

_____

_____

_____

_____

_____

Step 4. Configure **ISP** to use PPP encapsulation with **R3**.

a. Click the **Internet** cloud, then ISP. Enter the following commands:

```
Router(config)# interface s0/0/0
Router(config-if)# encapsulation ppp
```

b. Exit the **Internet** cloud by clicking **Back** in the upper left corner or by pressing **Alt+left arrow**.

Step 5. Test connectivity to the Web Server.

PC and **Laptop** should be able to ping the Web Server at 209.165.200.2. This may take some time as interfaces start working again and EIGRP reconverges.

Part 3: Configure PPP Authentication

Step 1.   Configure PPP PAP authentication between **R1** and **R3**.

Note: Instead of using the keyword **password** as shown in the curriculum, you will use the keyword **secret** to provide a better encryption of the password.

---

a.   Enter the following commands into **R1**:

```
R1(config)# username R3 secret class
R1(config)# interface s0/0/0
R1(config-if)# ppp authentication pap
R1(config-if)# ppp pap sent-username R1 password cisco
```

b.   Enter the following commands into **R3**:

```
R3(config)# username R1 secret cisco
R3(config)# interface s0/0/0
R3(config-if)# ppp authentication pap
R3(config-if)# ppp pap sent-username R3 password class
```

Step 2.   Configure PPP PAP authentication between **R2** and **R3**.

Repeat Step 1 to configure authentication between **R2** and **R3** changing the usernames as needed. Note that each password sent on each serial port matches the password expected by the opposite router.

_____

_____

_____

_____

_____

_____

_____

_____

Step 3.   Configure PPP CHAP authentication between **R3** and **ISP**.

a.   Enter the following commands into **ISP**. The hostname is sent as the username:

```
Router(config)# hostname ISP
ISP(config)# username R3 secret cisco
ISP(config)# interface s0/0/0
ISP(config-if)# ppp authentication chap
```

b.   Enter the following commands into **R3**. The passwords must match for CHAP authentication:

```
R3(config)# username ISP secret cisco
R3(config)# interface serial0/1/0
R3(config-if)# ppp authentication chap
```

Step 4.   Test connectivity between computers and the Web Server.

From **PC** and **Laptop**, ping the Web Server at 209.165.200.2. Both **ping** commands should be successful. Remember to give enough time for STP and EIGRP to converge.

2.3.2.7 Lab–Configuring Basic PPP with Authentication

Topology

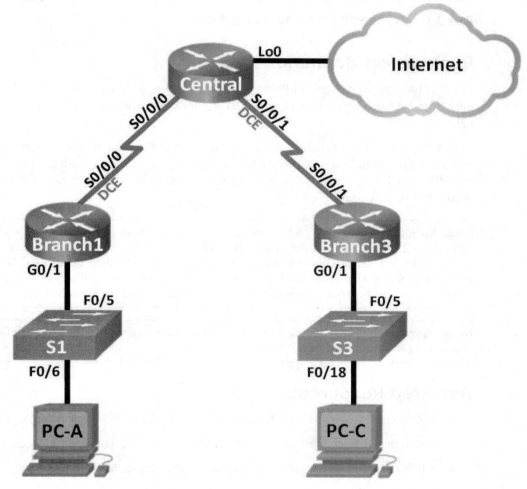

Addressing Table

Device	Interface	IP Address	Subnet Mask	Default Gateway
Branch1	G0/1	192.168.1.1	255.255.255.0	N/A
	S0/0/0 (DCE)	10.1.1.1	255.255.255.252	N/A
Central	S0/0/0	10.1.1.2	255.255.255.252	N/A
	S0/0/1 (DCE)	10.2.2.2	255.255.255.252	N/A
	Lo0	209.165.200.225	255.255.255.224	N/A
Branch3	G0/1	192.168.3.1	255.255.255.0	N/A
	S0/0/1	10.2.2.1	255.255.255.252	N/A
PC-A	NIC	192.168.1.3	255.255.255.0	192.168.1.1
PC-C	NIC	192.168.3.3	255.255.255.0	192.168.3.1

Objectives

Part 1: Configure Basic Device Settings

Part 2: Configure PPP Encapsulation

Part 3: Configure PPP CHAP Authentication

Background/Scenario

The Point-to-Point Protocol (PPP) is a very common Layer 2 WAN protocol. PPP can be used to connect from LANs to service provider WANs and for connection of LAN segments within an enterprise network.

In this lab, you will configure PPP encapsulation on dedicated serial links between the branch routers and a central router. You will configure PPP Challenge Handshake Authentication Protocol (CHAP) on the PPP serial links. You will also examine the effects of the encapsulation and authentication changes on the status of the serial link.

Note: The routers used with CCNA hands-on labs are Cisco 1941 Integrated Services Routers (ISRs) with Cisco IOS Release 15.2(4)M3 (universalk9 image). The switches used are Cisco Catalyst 2960s with Cisco IOS Release 15.0(2) (lanbasek9 image). Other routers, switches, and Cisco IOS versions can be used. Depending on the model and Cisco IOS version, the commands available and output produced might vary from what is shown in the labs. Refer to the Router Interface Summary Table at the end of this lab for the correct interface identifiers.

Note: Make sure that the routers and switches have been erased and have no startup configurations. If you are unsure, contact your instructor.

Required Resources

- 3 Routers (Cisco 1941 with Cisco IOS Release 15.2(4)M3 universal image or comparable)
- 2 Switches (Cisco 2960 with Cisco IOS Release 15.0(2) lanbasek9 image or comparable)
- 2 PCs (Windows with terminal emulation program, such as Tera Term)
- Console cables to configure the Cisco IOS devices via the console ports
- Ethernet and serial cables as shown in the topology

Part 1: Configure Basic Device Settings

In Part 1, you will set up the network topology and configure basic router settings, such as the interface IP addresses, routing, device access, and passwords.

Step 1.   Cable the network as shown in the topology.

Attach the devices as shown in the Topology, and cable as necessary.

Step 2.   Initialize and reload the routers and switches.

Step 3.   Configure basic settings for each router.

a.   Disable DNS lookup.

b.   Configure the device name.

c.   Encrypt plaintext passwords.

d. Create a message of the day (MOTD) banner warning users that unauthorized access is prohibited.

e. Assign **class** as the encrypted privileged EXEC mode password.

f. Assign **cisco** as the console and vty password and enable login.

g. Set console logging to synchronous mode.

h. Apply the IP addresses to Serial and Gigabit Ethernet interfaces according to the Addressing Table and activate the physical interfaces.

i. Set the clock rate to **128000** for DCE serial interfaces.

j. Create **Loopback0** on the Central router to simulate access to the Internet and assign an IP address according to the Addressing Table.

Step 4. Configure routing.

a. Enable single-area OSPF on the routers and use a process ID of 1. Add all the networks, except 209.165.200.224/27 into the OSPF process.

b. Configure a default route to the simulated Internet on the Central router using Lo0 as the exit interface and redistribute this route into the OSPF process.

c. Issue the **show ip route ospf**, **show ip ospf interface brief**, and **show ip ospf neighbor** commands on all routers to verify that OSPF is configured correctly. Take note of the router ID for each router.

Step 5. Configure the PCs.

Assign IP addresses and default gateways to the PCs according to the Addressing Table.

Step 6. Verify end-to-end connectivity.

All devices should be able to ping other devices in the Topology. If not, troubleshoot until you can establish end-to-end connectivity.

Note: It may be necessary to disable the PC firewall to ping between PCs.

Step 7. Save your configurations.

Part 2: Configure PPP Encapsulation

Step 1. Display the default serial encapsulation.

On the routers, issue **show interfaces serial** *interface-id* to display the current serial encapsulation.

```
Branch1# show interfaces s0/0/0
Serial0/0/0 is up, line protocol is up
  Hardware is WIC MBRD Serial
  Internet address is 10.1.1.1/30
  MTU 1500 bytes, BW 1544 Kbit/sec, DLY 20000 usec,
     reliability 255/255, txload 1/255, rxload 1/255
  Encapsulation HDLC, loopback not set
  Keepalive set (10 sec)
  Last input 00:00:02, output 00:00:05, output hang never
  Last clearing of "show interface" counters never
  Input queue: 0/75/0/0 (size/max/drops/flushes); Total output drops: 0
```

```
Queueing strategy: fifo
Output queue: 0/40 (size/max)
5 minute input rate 0 bits/sec, 0 packets/sec
5 minute output rate 0 bits/sec, 0 packets/sec
   1003 packets input, 78348 bytes, 0 no buffer
   Received 527 broadcasts (0 IP multicasts)
   0 runts, 0 giants, 0 throttles
   0 input errors, 0 CRC, 0 frame, 0 overrun, 0 ignored, 0 abort
   1090 packets output, 80262 bytes, 0 underruns
   0 output errors, 0 collisions, 3 interface resets
   0 unknown protocol drops
   0 output buffer failures, 0 output buffers swapped out
   2 carrier transitions
   DCD=up  DSR=up  DTR=up  RTS=up  CTS=up
```

What is the default serial encapsulation for a Cisco router? _____

Step 2.   Change the serial encapsulation to PPP.

   a.   Issue the **encapsulation ppp** command on the S0/0/0 interface for the Branch1 router to change the encapsulation from HDLC to PPP.

```
Branch1(config)# interface s0/0/0
Branch1(config-if)# encapsulation ppp
Branch1(config-if)#
Jun 19 06:02:33.687: %OSPF-5-ADJCHG: Process 1, Nbr 209.165.200.225 on
Serial0/0/0 from FULL to DOWN, Neighbor Down: Interface down or detached
Branch1(config-if)#
Jun 19 06:02:35.687: %LINEPROTO-5-UPDOWN: Line protocol on Interface
Serial0/0/0, changed state to down
```

   b.   Issue the command to display the line status and line protocol for interface S0/0/0 on the Branch1 router. Document the command issued. What is the current interface status for S0/0/0?

   _____

   c.   Issue the **encapsulation ppp** command on interface S0/0/0 for the Central router to correct the serial encapsulation mismatch.

```
Central(config)# interface s0/0/0
Central(config-if)# encapsulation ppp
Central(config-if)#
.Jun 19 06:03:41.186: %LINEPROTO-5-UPDOWN: Line protocol on Interface
Serial0/0/0, changed state to up
.Jun 19 06:03:41.274: %OSPF-5-ADJCHG: Process 1, Nbr 192.168.1.1 on Serial0/0/0
from LOADING to FULL, Loading Done
```

   d.   Verify that interface S0/0/0 on both Branch1 and Central routers is up/up and is configured with PPP encapsulation.

   What is the status of the PPP Link Control Protocol (LCP)? _____

   Which Network Control Protocol (NCP) protocols have been negotiated?

   _____

```
Branch1# show interfaces s0/0/0
Serial0/0/0 is up, line protocol is up
  Hardware is WIC MBRD Serial
```

```
  Internet address is 10.1.1.1/30
  MTU 1500 bytes, BW 1544 Kbit/sec, DLY 20000 usec,
     reliability 255/255, txload 1/255, rxload 1/255
  Encapsulation PPP, LCP Open
  Open: IPCP, CDPCP, loopback not set
  Keepalive set (10 sec)
  Last input 00:00:00, output 00:00:00, output hang never
  Last clearing of "show interface" counters 00:03:58
  Input queue: 0/75/0/0 (size/max/drops/flushes); Total output drops: 0
  Queueing strategy: fifo
  Output queue: 0/40 (size/max)
  5 minute input rate 0 bits/sec, 0 packets/sec
  5 minute output rate 0 bits/sec, 0 packets/sec
     77 packets input, 4636 bytes, 0 no buffer
     Received 0 broadcasts (0 IP multicasts)
     0 runts, 0 giants, 0 throttles
     0 input errors, 0 CRC, 0 frame, 0 overrun, 0 ignored, 0 abort
     117 packets output, 5800 bytes, 0 underruns
     0 output errors, 0 collisions, 8 interface resets
     22 unknown protocol drops
     0 output buffer failures, 0 output buffers swapped out
     18 carrier transitions
     DCD=up  DSR=up  DTR=up  RTS=up  CTS=up

Central# show interfaces s0/0/0
Serial0/0/0 is up, line protocol is up
  Hardware is WIC MBRD Serial
  Internet address is 10.1.1.2/30
  MTU 1500 bytes, BW 1544 Kbit/sec, DLY 20000 usec,
     reliability 255/255, txload 1/255, rxload 1/255
  Encapsulation PPP, LCP Open
  Open: IPCP, CDPCP, loopback not set
  Keepalive set (10 sec)
  Last input 00:00:02, output 00:00:03, output hang never
  Last clearing of "show interface" counters 00:01:20
  Input queue: 0/75/0/0 (size/max/drops/flushes); Total output drops: 0
  Queueing strategy: fifo
  Output queue: 0/40 (size/max)
  5 minute input rate 0 bits/sec, 0 packets/sec
  5 minute output rate 0 bits/sec, 0 packets/sec
     41 packets input, 2811 bytes, 0 no buffer
     Received 0 broadcasts (0 IP multicasts)
     0 runts, 0 giants, 0 throttles
     0 input errors, 0 CRC, 0 frame, 0 overrun, 0 ignored, 0 abort
     40 packets output, 2739 bytes, 0 underruns
     0 output errors, 0 collisions, 0 interface resets
     0 unknown protocol drops
     0 output buffer failures, 0 output buffers swapped out
     0 carrier transitions
     DCD=up  DSR=up  DTR=up  RTS=up  CTS=up
```

Step 3.   Intentionally break the serial connection.

a.   Issue the **debug ppp** commands to observe the effects of changing the PPP configuration on the Branch1 router and the Central router.

```
Branch1# debug ppp negotiation
PPP protocol negotiation debugging is on
Branch1# debug ppp packet
PPP packet display debugging is on

Central# debug ppp negotiation
PPP protocol negotiation debugging is on
Central# debug ppp packet
PPP packet display debugging is on
```

b.   Observe the debug PPP messages when traffic is flowing on the serial link between the Branch1 and Central routers.

```
Branch1#
Jun 20 02:20:45.795: Se0/0/0 PPP: O pkt type 0x0021, datagramsize 84
Jun 20 02:20:49.639: Se0/0/0 PPP: I pkt type 0x0021, datagramsize 84 link[ip]
Jun 20 02:20:50.147: Se0/0/0 LCP-FS: I ECHOREQ [Open] id 45 len 12 magic
0x73885AF2
Jun 20 02:20:50.147: Se0/0/0 LCP-FS: O ECHOREP [Open] id 45 len 12 magic
0x8CE1F65F
Jun 20 02:20:50.159: Se0/0/0 LCP: O ECHOREQ [Open] id 45 len 12 magic
0x8CE1F65F
Jun 20 02:20:50.159: Se0/0/0 LCP-FS: I ECHOREP [Open] id 45 len 12 magic
0x73885AF2
Jun 20 02:20:50.159: Se0/0/0 LCP-FS: Received id 45, sent id 45, line up

Central#
Jun 20 02:20:49.636: Se0/0/0 PPP: O pkt type 0x0021, datagramsize 84
Jun 20 02:20:50.148: Se0/0/0 LCP: O ECHOREQ [Open] id 45 len 12 magic
0x73885AF2
Jun 20 02:20:50.148: Se0/0/0 LCP-FS: I ECHOREP [Open] id 45 len 12 magic
0x8CE1F65F
Jun 20 02:20:50.148: Se0/0/0 LCP-FS: Received id 45, sent id 45, line up
Jun 20 02:20:50.160: Se0/0/0 LCP-FS: I ECHOREQ [Open] id 45 len 12 magic
0x8CE1F65F
Jun 20 02:20:50.160: Se0/0/0 LCP-FS: O ECHOREP [Open] id 45 len 12 magic
0x73885AF2
Jun 20 02:20:55.552: Se0/0/0 PPP: I pkt type 0x0021, datagramsize 84 link[ip]
```

c.   Break the serial connection by returning the serial encapsulation to HDLC for interface S0/0/0 on the Branch1 router. Record the command used to change the encapsulation to HDLC.

_____

d.   Observe the debug PPP messages on the Branch1 router. The serial connection has terminated, and the line protocol is down. The route to 10.1.1.2 (Central) has been removed from the routing table.

```
Jun 20 02:29:50.295: Se0/0/0 PPP DISC: Lower Layer disconnected
Jun 20 02:29:50.295: PPP: NET STOP send to AAA.
Jun 20 02:29:50.299: Se0/0/0 IPCP: Event[DOWN] State[Open to Starting]
Jun 20 02:29:50.299: Se0/0/0 IPCP: Event[CLOSE] State[Starting to Initial]
```

```
Jun 20 02:29:50.299: Se0/0/0 CDPCP: Event[DOWN] State[Open to Starting]
Jun 20 02:29:50.299: Se0/0/0 CDPCP: Event[CLOSE] State[Starting to Initial]
Jun 20 02:29:50.29
Branch1(config-if)#9: Se0/0/0 LCP: O TERMREQ [Open] id 7 len 4
Jun 20 02:29:50.299: Se0/0/0 LCP: Event[CLOSE] State[Open to Closing]
Jun 20 02:29:50.299: Se0/0/0 PPP: Phase is TERMINATING
Jun 20 02:29:50.299: Se0/0/0 Deleted neighbor route from AVL tree: topoid 0,
address 10.1.1.2
Jun 20 02:29:50.299: Se0/0/0 IPCP: Remove route to 10.1.1.2
Jun 20 02:29:50.299: Se0/0/0 LCP: Event[DOWN] State[Closing to Initial]
Jun 20 02:29:50.299: Se0/0/0 PPP: Phase is DOWN
Branch1(config-if)#
Jun 20 02:30:17.083: %LINEPROTO-5-UPDOWN: Line protocol on Interface
Serial0/0/0, changed state to down
Jun 20 02:30:17.083: %OSPF-5-ADJCHG: Process 1, Nbr 209.165.200.225 on
Serial0/0/0 from FULL to DOWN, Neighbor Down: Interface down or detached
```

e. Observe the debug PPP messages on the Central router. The Central router continues to attempt to establish a connection with Branch1 as indicated by the debug messages. When the interfaces are unable to establish a connection, the interfaces go back down again. Furthermore, OSPF cannot establish an adjacency with its neighbor due to the mismatched serial encapsulation.

```
Jun 20 02:29:50.296: Se0/0/0 PPP: Sending cstate DOWN notification
Jun 20 02:29:50.296: Se0/0/0 PPP: Processing CstateDown message
Jun 20 02:29:50.296: Se0/0/0 PPP DISC: Lower Layer disconnected
Jun 20 02:29:50.296: PPP: NET STOP send to AAA.
Jun 20 02:29:50.296: Se0/0/0 IPCP: Event[DOWN] State[Open to Starting]
Jun 20 02:29:50.296: Se0/0/0 IPCP: Event[CLOSE] State[Starting to Initial]
Jun 20 02:29:50.296: Se0/0/0 CDPCP: Event[DOWN] State[Open to Starting]
Jun 20 02:29:50.296: Se0/0/0 CDPCP: Event[CLOSE] State[Starting to Initial]
Jun 20 02:29:50.296: Se0/0/0 LCP: O TERMREQ [Open] id 2 len 4
Jun 20 02:29:50.296: Se0/0/0 LCP: Event[CLOSE] State[Open to Closing]
Jun 20 02:29:50.296: Se0/0/0 PPP: Phase is TERMINATING
Jun 20 02:29:50.296: Se0/0/0 Deleted neighbor route from AVL tree: topoid 0,
address 10.1.1.1
Jun 20 02:29:50.296: Se0/0/0 IPCP: Remove route to 10.1.1.1
Jun 20 02:29:50.296: %OSPF-5-ADJCHG: Process 1, Nbr 192.168.1.1 on Serial0/0/0
from FULL to DOWN, Neighbor Down: Interface down or detached
Jun 20 02:29:50.296: Se0/0/0 LCP: Event[DOWN] State[Closing to Initial]
Jun 20 02:29:50.296: Se0/0/0 PPP: Phase is DOWN
Jun 20 02:29:52.296: %LINEPROTO-5-UPDOWN: Line protocol on Interface
Serial0/0/0, changed state to down
.Jun 20 02:29:52.296: Se0/0/0 PPP: Sending cstate UP notification
.Jun 20 02:29:52.296: Se0/0/0 PPP: Processing CstateUp message
.Jun 20 02:29:52.296: PPP: Alloc Context [29F9F32C]
.Jun 20 02:29:52.296: ppp3 PPP: Phase is ESTABLISHING
.Jun 20 02:29:52.296: Se0/0/0 PPP: Using default call direction
.Jun 20 02:29:52.296: Se0/0/0 PPP: Treating connection as a dedicated line
.Jun 20 02:29:52.296: Se0/0/0 PPP: Session handle[60000003] Session id[3]
.Jun 20 02:29:52.296: Se0/0/0 LCP: Event[OPEN] State[Initial to Starting]
.Jun 20 02:29:52.296: Se0/0/0 LCP: O CONFREQ [Starting] id 1 len 10
.Jun 20 02:29:52.296: Se0/0/0 LCP:    MagicNumber 0x7397843B (0x05067397843B)
.Jun 20 02:29:52.296: Se0/0/0 LCP:Event[UP] State[Starting to REQsent]
```

```
.Jun 20 02:29:54.308: Se0/0/0 LCP: O CONFREQ [REQsent] id 2 len 10
.Jun 20 02:29:54.308: Se0/0/0 LCP:    MagicNumber 0x7397843B (0x05067397843B)
.Jun 20 02:29:54.308: Se0/0/0 LCP: Event[Timeout+] State[REQsent to REQsent]
.Jun 20 02:29:56.080: Se0/0/0 PPP: I pkt type 0x008F, datagramsize 24
link[illegal]
.Jun 20 02:29:56.080: Se0/0/0 UNKNOWN(0x008F): Non-NCP packet, discarding
<output omitted>
.Jun 20 02:30:10.436: Se0/0/0 LCP: O CONFREQ [REQsent] id 10 len 10
.Jun 20 02:30:10.436: Se0/0/0 LCP:    MagicNumber 0x7397843B (0x05067397843B)
.Jun 20 02:30:10.436: Se0/0/0 LCP: Event[Timeout+] State[REQsent to REQsent]
.Jun 20 02:30:12.452: Se0/0/0 PPP DISC: LCP failed to negotiate
.Jun 20 02:30:12.452: PPP: NET STOP send to AAA.
.Jun 20 02:30:12.452: Se0/0/0 LCP: Event[Timeout-] State[REQsent to Stopped]
.Jun 20 02:30:12.452: Se0/0/0 LCP: Event[DOWN] State[Stopped to Starting]
.Jun 20 02:30:12.452: Se0/0/0 PPP: Phase is DOWN
.Jun 20 02:30:14.452: PPP: Alloc Context [29F9F32C]
.Jun 20 02:30:14.452: ppp4 PPP: Phase is ESTABLISHING
.Jun 20 02:30:14.452: Se0/0/0 PPP: Using default call direction
.Jun 20 02:30:14.452: Se0/0/0 PPP: Treating connection as a dedicated line
.Jun 20 02:30:14.452: Se0/0/0 PPP: Session handle[6E000004] Session id[4]
.Jun 20 02:30:14.452: Se0/0/0 LCP: Event[OPEN] State[Initial to Starting]
.Jun 20 02:30:14.452: Se0/0/0 LCP: O CONFREQ [Starting] id 1 len 10
.Jun 20 02:30:14.452: Se0/0/0 LCP:    MagicNumber 0x7397DADA (0x05067397DADA)
.Jun 20 02:30:14.452: Se0/0/0 LCP: Event[UP] State[Starting to REQsent]
.Jun 20 02:30:16.080: Se0/0/0 PPP: I pkt type 0x008F, datagramsize 24
link[illegal]
.Jun 20 02:30:16.080: Se0/0/0 UNKNOWN(0x008F): Non-NCP packet, discarding
<output omitted>
.Jun 20 02:30:32.580: Se0/0/0 LCP: O CONFREQ [REQsent] id 10 len 10
.Jun 20 02:30:32.580: Se0/0/0 LCP:    MagicNumber 0x7397DADA (0x05067397DADA)
.Jun 20 02:30:32.580: Se0/0/0 LCP: Event[Timeout+] State[REQsent to REQsent]
.Jun 20 02:30:34.596: Se0/0/0 PPP DISC: LCP failed to negotiate
.Jun 20 02:30:34.596: PPP: NET STOP send to AAA.
.Jun 20 02:30:34.596: Se0/0/0 LCP: Event[Timeout-] State[REQsent to Stopped]
.Jun 20 02:30:34.596: Se0/0/0 LCP: Event[DOWN] State[Stopped to Starting]
.Jun 20 02:30:34.596: Se0/0/0 PPP: Phase is DOWN
.Jun 20 02:30:36.080: Se0/0/0 PPP: I pkt type 0x008F, discarded, PPP not
running
.Jun 20 02:30:36.596: PPP: Alloc Context [29F9F32C]
.Jun 20 02:30:36.596: ppp5 PPP: Phase is ESTABLISHING
.Jun 20 02:30:36.596: Se0/0/0 PPP: Using default call direction
.Jun 20 02:30:36.596: Se0/0/0 PPP: Treating connection as a dedicated line
.Jun 20 02:30:36.596: Se0/0/0 PPP: Session handle[34000005] Session id[5]
.Jun 20 02:30:36.596: Se0/0/0 LCP: Event[OPEN] State[Initial to Starting]
```

What happens when one end of the serial link is encapsulated with PPP and the other end of the link is encapsulated with HDLC?

_____

_____

_____

   f. Issue the **encapsulation ppp** command on the S0/0/0 interface for the Branch1 router to correct mismatched encapsulation.

```
Branch1(config)# interface s0/0/0
Branch1(config-if)# encapsulation ppp
```

   g. Observe the debug PPP messages from the Branch1 router as the Branch1 and Central routers establish a connection.

```
Branch1(config-if)#
Jun 20 03:01:57.399: %OSPF-5-ADJCHG: Process 1, Nbr 209.165.200.225 on
Serial0/0/0 from FULL to DOWN, Neighbor Down: Interface down or detached
Jun 20 03:01:59.399: %LINEPROTO-5-UPDOWN: Line protocol on Interface
Serial0/0/0, changed state to down
Jun 20 03:01:59.399: Se0/0/0 PPP: Sending cstate UP notification
Jun 20 03:01:59.399: Se0/0/0 PPP: Processing CstateUp message
Jun 20 03:01:59.399: PPP: Alloc Context [30F8D4F0]
Jun 20 03:01:59.399: ppp9 PPP: Phase is ESTABLISHING
Jun 20 03:01:59.399: Se0/0/0 PPP: Using default call direction
Jun 20 03:01:59.399: Se0/0/0 PPP: Treating connection as a dedicated line
Jun 20 03:01:59.399: Se0/0/0 PPP: Session handle[BA000009] Session id[9]
Jun 20 03:01:59.399: Se0/0/0 LCP: Event[OPEN] State[Initial to Starting]
Jun 20 03:01:59.399: Se0/0/0 LCP: O CONFREQ [Starting] id 1 len 10
Jun 20 03:01:59.399: Se0/0/0 LCP:    MagicNumber 0x8D0EAC44 (0x05068D0EAC44)
Jun 20 03:01:59.399: Se0/0/0 LCP: Event[UP] State[Starting to REQsent]
Jun 20 03:01:59.407: Se0/0/0 PPP: I pkt type 0xC021, datagramsize 14 link[ppp]
Jun 20 03:01:59.407: Se0/0/0 LCP: I CONFREQ [REQsent] id 1 len 10
Jun 20 03:01:59.407: Se0/0/0 LCP:    MagicNumber 0x73B4F1AF (0x050673B4F1AF)
Jun 20 03:01:59.407: Se0/0/0 LCP: O CONFACK [REQsent] id 1 len 10
Jun 20 03:01:59.407: Se0/0/0 LCP:    MagicNumber 0x73B4F1AF (0x050673B4F1AF)
Jun 20 03:01:59.407: Se0/0/0 LCP: Event[Receive ConfReq+] State[REQsent to
ACKsent]
Jun 20 03:01:59.407: Se0/0/0 PPP: I pkt type 0xC021, datagramsize 14 link[ppp]
Jun 20 03:01:59.407: Se0/0/0 LCP: I CONFACK [ACKsent] id 1 len 10
Jun 20 03:01:59.407: Se0/0/0 LCP:    MagicNumber 0x8D0EAC44 (0x05068D0EAC44)
Jun 20 03:01:59.407: Se0/0/0 LCP: Event[Receive ConfAck] State[ACKsent to Open]
Jun 20 03:01:59.439: Se0/0/0 PPP: Phase is FORWARDING, Attempting Forward
Jun 20 03:01:59.439: Se0/0/0 LCP: State is Open
Jun 20 03:01:59.439: Se0/0/0 PPP: Phase is ESTABLISHING, Finish LCP
Jun 20 03:01:59.439: %LINEPROTO-5-UPDOWN: Line protocol on Interface
Serial0/0/0, changed state to up
Jun 20 03:01:59.439: Se0/0/0 PPP: Outbound cdp packet dropped, line protocol
not up
Jun 20 03:01:59.439: Se0/0/0 PPP: Phase is UP
Jun 20 03:01:59.439: Se0/0/0 IPCP: Protocol configured, start CP.
state[Initial]
Jun 20 03:01:59.439: Se0/0/0 IPCP: Event[OPEN] State[Initial to Starting]
Jun 20 03:01:59.439: Se0/0/0 IPCP: O CONFREQ [Starting] id 1 len 10
Jun 20 03:01:59.439: Se0/0/0 IPCP:    Address 10.1.1.1 (0x03060A010101)
Jun 20 03:01:59.439: Se0/0/0 IPCP: Event[UP] State[Starting to REQsent]
Jun 20 03:01:59.439: Se0/0/0 CDPCP: Protocol configured, start CP.
state[Initial]
<output omitted>
Jun 20 03:01:59.471: Se0/0/0 Added to neighbor route AVL tree: topoid 0,
address 10.1.1.2
```

```
Jun 20 03:01:59.471: Se0/0/0 IPCP: Install route to 10.1.1.2
Jun 20 03:01:59.471: Se0/0/0 PPP: O pkt type 0x0021, datagramsize 80
Jun 20 03:01:59.479: Se0/0/0 PPP: I pkt type 0x0021, datagramsize 80 link[ip]
Jun 20 03:01:59.479: Se0/0/0 PPP: O pkt type 0x0021, datagramsize 84
Jun 20 03:01:59.483: Se0/0/0 PPP: I pkt type 0x0021, datagramsize 84 link[ip]
Jun 20 03:01:59.483: Se0/0/0 PPP: O pkt type 0x0021, datagramsize 68
Jun 20 03:01:59.491: Se0/0/0 PPP: I pkt type 0x0021, datagramsize 68 link[ip]
Jun 20 03:01:59.491: Se0/0/0 PPP: O pkt type 0x0021, datagramsize 148
Jun 20 03:01:59.511: Se0/0/0 PPP: I pkt type 0x0021, datagramsize 148 link[ip]
Jun 20 03:01:59.511: %OSPF-5-ADJCHG:Process 1, Nbr 209.165.200.225 on
Serial0/0/0 from LOADING to FULL, Loading Done
Jun 20 03:01:59.511: Se0/0/0 PPP: O pkt type 0x0021, datagramsize 68
Jun 20 03:01:59.519: Se0/0/0 PPP: I pkt type 0x0021, datagramsize 60 link[ip]
```

h. Observe the debug PPP messages from the Central router as the Branch1 and Central
    routers establish a connection.

```
Jun 20 03:01:59.393: Se0/0/0 PPP: I pkt type 0xC021, datagramsize 14 link[ppp]
Jun 20 03:01:59.393: Se0/0/0 LCP: I CONFREQ [Open] id 1 len 10
Jun 20 03:01:59.393: Se0/0/0 LCP:    MagicNumber 0x8D0EAC44 (0x05068D0EAC44)
Jun 20 03:01:59.393: Se0/0/0 PPP DISC: PPP Renegotiating
Jun 20 03:01:59.393: PPP: NET STOP send to AAA.
Jun 20 03:01:59.393: Se0/0/0 LCP: Event[LCP Reneg] State[Open to Open]
Jun 20 03:01:59.393: Se0/0/0 IPCP: Event[DOWN] State[Open to Starting]
Jun 20 03:01:59.393: Se0/0/0 IPCP: Event[CLOSE] State[Starting to Initial]
Jun 20 03:01:59.393: Se0/0/0 CDPCP: Event[DOWN] State[Open to Starting]
Jun 20 03:01:59.393: Se0/0/0 CDPCP: Event[CLOSE] State[Starting to Initial]
Jun 20 03:01:59.393: Se0/0/0 LCP: Event[DOWN] State[Open to Starting]
Jun 20 03:01:59.393: %LINEPROTO-5-UPDOWN: Line protocol on Interface
Serial0/0/0, changed state to down
Jun 20 03:01:59.393: Se0/0/0 PPP: Outbound cdp packet dropped, NCP not negoti-
ated
.Jun 20 03:01:59.393: Se0/0/0 PPP: Phase is DOWN
.Jun 20 03:01:59.393: Se0/0/0 Deleted neighbor route from AVL tree: topoid 0,
address 10.1.1.1
.Jun 20 03:01:59.393: Se0/0/0 IPCP: Remove route to 10.1.1.1
.Jun 20 03:01:59.393: %OSPF-5-ADJCHG: Process 1, Nbr 192.168.1.1 on Serial0/0/0
from FULL to DOWN, Neighbor Down: Interface down or detached
.Jun 20 03:01:59.397: PPP: Alloc Context [29F9F32C]
.Jun 20 03:01:59.397: ppp38 PPP: Phase is ESTABLISHING
.Jun 20 03:01:59.397: Se0/0/0 PPP: Using default call direction
.Jun 20 03:01:59.397: Se0/0/0 PPP: Treating connection as a dedicated line
<output omitted>
.Jun 20 03:01:59.401: Se0/0/0 LCP:    MagicNumber 0x73B4F1AF (0x050673B4F1AF)
.Jun 20 03:01:59.401: Se0/0/0 LCP: Event[Receive ConfAck] State[ACKsent to
Open]
.Jun 20 03:01:59.433: Se0/0/0 PPP: Phase is FORWARDING, Attempting Forward
.Jun 20 03:01:59.433: Se0/0/0 LCP: State is Open
.Jun 20 03:01:59.433: Se0/0/0 PPP: I pkt type 0x8021, datagramsize 14 link[ip]
.Jun 20 03:01:59.433: Se0/0/0 PPP: Queue IPCP code[1] id[1]
.Jun 20 03:01:59.433: Se0/0/0 PPP: I pkt type 0x8207, datagramsize 8 link[cdp]
.Jun 20 03:01:59.433: Se0/0/0 PPP: Discarded CDPCP code[1] id[1]
.Jun 20 03:01:59.433: Se0/0/0 PPP: Phase is ESTABLISHING, Finish LCP
.Jun 20 03:01:59.433: %LINEPROTO-5-UPDOWN: Line protocol on Interface
```

```
Serial0/0/0, changed state to up
.Jun 20 03:01:59.433: Se0/0/0 PPP: Outbound cdp packet dropped, line protocol
not up
.Jun 20 03:01:59.433: Se0/0/0 PPP: Phase is UP
.Jun 20 03:01:59.433: Se0/0/0 IPCP: Protocol configured, start CP.
state[Initial]
.Jun 20 03:01:59.433: Se0/0/0 IPCP: Event[OPEN] State[Initial to Starting]
.Jun 20 03:01:59.433: Se0/0/0 IPCP: O CONFREQ [Starting] id 1 len 10
.Jun 20 03:01:59.433: Se0/0/0 IPCP:    Address 10.1.1.2 (0x03060A010102)
.Jun 20 03:01:59.433: Se0/0/0 IPCP: Event[UP] State[Starting to REQsent]
.Jun 20 03:01:59.433: Se0/0/0 CDPCP: Protocol configured, start CP.
state[Initial]
.Jun 20 03:01:59.433: Se0/0/0 CDPCP: Event[OPEN] State[Initial to Starting]
.Jun 20 03:01:59.433: Se0/0/0 CDPCP: O CONFREQ [Starting] id 1 len 4
.Jun 20 03:01:59.433: Se0/0/0 CDPCP: Event[UP] State[Starting to REQsent]
<output omitted>
.Jun 20 03:01:59.465: Se0/0/0 IPCP: State is Open
.Jun 20 03:01:59.465: Se0/0/0 Added to neighbor route AVL tree: topoid 0,
address 10.1.1.1
.Jun 20 03:01:59.465: Se0/0/0 IPCP: Install route to 10.1.1.1
.Jun 20 03:01:59.465: Se0/0/0 PPP: O pkt type 0x0021, datagramsize 80
.Jun 20 03:01:59.465: Se0/0/0 PPP: I pkt type 0x0021, datagramsize 80 link[ip]
.Jun 20 03:01:59.469: Se0/0/0 PPP: O pkt type 0x0021, datagramsize 84
.Jun 20 03:01:59.477: Se0/0/0 PPP: I pkt type 0x0021, datagramsize 84 link[ip]
.Jun 20 03:01:59.477: Se0/0/0 PPP: O pkt type 0x0021, datagramsize 68
.Jun 20 03:01:59.481: Se0/0/0 PPP: I pkt type 0x0021, datagramsize 68 link[ip]
.Jun 20 03:01:59.489: Se0/0/0 PPP: I pkt type 0x0021, datagramsize 148 link[ip]
.Jun 20 03:01:59.493: Se0/0/0 PPP: O pkt type 0x0021, datagramsize 148
.Jun 20 03:01:59.505: Se0/0/0 PPP: I pkt type 0x0021, datagramsize 68 link[ip]
.Jun 20 03:01:59.505: Se0/0/0 PPP: O pkt type 0x0021, datagramsize 60
.Jun 20 03:01:59.517: Se0/0/0 PPP: I pkt type 0x0021, datagramsize 88 link[ip]
.Jun 20 03:01:59.517: %OSPF-5-ADJCHG: Process 1, Nbr 192.168.1.1 on Serial0/0/0
from LOADING to FULL, Loading Done
.Jun 20 03:01:59.561: Se0/0/0 PPP: O pkt type 0x0021, datagramsize 80
.Jun 20 03:01:59.569: Se0/0/0 PPP: I pkt type 0x0021, datagramsize 80 link[ip]
Jun 20 03:02:01.445: Se0/0/0 PPP: I pkt type 0x8207, datagramsize 8 link[cdp]
Jun 20 03:02:01.445: Se0/0/0 CDPCP: I CONFREQ [ACKrcvd] id 2 len 4
Jun 20 03:02:01.445: Se0/0/0 CDPCP: O CONFACK [ACKrcvd] id 2 len 4
Jun 20 03:02:01.445: Se0/0/0 CDPCP: Event[Receive ConfReq+] State[ACKrcvd to
Open]
Jun 20 03:02:01.449: Se0/0/0 CDPCP: State is Open
Jun 20 03:02:01.561: Se0/0/0 PPP: O pkt type 0x0021, datagramsize 80
Jun 20 03:02:01.569: Se0/0/0 PPP: I pkt type 0x0021, datagramsize 80 link[ip]
Jun 20 03:02:02.017: Se0/0/0 PPP: O pkt type 0x0021, datagramsize 68
Jun 20 03:02:02.897: Se0/0/0 PPP: I pkt type 0x0021, datagramsize 112 link[ip]
Jun 20 03:02:03.561: Se0/0/0 PPP: O pkt type 0x0021, datagramsize 80
```

From the debug message, what phases does PPP go through when the other end of the
serial link on the Central router is configured with PPP encapsulation?

What happens when PPP encapsulation is configured on each end of the serial link?

_____

i. Issue the **undebug all** (or **u all**) command on the Branch1 and Central routers to turn off all debugging on both routers.

j. Issue the **show ip interface brief** command on the Branch1 and Central routers after the network converges. What is the status for interface S0/0/0 on both routers?

_____

k. Verify that the interface S0/0/0 on both Branch1 and Central routers are configured for PPP encapsulation.

Record the command to verify the PPP encapsulation in the space provided below.

_____

l. Change the serial encapsulation for the link between the Central and Branch3 routers to PPP encapsulation.

```
Central(config)# interface s0/0/1
Central(config-if)# encapsulation ppp
Central(config-if)#
Jun 20 03:17:15.933: %OSPF-5-ADJCHG: Process 1, Nbr 192.168.3.1 on Serial0/0/1
from FULL to DOWN, Neighbor Down: Interface down or detached
Jun 20 03:17:17.933: %LINEPROTO-5-UPDOWN: Line protocol on Interface
Serial0/0/1, changed state to down
Jun 20 03:17:23.741: %LINEPROTO-5-UPDOWN: Line protocol on Interface
Serial0/0/1, changed state to up
Jun 20 03:17:23.825: %OSPF-5-ADJCHG: Process 1, Nbr 192.168.3.1 on Serial0/0/1
from LOADING to FULL, Loading Done


Branch3(config)# interface s0/0/1
Branch3(config-if)# encapsulation ppp
Branch3(config-if)#
Jun 20 03:17:21.744: %OSPF-5-ADJCHG: Process 1, Nbr 209.165.200.225 on
Serial0/0/1 from FULL to DOWN, Neighbor Down: Interface down or detached
Jun 20 03:17:21.948: %LINEPROTO-5-UPDOWN: Line protocol on Interface
Serial0/0/1, changed state to down
.Jun 20 03:17:21.964: %LINEPROTO-5-UPDOWN: Line protocol on Interface
Serial0/0/1, changed state to up
.Jun 20 03:17:23.812: %OSPF-5-ADJCHG: Process 1, Nbr 209.165.200.225 on
Serial0/0/1 from LOADING to FULL, Loading Done
```

m. Verify that end-to-end connectivity is restored before continuing to Part 3.

Part 3: Configure PPP CHAP Authentication

Step 1. Verify that PPP encapsulation is configured on all serial interfaces.

Record the command used to verify that PPP encapsulation is configured.

_____

Step 2. Configure PPP CHAP authentication for the link between the Central router and the Branch3 router.

    a. Configure a username for CHAP authentication.

```
Central(config)# username Branch3 password cisco
Branch3(config)# username Central password cisco
```

    b. Issue the **debug ppp** commands on the Branch3 router to observe the process, which is associated with authentication.

```
Branch3# debug ppp negotiation
PPP protocol negotiation debugging is on
Branch3# debug ppp packet
PPP packet display debugging is on
```

    c. Configure the interface S0/0/1 on Branch3 for CHAP authentication.

```
Branch3(config)# interface s0/0/1
Branch3(config-if)# ppp authentication chap
```

    d. Examine the debug PPP messages on the Branch3 router during the negotiation with the Central router.

```
Branch3(config-if)#
Jun 20 04:25:02.079: Se0/0/1 PPP DISC: Authentication configuration changed
Jun 20 04:25:02.079: PPP: NET STOP send to AAA.
Jun 20 04:25:02.079: Se0/0/1 IPCP: Event[DOWN] State[Open to Starting]
Jun 20 04:25:02.079: Se0/0/1 IPCP: Event[CLOSE] State[Starting to Initial]
Jun 20 04:25:02.079: Se0/0/1 CDPCP: Event[DOWN] State[Open to Starting]
Jun 20 04:25:02.079: Se0/0/1 CDPCP: Event[CLOSE] State[Starting to Initial]
Jun 20 04:25:02.079: Se0/0/1 LCP: Event[DOWN] State[Open to Starting]
Jun 20 04:25:02.079: %LINEPROTO-5-UPDOWN: Line protocol on Interface
Serial0/0/1, changed state to down
Jun 20 04:25:02.079: Se0/0/1 PPP: Outbound cdp packet dropped, NCP not
negotiated
.Jun 20 04:25:02.079: Se0/0/1 PPP: Phase is DOWN
.Jun 20 04:25:02.079: Se0/0/1 Deleted neighbor route from AVL tree: topoid 0,
address 10.2.2.2
.Jun 20 04:25:02.079: Se0/0/1 IPCP: Remove route to 10.2.2.2
.Jun 20 04:25:02.079: %OSPF-5-ADJCHG: Process 1, Nbr 209.165.200.225 on
Serial0/0/1 from FULL to DOWN, Neighbor Down: Interface down or detached
.Jun 20 04:25:02.083: PPP: Alloc Context [29F4DA8C]
.Jun 20 04:25:02.083: ppp73 PPP: Phase is ESTABLISHING
.Jun 20 04:25:02.083: Se0/0/1 PPP: Using default call direction
.Jun 20 04:25:02.083: Se0/0/1 PPP: Treating connection as a dedicated line
.Jun 20 04:25:02.083: Se0/0/1 PPP: Session handle[2700004D] Session id[73]
<output omitted>
.Jun 20 04:25:02.091: Se0/0/1 PPP: I pkt type 0xC021, datagramsize 19 link[ppp]
.Jun 20 04:25:02.091: Se0/0/1 LCP: I CONFACK [ACKsent] id 1 len 15
.Jun 20 04:25:02.091: Se0/0/1 LCP:    AuthProto CHAP (0x0305C22305)
.Jun 20 04:25:02.091: Se0/0/1 LCP:    MagicNumber 0xF7B20F10 (0x0506F7B20F10)
.Jun 20 04:25:02.091: Se0/0/1 LCP: Event[Receive ConfAck] State[ACKsent to
Open]
.Jun 20 04:25:02.123: Se0/0/1 PPP: Phase is AUTHENTICATING, by this end
.Jun 20 04:25:02.123: Se0/0/1 CHAP: O CHALLENGE id 1 len 28 from "Branch3"
.Jun 20 04:25:02.123: Se0/0/1 LCP: State is Open
.Jun 20 04:25:02.127: Se0/0/1 PPP: I pkt type 0xC223, datagramsize 32 link[ppp]
```

```
.Jun 20 04:25:02.127: Se0/0/1 CHAP: I RESPONSE id 1 len 28 from "Central"
.Jun 20 04:25:02.127: Se0/0/1 PPP: Phase is FORWARDING, Attempting Forward
.Jun 20 04:25:02.127: Se0/0/1 PPP: Phase is AUTHENTICATING, Unauthenticated
User
.Jun 20 04:25:02.127: Se0/0/1 PPP: Sent CHAP LOGIN Request
.Jun 20 04:25:02.127: Se0/0/1 PPP: Received LOGIN Response PASS
.Jun 20 04:25:02.127: Se0/0/1 IPCP: Authorizing CP
.Jun 20 04:25:02.127: Se0/0/1 IPCP: CP stalled on event[Authorize CP]
.Jun 20 04:25:02.127: Se0/0/1 IPCP: CP unstall
.Jun 20 04:25:02.127: Se0/0/1 PPP: Phase is FORWARDING, Attempting Forward
.Jun 20 04:25:02.135: Se0/0/1 PPP: Phase is AUTHENTICATING, Authenticated User
.Jun 20 04:25:02.135: Se0/0/1 CHAP: O SUCCESS id 1 len 4
.Jun 20 04:25:02.135: %LINEPROTO-5-UPDOWN: Line protocol on Interface
Serial0/0/1, changed state to up
.Jun 20 04:25:02.135: Se0/0/1 PPP: Outbound cdp packet dropped, line protocol
not up
.Jun 20 04:25:02.135: Se0/0/1 PPP: Phase is UP
.Jun 20 04:25:02.135: Se0/0/1 IPCP: Protocol configured, start CP.
state[Initial]
.Jun 20 04:25:02.135: Se0/0/1 IPCP: Event[OPEN] State[Initial to Starting]
.Jun 20 04:25:02.135: Se0/0/1 IPCP: O CONFREQ [Starting] id 1 len 10
<output omitted>
.Jun 20 04:25:02.143: Se0/0/1 CDPCP: I CONFACK [ACKsent] id 1 len 4
.Jun 20 04:25:02.143: Se0/0/1 CDPCP: Event[Receive ConfAck] State[ACKsent to
Open]
.Jun 20 04:25:02.155: Se0/0/1 IPCP: State is Open
.Jun 20 04:25:02.155: Se0/0/1 CDPCP: State is Open
.Jun 20 04:25:02.155: Se0/0/1 Added to neighbor route AVL tree: topoid 0,
address 10.2.2.2
.Jun 20 04:25:02.155: Se0/0/1 IPCP: Install route to 10.2.2.2
.Jun 20 04:25:02.155: Se0/0/1 PPP: O pkt type 0x0021, datagramsize 80
.Jun 20 04:25:02.155: Se0/0/1 PPP: I pkt type 0x0021, datagramsize 80 link[ip]
.Jun 20 04:25:02.155: Se0/0/1 PPP: O pkt type 0x0021, datagramsize 84
.Jun 20 04:25:02.167: Se0/0/1 PPP: I pkt type 0x0021, datagramsize 84 link[ip]
.Jun 20 04:25:02.167: Se0/0/1 PPP: O pkt type 0x0021, datagramsize 68
.Jun 20 04:25:02.171: Se0/0/1 PPP: I pkt type 0x0021, datagramsize 68 link[ip]
.Jun 20 04:25:02.171: Se0/0/1 PPP: O pkt type 0x0021, datagramsize 148
.Jun 20 04:25:02.191: Se0/0/1 PPP: I pkt type 0x0021, datagramsize 148 link[ip]
.Jun 20 04:25:02.191: %OSPF-5-ADJCHG: Process 1, Nbr 209.165.200.225 on
Serial0/0/1 from LOADING to FULL, Loading Done
.Jun 20 04:25:02.191: Se0/0/1 PPP: O pkt type 0x0021, datagramsize 68
.Jun 20 04:25:02.571: Se0/0/1 PPP: O pkt type 0x0021, datagramsize 80
.Jun 20 04:25:03.155: Se0/0/1 PPP: I pkt type 0x0207, datagramsize 333
link[cdp]
.Jun 20 04:25:03.155: Se0/0/1 PPP: O pkt type 0x0207, datagramsize 339
.Jun 20 04:25:04.155: Se0/0/1 PPP: O pkt type 0x0207, datagramsize 339
```

From the PPP debug messages, what phases did the Branch3 router go through before the link is up with the Central router?

_____

_____

e. Issue the **debug ppp authentication** command to observe the CHAP authentication messages on the Central router.

```
Central# debug ppp authentication
PPP authentication debugging is on
```

f. Configure CHAP authentication on S0/0/1 on the Central router.

_____

_____

g. Observe the debug PPP messages relating to CHAP authentication on the Central router.

```
Central(config-if)#
.Jun 20 05:05:16.057: %LINEPROTO-5-UPDOWN: Line protocol on Interface
Serial0/0/1, changed state to down
.Jun 20 05:05:16.061: %OSPF-5-ADJCHG: Process 1, Nbr 192.168.3.1 on Serial0/0/1
from FULL to DOWN, Neighbor Down: Interface down or detached
.Jun 20 05:05:16.061: Se0/0/1 PPP: Using default call direction
.Jun 20 05:05:16.061: Se0/0/1 PPP: Treating connection as a dedicated line
.Jun 20 05:05:16.061: Se0/0/1 PPP: Session handle[12000078] Session id[112]
.Jun 20 05:05:16.081: Se0/0/1 CHAP: O CHALLENGE id 1 len 28 from "Central"
.Jun 20 05:05:16.089: Se0/0/1 CHAP: I CHALLENGE id 1 len 28 from "Branch3"
.Jun 20 05:05:16.089: Se0/0/1 PPP: Sent CHAP SENDAUTH Request
.Jun 20 05:05:16.089: Se0/0/1 PPP: Received SENDAUTH Response PASS
.Jun 20 05:05:16.089: Se0/0/1 CHAP: Using hostname from configured hostname
.Jun 20 05:05:16.089: Se0/0/1 CHAP: Using password from AAA
.Jun 20 05:05:16.089: Se0/0/1 CHAP: O RESPONSE id 1 len 28 from "Central"
.Jun 20 05:05:16.093: Se0/0/1 CHAP: I RESPONSE id 1 len 28 from "Branch3"
.Jun 20 05:05:16.093: Se0/0/1 PPP: Sent CHAP LOGIN Request
.Jun 20 05:05:16.093: Se0/0/1 PPP: Received LOGIN Response PASS
.Jun 20 05:05:16.093: Se0/0/1 CHAP: O SUCCESS id 1 len 4
.Jun 20 05:05:16.097: Se0/0/1 CHAP: I SUCCESS id 1 len 4
.Jun 20 05:05:16.097: %LINEPROTO-5-UPDOWN: Line protocol on Interface
Serial0/0/1, changed state to up
.Jun 20 05:05:16.165: %OSPF-5-ADJCHG: Process 1, Nbr 192.168.3.1 on Serial0/0/1
from LOADING to FULL, Loading Done
```

h. Issue the **undebug all** (or **u all**) command on the Central and Branch3 routers to turn off all debugging.

```
Central# undebug all
All possible debugging has been turned off
```

Step 3. Intentionally break the serial link configured with authentication.

a. On the Central router, configure a username for use with Branch1. Assign **cisco** as the password.

```
Central(config)# username Branch1 password cisco
```

b. On the Central and Branch1 routers, configure CHAP authentication on interface S0/0/0. What is happening with the interface?

_____

_____

Note: To speed up the process, shut down the interface and enable it again.

c. Use a **debug ppp negotiation** command to examine what is happening.

```
Central# debug ppp negotiation
PPP protocol negotiation debugging is on
Central(config-if)#
.Jun 20 05:25:26.229: Se0/0/0 PPP: Missed a Link-Up transition, starting PPP
.Jun 20 05:25:26.229: Se0/0/0 PPP: Processing FastStart message
.Jun 20 05:25:26.229: PPP: Alloc Context [29F9F32C]
.Jun 20 05:25:26.229: ppp145 PPP: Phase is ESTABLISHING
.Jun 20 05:25:26.229: Se0/0/0 PPP: Using default call direction
.Jun 20 05:25:26.229: Se0/0/0 PPP: Treating connection as a dedicated line
.Jun 20 05:25:26.229: Se0/0/0 PPP: Session handle[6000009C] Session id[145]
.Jun 20 05:25:26.229: Se0/0/0 LCP: Event[OPEN] State[Initial to Starting]
.Jun 20 05:25:26.229: Se0/0/0 LCP: O CONFREQ [Starting] id 1 len 15
.Jun 20 05:25:26.229: Se0/0/0 LCP:    AuthProto CHAP (0x0305C22305)
.Jun 20 05:25:26.229: Se0/0/0 LCP:    MagicNumber 0x74385C31 (0x050674385C31)
.Jun 20 05:25:26.229: Se0/0/0 LCP: Event[UP] State[Starting to REQsent]
.Jun 20 05:25:26.229: Se0/0/0 LCP: I CONFREQ [REQsent] id 1 len 10
.Jun 20 05:25:26.229: Se0/0/0 LCP:    MagicNumber 0x8D920101 (0x05068D920101)
.Jun 20 05:25:26.229: Se0/0/0 LCP: O CONFACK [REQsent] id 1 len 10
.Jun 20 05:25:26.229: Se0/0/0 LCP:    MagicNumber 0x8D920101 (0x05068D920101)
.Jun 20 05:25:26.229: Se0/0/0 LCP: Event[Receive ConfReq+] State[REQsent to
ACKsent]
.Jun 20 05:25:26.233: Se0/0/0 LCP: I CONFACK [ACKsent] id 1 len 15
.Jun 20 05:25:26.233: Se0/0/0 LCP:    AuthProto CHAP (0x0305C22305)
.Jun 20 05:25:26.233: Se0/0/0 LCP:    MagicNumber 0x74385C31 (0x050674385C31)
.Jun 20 05:25:26.233: Se0/0/0 LCP: Event[Receive ConfAck] State[ACKsent to
Open]
.Jun 20 05:25:26.261: Se0/0/0 PPP: Phase is AUTHENTICATING, by this end
.Jun 20 05:25:26.261: Se0/0/0 CHAP: O CHALLENGE id 1 len 28 from "Central"
.Jun 20 05:25:26.261: Se0/0/0 LCP: State is Open
.Jun 20 05:25:26.265: Se0/0/0 LCP: I TERMREQ [Open] id 2 len 4
.Jun 20 05:25:26.265: Se0/0/0 PPP DISC: Received LCP TERMREQ from peer
.Jun 20 05:25:26.265: PPP: NET STOP send to AAA.
.Jun 20 05:25:26.265: Se0/0/0 PPP: Phase is TERMINATING
.Jun 20 05:25:26.265: Se0/0/0 LCP: O TERMACK [Open] id 2 len 4
.Jun 20 05:25:26.265: Se0/0/0 LCP: Event[Receive TermReq] State[Open to
Stopping]
.Jun 20 05:25:26.265: Se0/0/0 PPP: Sending cstate DOWN notification
.Jun 20 05:25:26.265: Se0/0/0 PPP: Processing CstateDown message
.Jun 20 05:25:26.265: Se0/0/0 LCP: Event[CLOSE] State[Stopping to Closing]
.Jun 20 05:25:26.265: Se0/0/0 LCP: Event[DOWN] State[Closing to Initial]
.Jun 20 05:25:26.265: Se0/0/0 PPP: Phase is DOWN
```

Explain what is causing the link to terminate. Correct the issue and document the command issued to correct the issue in the space provided below.

_____

_____

_____

    d.   Issue the **undebug all** command on all routers to turn off debugging.

    e.   Verify end-to-end connectivity.

Reflection

1. What are the indicators that you may have a serial encapsulation mismatch on a serial link?

_____

2. What are the indicators that you may have an authentication mismatch on a serial link?

_____

Router Interface Summary Table

Router Interface Summary				
Router Model	**Ethernet Interface #1**	**Ethernet Interface #2**	**Serial Interface #1**	**Serial Interface #2**
1800	Fast Ethernet 0/0 (F0/0)	Fast Ethernet 0/1 (F0/1)	Serial 0/0/0 (S0/0/0)	Serial 0/0/1 (S0/0/1)
1900	Gigabit Ethernet 0/0 (G0/0)	Gigabit Ethernet 0/1 (G0/1)	Serial 0/0/0 (S0/0/0)	Serial 0/0/1 (S0/0/1)
2801	Fast Ethernet 0/0 (F0/0)	Fast Ethernet 0/1 (F0/1)	Serial 0/1/0 (S0/1/0)	Serial 0/1/1 (S0/1/1)
2811	Fast Ethernet 0/0 (F0/0)	Fast Ethernet 0/1 (F0/1)	Serial 0/0/0 (S0/0/0)	Serial 0/0/1 (S0/0/1)
2900	Gigabit Ethernet 0/0 (G0/0)	Gigabit Ethernet 0/1 (G0/1)	Serial 0/0/0 (S0/0/0)	Serial 0/0/1 (S0/0/1)

Note: To find out how the router is configured, look at the interfaces to identify the type of router and how many interfaces the router has. There is no way to effectively list all the combinations of configurations for each router class. This table includes identifiers for the possible combinations of Ethernet and Serial interfaces in the device. The table does not include any other type of interface, even though a specific router may contain one. An example of this might be an ISDN BRI interface. The string in parentheses is the legal abbreviation that can be used in Cisco IOS commands to represent the interface.

2.4.1.4 Packet Tracer–Troubleshooting PPP with Authentication

Topology

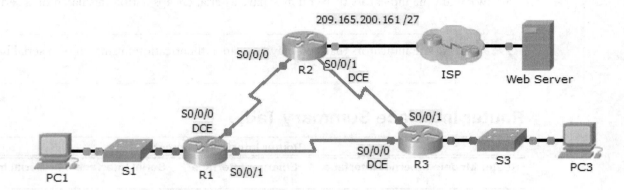

Addressing Table

Device	Interface	IP Address	Subnet Mask	Default Gateway
R1	G0/1	10.0.0.1	255.255.255.128	N/A
	S0/0/0	172.16.0.1	255.255.255.252	N/A
	S0/0/1	172.16.0.9	255.255.255.252	N/A
R2	G0/1	209.165.200.161	255.255.255.224	N/A
	S0/0/0	172.16.0.2	255.255.255.252	N/A
	S0/0/1	172.16.0.5	255.255.255.252	N/A
R3	G0/1	10.0.0.129	255.255.255.128	N/A
	S0/0/0	172.16.0.10	255.255.255.252	N/A
	S0/0/1	172.16.0.6	255.255.255.252	N/A
ISP	G0/1	209.165.200.162	255.255.255.224	N/A
PC1	NIC	10.0.0.10	255.255.255.128	10.0.0.1
PC3	NIC	10.0.0.139	255.255.255.128	10.0.0.129
Web Server	NIC	209.165.200.2	255.255.255.252	209.165.200.1

Objectives

Part 1: Diagnose and Repair the Physical Layer

Part 2: Diagnose and Repair the Data Link Layer

Part 3: Diagnose and Repair the Network Layer

Scenario

The routers at your company were configured by an inexperienced network engineer. Several errors in the configuration have resulted in connectivity issues. Your boss has asked you to troubleshoot and correct the configuration errors and document your work. Using your knowledge of PPP and standard testing methods, find and correct the errors. Make sure that all of the serial links use PPP CHAP authentication, and that all of the networks are reachable. The passwords are **cisco** and **class**.

Part 1: Diagnose and Repair the Physical Layer

Step 1.   Diagnose and repair the cabling.

    a.   Examine the **Addressing Table** to determine the location of all the connections.

    b.   Verify cables are connected as specified.

    c.   Diagnose and repair any inactive interfaces.

_____

_____

_____

_____

_____

_____

_____

_____

_____

_____

_____

_____

_____

_____

_____

_____

Part 2: Diagnose and Repair the Data Link Layer

Step 1.   Examine and set clock rates on the DCE equipment.

Examine the configuration of each router to verify that a clock rate has been set on appropriate interfaces. Set the clock rate of any serial interface that requires it.

_____

_____

Step 2. Examine the encapsulation on the DCE equipment.

All of the serial interfaces should be using PPP as the encapsulation type. Change the encapsulation type to PPP for any interface that is set otherwise.

_____

_____

_____

_____

_____

_____

Step 3. Examine and set CHAP usernames and passwords.

Examine each link to verify that routers are logging into each other correctly. All CHAP passwords are set to **cisco**. Use the **debug ppp authentication** command if needed. Correct or set any usernames and passwords that need it.

_____

_____

_____

_____

_____

_____

_____

_____

_____

_____

_____

_____

_____

_____

_____

Part 3: Diagnose and Repair the Network Layer

Step 1.   Verify the IP addressing.

Check IP addresses against the Addressing Table and ensure that they are in the correct subnet with their connecting interface. Correct any IP addresses that overlap, are on the wrong interface, have the wrong subnet address, or are set to the host or broadcast address.

_____

_____

_____

_____

_____

_____

_____

_____

_____

_____

_____

Step 2.   Verify full connectivity by tracing a path from **PC1** and **PC3** to the Web Server.

2.4.1.5 Lab–Troubleshooting Basic PPP with Authentication

Topology

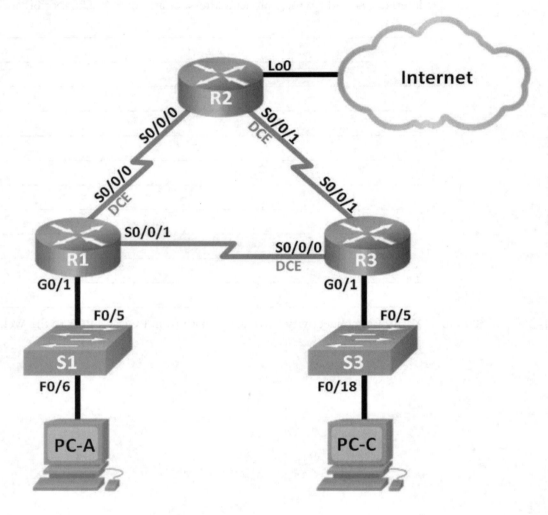

Addressing Table

Device	Interface	IP Address	Subnet Mask	Default Gateway
R1	G0/1	192.168.1.1	255.255.255.0	N/A
	S0/0/0 (DCE)	192.168.12.1	255.255.255.252	N/A
	S0/0/1	192.168.13.1	255.255.255.252	N/A
R2	Lo0	209.165.200.225	255.255.255.252	N/A
	S0/0/0	192.168.12.2	255.255.255.252	N/A
	S0/0/1 (DCE)	192.168.23.1	255.255.255.252	N/A
R3	G0/1	192.168.3.1	255.255.255.0	N/A
	S0/0/0 (DCE)	192.168.13.2	255.255.255.252	N/A
	S0/0/1	192.168.23.2	255.255.255.252	N/A

Device	Interface	IP Address	Subnet Mask	Default Gateway
PC-A	NIC	192.168.1.3	255.255.255.0	192.168.1.1
PC-C	NIC	192.168.3.3	255.255.255.0	192.168.3.1

Objectives

Part 1: Build the Network and Load Device Configurations

Part 2: Troubleshoot the Data Link Layer

Part 3: Troubleshoot the Network Layer

Background/Scenario

The routers at your company were configured by an inexperienced network engineer. Several errors in the configuration have resulted in connectivity issues. Your manager has asked you to troubleshoot and correct the configuration errors and document your work. Using your knowledge of PPP and standard testing methods, find and correct the errors. Ensure that all of the serial links use PPP CHAP authentication, and that all of the networks are reachable.

Note: The routers used with CCNA hands-on labs are Cisco 1941 Integrated Services Routers (ISRs) with Cisco IOS Release 15.2(4)M3 (universalk9 image). The switches used are Cisco Catalyst 2960s with Cisco IOS Release 15.0(2) (lanbasek9 image). Other routers, switches, and Cisco IOS versions can be used. Depending on the model and Cisco IOS version, the commands available and output produced might vary from what is shown in the labs. Refer to the Router Interface Summary Table at the end of this lab for the correct interface identifiers.

Note: Make sure that the routers and switches have been erased and have no startup configurations. If you are unsure, contact your instructor.

Required Resources

- 3 Routers (Cisco 1941 with Cisco IOS Release 15.2(4)M3 universal image or comparable)
- 2 Switches (Cisco 2960 with Cisco IOS Release 15.0(2) lanbasek9 image or comparable)
- 2 PCs (Windows with a terminal emulation program, such as Tera Term)
- Console cables to configure the Cisco IOS devices via the console ports
- Ethernet and serial cables as shown in the topology

Part 1: Build the Network and Load Device Configurations

In Part 1, you will set up the network topology, configure basic settings on the PC hosts, and load configurations on the routers.

Step 1.   Cable the network as shown in the topology.

Step 2.   Configure the PC hosts.

Step 3.   Load router configurations.

Load the following configurations into the appropriate router. All routers have the same passwords. The privileged EXEC mode password is **class**. The password for console and vty access is **cisco**. All serial interfaces should be configured with PPP encapsulation and authenticated with CHAP using the password of **chap123**.

Router R1 Configuration:

```
hostname R1
enable secret class
no ip domain lookup
banner motd #Unauthorized Access is Prohibited!#
username R2 password chap123
username R3 password chap123
interface g0/1
 ip address 192.168.1.1 255.255.255.0
 no shutdown
interface s0/0/0
 ip address 192.168.12.1 255.255.255.252
 clock rate 128000
 encapsulation ppp
 ppp authentication chap
interface s0/0/1
 ip address 192.168.31.1 255.255.255.252
 encapsulation ppp
 ppp authentication pap
exit
router ospf 1
 router-id 1.1.1.1
 network 192.168.1.0 0.0.0.255 area 0
 network 192.168.12.0 0.0.0.3 area 0
 network 192.168.13.0 0.0.0.3 area 0
 passive-interface g0/1
 exit
line con 0
 password cisco
 logging synchronous
 login
line vty 0 4
 password cisco
 login
```

Router R2 Configuration:

```
hostname R2
enable secret class
no ip domain lookup
banner motd #Unauthorized Access is Prohibited!#
username R1 password chap123
username r3 password chap123
```

```
interface lo0
 ip address 209.165.200.225 255.255.255.252
interface s0/0/0
 ip address 192.168.12.2 255.255.255.252
 encapsulation ppp
 ppp authentication chap
 no shutdown
interface s0/0/1
 ip address 192.168.23.1 255.255.255.252
 clock rate 128000
 no shutdown
 exit
router ospf 1
 router-id 2.2.2.2
 network 192.168.12.0 0.0.0.3 area 0
 network 192.168.23.0 0.0.0.3 area 0
 default-information originate
 exit
ip route 0.0.0.0 0.0.0.0 loopback0
line con 0
 password cisco
 logging synchronous
 login
line vty 0 4
 password cisco
 login
```

Router R3 Configuration:

```
hostname R3
enable secret class
no ip domain lookup
banner motd #Unauthorized Access is Prohibited!#
username R2 password chap123
username R3 password chap123
interface g0/1
 ip address 192.168.3.1 255.255.255.0
 no shutdown
interface s0/0/0
 ip address 192.168.13.2 255.255.255.252
 clock rate 128000
 encapsulation ppp
 ppp authentication chap
 no shutdown
interface s0/0/1
 ip address 192.168.23.2 255.255.255.252
 encapsulation ppp
 ppp authentication chap
 no shutdown
 exit
router ospf 1
 router-id 3.3.3.3
```

```
            network 192.168.13.0 0.0.0.3 area 0
            network 192.168.23.0 0.0.0.3 area 0
            passive-interface g0/1
        line con 0
            password cisco
            logging synchronous
            login
        line vty 0 4
            password cisco
            login
```

Step 4.   Save your running configuration.

Part 2: Troubleshoot the Data Link Layer

In Part 2, you will use **show** commands to troubleshoot data link layer issues. Be sure to verify settings, such as clock rate, encapsulation, CHAP, and usernames/passwords.

Step 1.   Examine the R1 configuration.

   a.   Use the **show interfaces** command to determine whether PPP has been established on both serial links.

   From the **show interfaces** results for S0/0/0 and S0/0/1, what are possible issues with the PPP links?

   _____

   _____

   _____

   b.   Use the **debug ppp authentication** command to view real-time PPP authentication output during troubleshooting.

   ```
   R1# debug ppp authentication
   PPP authentication debugging is on
   ```

   c.   Use the **show run interface s0/0/0** command to examine the settings on S0/0/0.

   Resolve all problems found for S0/0/0. Record the commands used to correct the configuration.

   _____

   _____

   After correcting the issue, what information does the debug output provide?

   _____

   _____

d. Use the **show run interface s0/0/1** command to examine the settings on S0/0/1.

Resolve all problems found for S0/0/1. Record the commands used to correct the configuration.

_____

_____

_____

After correcting the issue, what information does the debug output provide?

_____

_____

_____

e. Use the **no debug ppp authentication** or **undebug all** command to turn off the debug PPP output.

f. Use the **show running-config | include username** command to verify the correct username and password configurations.

Resolve all problems found. Record the commands used to correct the configuration.

_____

Step 2. Examine the R2 configuration.

a. Use the **show interfaces** command to determine if PPP has been established on both serial links.

Have all links been established? _____

If the answer is no, which links need to be examined? What are the possible issues?

_____

_____

_____

b. Use the **show run interface** command to examine links that have not been established.

Resolve all problems found for the interfaces. Record the commands used to correct the configuration.

_____

_____

_____

c. Use the **show running-config | include username** command to verify the correct username and password configurations.

Resolve all problems found. Record the commands used to correct the configuration.

_____

_____

d. Use the **show ppp interface serial** command for the serial interface that you are troubleshooting.

Has the link been established? _____

Step 3. Examine the R3 configuration.

a. Use the **show interfaces** command to determine whether PPP has been established on both serial links.

Have all links been established? _____

If the answer is no, which links need to be examined? What are the possible issues?

_____

_____

b. Use the **show run interface** command to examine any serial link that has not been established.

Resolve all problems found on the interfaces. Record the commands used to correct the configuration.

_____

_____

c. Use the **show running-config | include username** command to verify the correct user-name and password configurations.

Resolve all problems found. Record the commands used to correct the configuration.

_____

_____

d. Use the **show interface** command to verify that serial links have been established.

e. Have all PPP links been established? _____

f. Can PC-A ping Lo0? _____

g. Can PC-A ping PC-C? _____

Note: It may be necessary to disable the PC firewall for pings between the PCs to succeed.

Part 3: Troubleshoot the Network Layer

In Part 3, you will verify that Layer 3 connectivity is established on all interfaces by examining IPv4 and OSPF configurations.

Step 1. Verify that the interfaces listed in the Addressing Table are active and configured with the correct IP address information.

Issue the **show ip interface brief** command on all routers to verify that the interfaces are in an up/up state.

Resolve all problems found. Record the commands used to correct the configuration.

_____

_____

Step 2. Verify OSPF Routing

Issue the **show ip protocols** command to verify that OSPF is running and that all networks are advertised.

Resolve all problems found. Record the commands used to correct the configuration.

_____

_____

Can PC-A ping PC-C? _____

If connectivity does not exist between all hosts, then continue troubleshooting to resolve any remaining issues.

Note: It may be necessary to disable the PC firewall for pings between the PCs to succeed.

Router Interface Summary Table

Router Interface Summary				
Router Model	**Ethernet Interface #1**	**Ethernet Interface #2**	**Serial Interface #1**	**Serial Interface #2**
1800	Fast Ethernet 0/0 (F0/0)	Fast Ethernet 0/1 (F0/1)	Serial 0/0/0 (S0/0/0)	Serial 0/0/1 (S0/0/1)
1900	Gigabit Ethernet 0/0 (G0/0)	Gigabit Ethernet 0/1 (G0/1)	Serial 0/0/0 (S0/0/0)	Serial 0/0/1 (S0/0/1)
2801	Fast Ethernet 0/0 (F0/0)	Fast Ethernet 0/1 (F0/1)	Serial 0/1/0 (S0/1/0)	Serial 0/1/1 (S0/1/1)
2811	Fast Ethernet 0/0 (F0/0)	Fast Ethernet 0/1 (F0/1)	Serial 0/0/0 (S0/0/0)	Serial 0/0/1 (S0/0/1)
2900	Gigabit Ethernet 0/0 (G0/0)	Gigabit Ethernet 0/1 (G0/1)	Serial 0/0/0 (S0/0/0)	Serial 0/0/1 (S0/0/1)

Note: To find out how the router is configured, look at the interfaces to identify the type of router and how many interfaces the router has. There is no way to effectively list all the combinations of configurations for each router class. This table includes identifiers for the possible combinations of Ethernet and Serial interfaces in the device. The table does not include any other type of interface, even though a specific router may contain one. An example of this might be an ISDN BRI interface. The string in parentheses is the legal abbreviation that can be used in Cisco IOS commands to represent the interface.

2.5.1.1 Class Activity–PPP Validation

Objective

Use **show** and **debug** commands to troubleshoot PPP.

Scenario

Three friends who are enrolled in the Cisco Networking Academy want to check their knowledge of PPP network configuration.

They set up a contest where each person will be tested on configuring PPP with defined PPP scenario requirements and varying options. Each person devises a different configuration scenario.

Below are some suggested scenarios:

Scenario 1

- Address the topology using IPv4.
- Configure PPP encapsulation with CHAP.
- Configure OSPF routing.
- Configure the clock to read today's date.
- Change the OSPF router priorities on both serial interfaces.

Scenario 2

- Address the topology using IPv6.
- Configure PPP encapsulation with PAP.
- Configure EIGRP routing.
- Configure the clock to read the current time.
- Place a description on both connected serial interfaces.

Scenario 3

- Address the topology using IPv6.
- Configure a Message of the Day.
- Configure PPP with CHAP.
- Configure OSPF routing.
- Configure the clock to read today's time and date.

Resources

- Packet Tracer software
- Stopwatch or timer

Step 1.   Open Packet Tracer.

     a.   Create a two-router topology with a serial connection.

     b.   Include one PC and switch attached to each router.

Step 2.   Complete the first scenario.

     a.   Start the assigned scenario.

     b.   The instructor calls the time when the scenario is completed; all students and groups must stop their configuration work at that time.

     c.   The instructor checks the validity of the completed scenario configuration.

          1)   The devices must be able to successfully ping from one end of the topology to the other.

          2)   All scenario options requested must be present in the final topology.

          3)   The instructor may ask you to prove your work by choosing different **show** and **debug** commands to display the configuration output.

     d.   Begin the same process for the second scenario assigned by the instructor.

          1)   Delete the configurations from the first scenario, but you can re-use the same configurations.

          2)   Complete Steps 1 and 2 again using the next scenario's requirements.

Packet Tracer
☐ Activity

2.5.1.2 Packet Tracer–Skills Integration Challenge

Topology

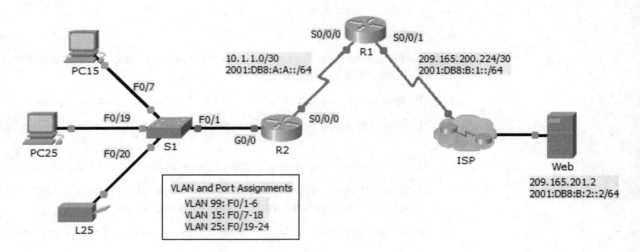

Addressing Table

Device	Interface	IPv4 Address	Subnet Mask	IPv4 and IPv6 Default Gateway
		IPv6 Address/Prefix		
R1	S0/0/0	10.1.1.2	255.255.255.252	N/A
		2001:DB8:A:A::2/64		FE80::1
	S0/0/1	209.165.200.226	255.255.255.252	N/A
		2001:DB8:B:1::2/64		FE80::1
R2	G0/0.1	192.168.1.193	255.255.255.224	N/A
		2001:DB8:A:1::1/64		FE80::2
	G0/0.15	192.168.1.1	255.255.255.128	N/A
		2001:DB8:A:15::1/64		FE80::2
	G0/0.25			N/A
		2001:DB8:A:25::1/64		FE80::2
	G0/0.99	192.168.1.225	255.255.255.224	N/A
		2001:DB8:A:99::1/64		FE80::2
	S0/0/0	10.1.1.1	255.255.255.252	N/A
		2001:DB8:A:A::1/64		FE80::2
S1	VLAN 99	192.168.1.226	255.255.255.224	192.168.1.225
PC15	NIC	192.168.1.2	255.255.255.128	192.168.1.1
		2001:DB8:A:15::2/64		FE80::2
PC25	NIC			
		2001:DB8:A:25::2/64		FE80::2
L25	NIC			
		2001:DB8:A:25::A/64		FE80::2

Background

This activity allows you to practice a variety of skills including configuring VLANs, PPP with CHAP, static and default routing, using IPv4 and IPv6. Due to the sheer number of graded elements, you can click **Check Results** and **Assessment Items** to see if you correctly entered a graded command. Use the **cisco** and **class** passwords to access privileged EXEC modes of the CLI for routers and switches.

Requirements

Addressing

- The addressing scheme uses the 192.168.1.0/24 address space. Additional address space is available between VLAN 15 and VLAN 1. VLAN 25 needs enough addresses for 50 hosts. Determine the subnet and complete the subnet table below.

VLAN	IPv4 Subnet Address	Subnet Mask	Hosts
1	192.168.1.192	255.255.255.224	20
15	192.168.1.0	255.255.255.128	100
25			50
99	192.168.1.224	255.255.255.224	20

- Complete the **Addressing Table** by assigning the following addresses to VLAN 25:
  - **R2 G0/0.25** - First IPv4 address
  - **PC25** - 2nd IPv4 address
  - **L25** - Last IPv4 address
- Configure IPv4 addressing on the necessary end devices.
- On **R2**, create and apply IPv4 and IPv6 addressing to the G0/0.25 subinterface.

VLANs

- On **S1**, create VLAN 86 and name it **BlackHole**.
- Configure **S1** ports in static mode with the following requirements:
  - **F0/1** is the native trunk for VLAN 99.
  - **F0/7 - F0/18** as access ports in VLAN 15.
  - **F0/19 - F0/24** as access ports in VLAN 25.
  - **G0/1 - 2** and **F0/2 - F0/6** are unused. They should be properly secured and assigned to the **BlackHole** VLAN.
- On **R2**, configure inter-VLAN routing. VLAN 99 is the native VLAN.

PPP

- Configure **R1** and **R2** to use PPP with CHAP for the shared link. The password for CHAP is **cisco**.

Routing

- On **R1**, configure IPv4 and IPv6 default routes using the appropriate exit interface.
- On **R2**, configure an IPv6 default route using the appropriate exit interface.
- Configure IPv4 OSPF using the following requirements:
    - Use process ID 1.
    - Routers **R1** and **R2** are in area 0.
    - **R1** uses router ID 1.1.1.1.
    - **R2** uses router ID 2.2.2.2.
    - Advertise specific subnets.
    - On **R1**, propagate the IPv4 default route created.
- Configure IPv6 OSPF using the following requirements:
    - Use process ID 1.
    - Routers **R1** and **R2** are in area 0.
    - Configure OSPF on appropriate interfaces on **R1** and **R2**.
    - **R1** uses router ID 1.1.1.1.
    - **R2** uses router ID 2.2.2.2.

Connectivity

- All devices should be able to ping the Web Server.

CHAPTER 3

Branch Connections

With the advent of broadband technologies like digital subscriber line (DSL) and cable, working from home has become a popular option for both employees and companies alike. Virtual private networks (VPN) allow workers to securely connect to the business from remote locations. There are several factors to consider when choosing a broadband solution. This chapter reviews DSL, cable, wireless, VPN, and the factors to consider when implementing broadband solutions. In addition, the protocols Generic Routing Encapsulation (GRE) and Border Gateway Protocol (BGP) are reviewed.

Broadband Connections

Depending on the location of the teleworker, connecting to the corporate network can be done in one of three ways: cable, DSL, or broadband wireless.

Cable

Cable broadband uses a coaxial cable that carries _____ signals across the network. What portion of the electromagnetic spectrum do these signals occupy?

_____

Traditionally, cable communication was one way. Modern cable systems now provide two-way communication. What three main telecommunication services are offered by today's cable companies?

_____

Two-way communications occur downstream in the 50- to 860-MHz range and upstream in the 5- to 42-MHz range.

The _____ is the international standard developed by CableLabs that cable operators use to provide Internet access over their existing _____ infrastructure.

What two types of equipment are required to send digital modem signals upstream and downstream on a cable system?

_____

_____

Match the definition on the left with a term on the right. Terms are only used once.

Definitions

   a. Combining both fiber-optic and coax cabling together into a hybrid cabling infrastructure

   b. Defines the communications and operation support interface that permits the addition of high-speed data transfer to a traditional cable TV system

   c. The direction of a signal transmission from the headend to subscribers

   d. Located in the headend (and communicates with CMs located in subscriber homes)

   e. The rate at which current (voltage) cycles (computed as the number of waves per second)

   f. The direction of a signal transmission from subscribers to the headend

Terms

___ CMTS

___ DOCSIS

___ Downstream

___ Frequency

___ HFC

___ Upstream

DSL

Digital subscriber line (DSL) technology takes advantage of the additional bandwidth available in telephone networks between 3 KHz and 1 MHz.

Briefly describe the two main types of DSL.

_____

_____

The local loop connection to the CO must be less than 3.39 miles (5.46 km).

What two components are required to provide a DSL connection to the teleworker?

_____

_____

_____

The analog voice and ADSL signals must be separated to avoid interference. What two devices can separate the signals?

_____

_____

Match the definition on the left with a term on the right. Terms are only used once.

Definitions

a. Located at the CO, a device that combines individual DSL connections from subscribers into one high-capacity link to an ISP

b. Sometimes referred to as the DSL modem, a device that connects the subscriber to the DSL network

c. The category of DSL technology that provides high-speed downstream data capacity value with a lower upstream capacity value

d. Device with one end connecting to a telephone device and the other end connecting to the telephony wall jack

e. Category of DSL technology that provides equal high-speed downstream and upstream data capacities

f. A means of providing high-speed connections over pre-existing installed copper wire infrastructure

Terms

___ ADSL

___ DSL

___ DSLAM

___ Microfilter

___ SDSL

___ Transceiver

Broadband Wireless

Of the three broadband technologies, wireless offers the largest variety of ways to connect. Whether from your laptop or from a smartphone, urban or rural, broadband wireless has a solution.

Match the definition on the left with a term on the right. Terms are only used once.

Definitions

a. Uses a point-to-multipoint topology to provide wireless cellular broadband access at speeds up to 1 Gbps

b. Newer and faster technology for high-speed cellular data (considered to be part of 4G)

c. Cellular broadband access that gets faster with each generation

d. Employs a mesh network with an access point at each node for 802.11 connections

e. A general term for Internet service from a mobile phone or any other mobile device that uses the same technology

f. Two-way satellite Internet using IP multicasting technology

Terms

___ 3G/4G Wireless

___ LTE

___ Municipal WiFi

___ VSAT

___ WiMAX

___ Wireless Internet

Select a Broadband Solution Connection

Ideally, a teleworker would have a fiber-optic cable directly connected to the home office. When selecting the broadband solution that is right for you, you want to consider several factors. In Table 3-1, indicate the factors for each broadband solution.

Table 3-1   Broadband Solutions: Factors to Consider

Factor to Consider	Cable	DSL	Fiber-to-the-Home	Cellular/Mobile	Wi-Fi Mesh	WiMAX	Satellite
Requires fiber installation directly to the home.							
Coverage is often an issue, bandwidth is limited, and data may not be unlimited.							
Bit rate is limited to 2 Mbps per subscriber, cell size is 1 to 2 km (1.25 mi).							
Bandwidth is shared by many users, and upstream data rates are often slow.							
Limited bandwidth that is distance sensitive, and the upstream rate is proportionally quite small compared to downstream rate.							
Expensive, limited capacity per subscriber; often provides access where no other access is possible.							
Most municipalities do not have a mesh network deployed; if it is available and the SOHO is in range, it is a viable option.							

PPPoE

The underlying data link protocol commonly used by Internet service providers (ISPs) to send and receive data across DSL links is PPP over Ethernet (PPPoE).

PPPoE Overview

For the ISP, what are the benefits of using PPP?

_____

_____

What are the three stages of evolution in teleworker connections from the home that use PPP?

_____

Configuring PPPoE

Although PPPoE configuration is beyond the scope of the course, understanding how PPPoE is implemented will help solidify your skills in configuring PPP.

The two steps to configure PPPoE are as follows:

Step 1.   Create a PPP tunnel using dialer interface with the following settings:

- Encapsulation is PPP.

- IP address is negotiated.

- MTU size is set to 1492. Why?

_____

_____

- Dialer interface is assigned a pool.

- CHAP authentication with username and password assigned by ISP.

Step 2.   Enable PPPoE on the interface attached to the DSL modem and assign it as a PPPoE client using the dialer pool defined in Step 1.

You can verify the dialer interface was assigned an IP address with the **show ip interface brief** command.

In Figure 3-1, the ISP router is already configured. Record the commands to configure the Customer router using the following CHAP information:

Figure 3-1   PPPoE Configuration Topology

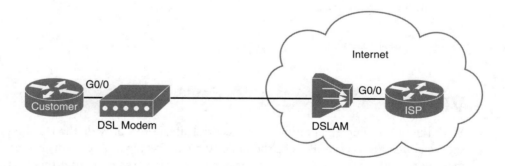

- Username is CustomerBob.
- Password is Bob$connect.

_____

_____

_____

_____

_____

_____

_____

_____

_____

_____

_____

_____

_____

If you want to configure this on lab equipment, connect two routers through a switch or with a cross-over cable and use the following configuration for ISP:

```
username CustomerBob password Bob$connect
!
bba-group pppoe global
 virtual-template 1
!
interface GigabitEthernet0/0
 no ip address
 pppoe enable group global
 no shutdown
!
interface Virtual-Template1
 mtu 1492
 ip address 64.100.1.254 255.255.255.0
 peer default ip address pool CUSTOMER_POOL
 ppp authentication chap callin
!
ip local pool CUSTOMER_POOL 64.100.1.1 64.100.1.253
```

VPNs

With the proper implementation at that central site, VPNs provide the flexibility of having safe and secure connections regardless of the underlying access technology. This is increasingly important as more users need or want access to their corporate networks no matter their current location.

Fundamentals of VPNs

VPNs are used to create a private tunnel over the Internet regardless of the WAN access option used to make the connection.

Briefly describe three different scenarios in which VPNs are a viable solution.

_____

_____

What is the difference between VPN and secure VPN?

_____

To implement a VPN, a VPN gateway is needed. List three devices that can serve as a VPN gateway.

_____

Briefly describe four benefits to using VPNs.

_____
_____
_____
_____
_____
_____

Types of VPNs

There are two main types of VPN networks. Site-to-site VPNs support connections where the two locations are permanent and contain more than one user. For example, a branch site or a business partner site most likely would benefit from a site-to-site VPN. Remote-access VPNs are best used for single user connection needs such as teleworkers and mobile users.

In Table 3-2, indicate the type of VPN described by each characteristic.

Table 3-2 Comparing Site-to-Site and Remote-Access VPNs

Characteristic	Site-to-Site VPN	Remote-Access VPNs
VPN is dynamically enabled when needed.		
Most likely uses VPN client software to establish VPN connection and encrypt data.		
Users have no knowledge of the VPN.		
Connects networks together through peer VPN gateways.		
Uses a client/server model.		
Connects teleworkers and mobile users.		
VPN connection is static.		

Dynamic Multipoint VPN (DMVPN) is a Cisco software solution for building multiple VPNs in an easy, dynamic, and scalable manner. Multiple branch VPNs can be connected easily to the central office in a hub-and-spoke topology. Spoke-to-spoke VPNs can be dynamically created as needed when branches offices need to communicate directly.

List and define the three main technologies that are used to create DMVPNs:

_____
_____
_____
_____
_____
_____

GRE

Generic routing encapsulation (GRE) is a site-to-site VPN tunneling protocol developed by Cisco. GRE can encapsulate a wide variety of protocol packet types inside IP tunnels.

Fundamentals of Generic Routing Encapsulation

List three protocols that GRE can encapsulate.

_____

Figure 3-2 shows the basic fields in a GRE encapsulated packet.

Figure 3-2   GRE Encapsulated Packet

Figure 3-3 shows the topology we will use to configure GRE later in this section. Notice how the protocol packet, IP, is encapsulated with GRE, then encapsulated in an IP packet for transport across the Internet. The inside IP packet is using private addressing and the outside IP packet is using public addressing.

Note: The public addressing is on the same subnet. This is uncommon on real networks. However, we are doing it here so that you can easily attach to routers and use this configuration for practice.

Figure 3-3   GRE Topology

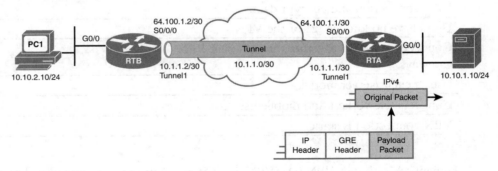

GRE is defined by IETF RFC _____. In the outer IP header, _____ is used in the Protocol field to indicate that a GRE header follows. In the GRE header, a Protocol _____ field specifies the OSI Layer 3 protocol that is encapsulated (IP in Figure 3-3). GRE is _____, meaning that it does not include any flow-control mechanisms. Also, GRE does not include any _____ mechanisms to protect the payload. The GRE header and additional IP header create at least _____ bytes of additional overhead for tunneled packets.

Configuring GRE Tunnels

In Figure 3-3 shown earlier, assume the physical interfaces on RTA and RTB are configured and active. Also assume that RTA is already configured with a GRE tunnel and OSPF routing. To configure GRE on RTB, complete the following steps:

Step 1. Create a tunnel interface using the **interface tunnel** *number* command. The interface numbers do not have to match between RTA and RTB.

Step 2. Configure an IP address for the tunnel interface. The two routers on the tunnel should use addresses from the same subnet. In our topology, the subnet is 10.1.1.0/30.

Step 3. Specify the tunnel's source IP address in the public part of the network with the **tunnel source** *ip-address* command. The IP address must match the other side's configuration for **tunnel destination** *ip-address*. For RTB, this address is the 64.100.1.2 IP address configured on its S0/0/0 interface.

Step 4. Specify the tunnel's destination IP address in the public part of the network with the **tunnel destination** *ip-address* command. The IP address must match the other side's **tunnel source** *ip-address*. For RTB, this address is the 64.100.1.1 IP address configured on RTA's S0/0/0.

Step 5. Configure routing to use the tunnel to advertise the private LANs at each site.

Note: These steps do not include configuring the **tunnel mode** command because the default, GRE IP, is what is needed here. However, in the future, the GRE tunnel will most likely be IPv6.

Using these steps, record the commands including the router prompt to configure RTB with a GRE tunnel to RTA.

_____

_____

_____

_____

_____

_____

_____

A number of commands can be used to verify the GRE tunnel is operational. Of course, the ultimate test is that PC1 should now be able to ping the server attached to the RTA LAN. If connectivity fails, use the following commands to troubleshoot the issue.

Record the commands and command filtering used to generate the following output.

```
RTB# _____

Neighbor ID    Pri   State        Dead Time    Address       Interface
64.100.1.1      0    FULL/  -     00:00:34     10.1.1.1      Tunnel1
RTB# _____
Tunnel1                  10.1.1.2        YES manual up              up
RTB# _____
Gateway of last resort is not set
```

```
        10.0.0.0/8 is variably subnetted, 5 subnets, 3 masks
O          10.10.1.0/24 [110/1001] via 10.1.1.1, 00:23:49, Tunnel1
RTB# _____
Tunnel1 is up, line protocol is up
  Hardware is Tunnel
  Internet address is 10.1.1.2/30
  MTU 17916 bytes, BW 100 Kbit/sec, DLY 50000 usec,
     reliability 255/255, txload 1/255, rxload 1/255
  Encapsulation TUNNEL, loopback not set
  Keepalive not set
  Tunnel source 64.100.1.2, destination 64.100.1.1
  Tunnel protocol/transport GRE/IP
    Key disabled, sequencing disabled
    Checksumming of packets disabled
  Tunnel TTL 255, Fast tunneling enabled
  Tunnel transport MTU 1476 bytes
<output omitted>
RTB#
```

In the output from the last command shown, why is the maximum transmission unit (MTU) set at 1476 bytes?

_____

_____

List three common GRE misconfiguration issues.

_____

_____

_____

_____

_____

Packet Tracer Exercise 3-1: GRE Implementation

Download and open the file LSG04-0301.pka found at the companion website for this book. Refer to the Introduction of this book for specifics on accessing files.

Note: The following instructions are also contained within the Packet Tracer Exercise.

In this Packet Tracer activity, you will configure the RTA and RTB routers to pass OSPF updates over a GRE tunnel.

Requirements

- Use OSPF process ID 1 to configure the routers to advertise the LAN and tunnel networks. Do not advertise the 64.100.1.0/30 network.

- Configure a GRE tunnel with the following:
    - Configure the tunnel interfaces according to the topology.
    - The mode is IP.
    - The tunnel source is the outbound interface number. Packet Tracer does support configuring the IP address as the tunnel source.

After OSPF converges, PC1 should be able to ping the Server. Your completion percentage should be 100%. All the connectivity tests should show a status of "successful." If not, click **Check Results** to see which required components are not yet completed.

eBGP

Border Gateway Protocol (BGP) is an Exterior Gateway Protocol (EGP) used for the exchange of routing information between autonomous systems, such as ISPs, companies, and content providers.

BGP Overview

BGP exchanges routing information with another router, called a BGP _____ or BGP _____, which are routers in other companies, not routers in the same company. This distinguishes BGP from interior gateway protocols (IGP) such as OSPF and EIGRP that exchange routing information with routers in the same company.

BGP updates are encapsulated over TCP on port _____. Therefore, BGP inherits the connection-oriented properties of TCP, which ensures that BGP updates are transmitted reliably.

Describe the two types of BGP:

- eBGP: _____
- iBGP: _____

eBGP Branch Configuration

To implement eBGP for this course, you will need to complete the following tasks:

Step 1.   Enable BGP routing.

Step 2.   Configure BGP neighbor(s) (peering).

Step 3.   Advertise network(s) originating from this AS.

Figure 3-4 shows the BGP configuration topology.

Figure 3-4   BGP Topology

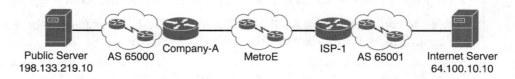

Public Server
198.133.219.10   AS 65000   Company-A   MetroE   ISP-1   AS 65001   Internet Server
64.100.10.10

List the commands to configure the Company-A router for single-homed BGP. ISP-1 is at 209.165.201.1. Advertise the 198.133.219.0/24 network to ISP-1.

_____

_____

_____

Record the commands to generate the following output.

```
Company-A#  _____

B*    0.0.0.0 [20/0] via 209.165.201.1, 00:25:09


Company-A#  _____

BGP table version is 4, local router ID is 209.165.201.2

Status codes: s suppressed, d damped, h history, * valid, > best, i - internal,
              r RIB-failure, S Stale

Origin codes: i - IGP, e - EGP, ? - incomplete


   Network          Next Hop          Metric LocPrf Weight Path
*> 0.0.0.0/32       209.165.201.1          0      0      0 65001 i
*> 198.133.219.0/24 0.0.0.0                0         32768 i


Company-A#  _____

BGP router identifier 209.165.201.2, local AS number 65000

BGP table version is 4, main routing table version 6

2 network entries using 264 bytes of memory

2 path entries using 104 bytes of memory

1/1 BGP path/bestpath attribute entries using 184 bytes of memory

2 BGP AS-PATH entries using 48 bytes of memory

0 BGP route-map cache entries using 0 bytes of memory

0 BGP filter-list cache entries using 0 bytes of memory

Bitfield cache entries: current 1 (at peak 1) using 32 bytes of memory

BGP using 632 total bytes of memory

BGP activity 2/0 prefixes, 2/0 paths, scan interval 60 secs


Neighbor        V    AS MsgRcvd MsgSent   TblVer  InQ OutQ Up/Down   State/PfxRcd
209.165.201.1   4 65001      30      28        4    0    0 00:23:08            4
```

Packet Tracer Exercise 3-2: BGP Branch Configuration

Download and open the file LSG04-0302.pka found at the companion website for this book. Refer to the Introduction of this book for specifics on accessing files.

_____

Note: The following instructions are also contained within the Packet Tracer Exercise.

_____

In this Packet Tracer activity, you will configure the Company-A router to send BGP updates to the ISP-1 router.

Requirements

- Use AS 65000.
- Configure the **neighbor** command.
- Advertise the 198.133.219.0/24 network.

After BGP converges, the Public Server should be able to ping the Internet Server. Your completion percentage should be 100%. If not, click **Check Results** to see which required components are not yet completed.

Labs and Activities

Command Reference

In Table 3-3, record the command, including the correct router prompt, that fits the description. Fill in any blanks with the appropriate missing information.

Table 3-3   Commands for Chapter 3, Branch Connections

Command	Description
	Configure a dialer interface to use an MTU of 1492.
	Configure an interface to use PPPoE.
	Configure an interface as a PPPoE client mapped to dialer pool 1.
	Create Tunnel 1.
	Configure a tunnel to use s0/0/0 as the source.
	Configure a tunnel to use the destination address 64.100.1.1.
	Enter the command to verify a tunnel interface.
	Configure a router with a BGP peer 64.100.1.1 that belongs to AS 65001.
	Configure a router to advertise 192.0.2.0/24 to its BGP peer.

3.0.1.2 Class Activity–Broadband Varieties

Objective

Select broadband solutions to support remote connectivity in a small- to medium-sized business network.

Scenario

Telework employment opportunities are expanding in your local area every day. You have been offered employment as a teleworker for a major corporation. The new employer requires teleworkers to have access to the Internet to fulfill their job responsibilities.

Research the following broadband Internet connection types that are available in your geographic area:

- DSL
- Cable
- Satellite

Consider the advantages and disadvantages of each broadband variation as you notate your research, which may include cost, speed, security, and ease of implementation or installation.

Resources

- World Wide Web access
- Word processing software

Step 1.   Research three major types of broadband Internet connections:

- DSL
- Cable
- Satellite

Step 2.   Decide which broadband options would be important to you as a teleworker in your small or home office:

- Cost
- Speed
- Security
- Ease of implementation
- Reliability

Step 3.   Using the options from Step 2, create a matrix that lists the advantages and disadvantages of each broadband type.

Step 4.   Share your research with the class or another group.

3.1.2.2 Lab–Researching Broadband Internet Access Technologies

Objectives

Part 1: Investigate Broadband Distribution

Part 2: Research Broadband Access Options for Specific Scenarios

Background/Scenario

Although broadband Internet access options have increased dramatically in recent years, broadband access varies greatly depending on location. In this lab, you will investigate current broadband distribution and research broadband access options for specific scenarios.

Required Resources

Device with Internet access

Part 1: Investigate Broadband Distribution

In Part 1, you will research broadband distribution in a geographical location.

Step 1.   Research broadband distribution.

Use the Internet to research the following questions:

   a.   For the country in which you reside, what percentage of the population has broadband Internet subscriptions?

   _____

   b.   What percentage of the population is without broadband Internet options?

   _____

Step 2.   Research broadband distribution in the United States.

Navigate to the website www.broadbandmap.gov. The National Broadband Map allows users to search and map broadband availability across the United States.

Note: For access options and ISPs for locations outside the United States, perform an Internet search using the keywords "broadband access XYZ," where XYZ is the name of the country.

---

   a.   Enter your zip code, city, and country that you would like to explore and click **Find Broadband**. List the zip code or city in the space provided.

   _____

   b.   Click **Show Wired** and **Expand All**. What, if any, wired broadband Internet connections are available at this location? Complete the table below.

   _____

ISP	Connection Type	Download Speed

c. Click **Show Wireless** and **Expand All**. What, if any, wireless broadband Internet connections are available in this location? Complete the table below.

ISP	Connection Type	Download Speed

d. Return to the home page and click **Explore the Maps**. The interactive map allows you to explore the geographical availability of a number of broadband Internet options.

e. Highlight each of the wired connections independently (DSL, cable, and fiber). Selections are highlighted in dark blue.

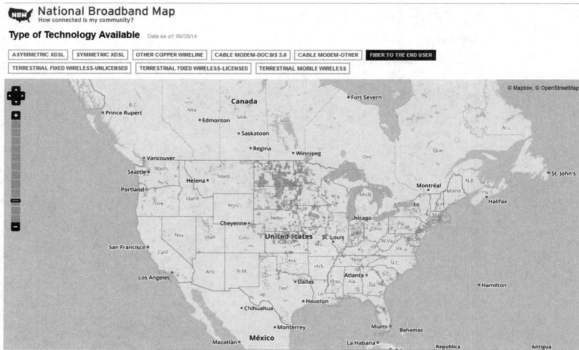

For wired connections, order the wired broadband connections from least to greatest in terms of geographical area covered. List your answer in the space provided.

_____

f. In the gallery of maps at the bottom of the web page, select **Broadband Availability Demographics**. Display the population by **density** and compare the broadband connection to the population distribution of the United States. What correlations can be drawn?

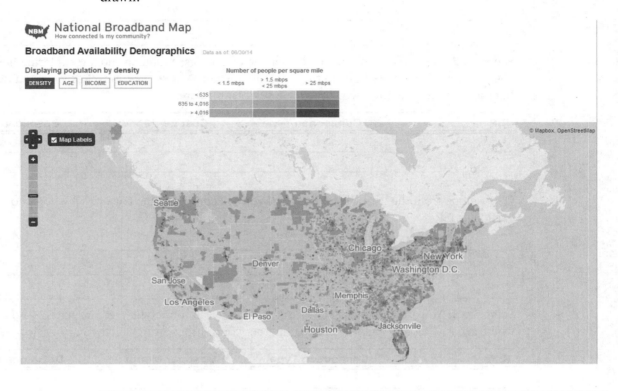

_____

_____

_____

Part 2: Research Broadband Access Options for Specific Scenarios

In Part 2, you will research and detail broadband options for the following scenarios and select the best last-mile technology to meet the needs of the consumer. You can use the http://www.broadbandmap. gov site as a starting point for your research.

Scenario 1: You are moving to Kansas City, Missouri and are exploring home Internet connections. Research and detail two Internet connections from which you can select in this metropolitan area.

ISP	Connection Type	Cost per Month	Download Speed

Choose one from the list of local ISPs that you selected. Give the reasons why you chose that particular ISP.

_____

_____

_____

Scenario 2: You are moving to an area outside of Billings, Montana and are exploring home Internet connections. You will be beyond the reach of cable or DSL connections. Research and detail two Internet connections from which you can select in this area.

ISP	Connection Type	Cost per Month	Download Speed

Choose one from the list of local ISPs that you selected. Give the reasons why you chose that particular ISP.

_____

_____

_____

Scenario 3: You are moving to New York City and your job requires you to have 24 hours anytime/anywhere access. Research and detail two Internet connections from which you can select in this area.

ISP	Connection Type	Cost per Month	Download Speed

Choose one from the list of local ISPs that you selected. Give the reasons why you chose that particular ISP.

_____

_____

_____

Scenario 4: You are a small business owner with 10 employees who telecommute in the Fargo, North Dakota area. The teleworkers live beyond the reach of cable Internet connections. Research and detail two Internet connections from which you can select in this area.

ISP	Connection Type	Cost per Month	Download Speed

Choose one from the list of local ISPs that you selected. Give the reasons why you chose that particular ISP.

_____

_____

_____

Scenario 5: Your business in Washington, D.C. is expanding to 25 employees and you will need to upgrade your broadband access to include equipment colocation and web hosting. Research and detail two Internet connections from which you can select in this area.

ISP	Connection Type	Cost per Month	Download Speed

Choose one from the list of local ISPs that you selected. Give the reasons why you chose that particular ISP.

_____

_____

_____

Reflection

How do you think broadband Internet access will change in the future?

_____

_____

_____

3.2.2.7 Lab–Configuring a Router as a PPPoE Client for DSL Connectivity

Topology

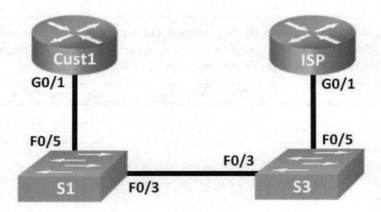

Addressing Table

Device	Interface	IP Address	Subnet Mask	Default Gateway
Cust1	G0/1	Learned via PPP	Learned via PPP	Learned via PPP
ISP	G0/1	N/A	N/A	N/A

Objectives

Part 1: Build the Network

Part 2: Configure the ISP Router

Part 3: Configure the Cust1 Router

Background/Scenario

ISPs often use Point-to-Point Protocol over Ethernet (PPPoE) on DSL links to their customers. PPP supports the assignment of IP address information to a device at the remote end of a PPP link. More importantly, PPP supports CHAP authentication. ISPs can check accounting records to see if a customer's bill has been paid, before letting them connect to the Internet.

In this lab, you will configure both the client and ISP side of the connection to set up PPPoE. Typically, you would only configure the client end.

Note: The routers used with CCNA hands-on labs are Cisco 1941 Integrated Services Routers (ISRs) with Cisco IOS Release 15.2(4)M3 (universalk9 image). The switches used are Cisco Catalyst 2960s with Cisco IOS Release 15.0(2) (lanbasek9 image). Other routers, switches, and Cisco IOS versions can be used. Depending on the model and Cisco IOS version, the commands available and output produced might vary from what is shown in the labs. Refer to the Router Interface Summary Table at the end of this lab for the correct interface identifiers.

Note: Ensure that the routers and switches have been erased and have no startup configurations. If you are unsure, contact your instructor.

Required Resources

- 2 Routers (Cisco 1941 with Cisco IOS Release 15.2(4)M3 universal image or comparable)
- 2 Switches (Cisco 2960 with Cisco IOS Release 15.0(2) lanbasek9 image or comparable)
- Console cables to configure the Cisco IOS devices via the console ports
- Ethernet cables as shown in the topology

Part 1: Build the Network

Step 1. Cable the network as shown in the topology.

Step 2. Initialize and reload the routers and switches.

Step 3. Configure basic settings for each router.

    a. Disable DNS lookup.

    b. Configure device name as shown in the topology.

    c. Encrypt plaintext passwords.

    d. Create a message of the day (MOTD) banner warning users that unauthorized access is prohibited.

    e. Assign **class** as the encrypted privileged EXEC mode password.

    f. Assign **cisco** as the console and vty password and enable login.

    g. Set console logging to synchronous mode.

    h. Save your configuration.

Part 2: Configure the ISP Router

In Part 2, you configure the ISP router with PPPoE parameters for connection from the Cust1 router.

Note: Many of the ISP router PPPoE configuration commands are beyond the scope of the course; however, they are necessary for completion of the lab. They can be copied and pasted into the ISP router at the global configuration mode prompt.

    a. Create a local database username **Cust1** with a password of **ciscopppoe**.

```
ISP(config)# username Cust1 password ciscopppoe
```

    b. Create a pool of addresses that will be assigned to customers.

```
ISP(config)# ip local pool PPPoEPOOL 10.0.0.1 10.0.0.10
```

    c. Create the Virtual Template and associate the IP address of G0/1 with it. Associate the Virtual Template with the pool of addresses. Configure CHAP to authenticate customers.

```
ISP(config)# interface virtual-template 1
ISP(config-if)# ip address 10.0.0.254 255.255.255.0
ISP(config-if)# mtu 1492
```

```
ISP(config-if)# peer default ip address pool PPPoEPOOL
ISP(config-if)# ppp authentication chap callin
ISP(config-if)# exit
```

d. Assign the template to the PPPoE group.

```
ISP(config)# bba-group pppoe global
ISP(config-bba-group)# virtual-template 1
ISP(config-bba-group)# exit
```

e. Associate the bba-group with the G0/1 physical interface.

```
ISP(config)# interface g0/1
ISP(config-if# pppoe enable group global
ISP(config-if)# no shutdown
```

Part 3: Configure the Cust1 Router

In Part 3, you will configure the Cust1 router with PPPoE parameters.

a. Configure G0/1 interface for PPPoE connectivity.

```
Cust1(config)# interface g0/1
Cust1(config-if)# pppoe enable
Cust1(config-if)# pppoe-client dial-pool-number 1
Cust1(config-if)# exit
```

b. Associate the G0/1 interface with a dialer interface. Use the username **Cust1** and password **ciscopppoe** configured in Part 2.

```
Cust1(config)# interface dialer 1
Cust1(config-if)# mtu 1492
Cust1(config-if)# ip address negotiated
Cust1(config-if)# encapsulation ppp
Cust1(config-if)# dialer pool 1
Cust1(config-if)# ppp authentication chap callin
Cust1(config-if)# ppp chap hostname Cust1
Cust1(config-if)# ppp chap password ciscopppoe
Cust1(config-if)# exit
```

c. Set up a static default route pointing to the Dialer interface.

```
Cust1(config)# ip route 0.0.0.0 0.0.0.0 dialer 1
```

d. Set up debugging on the Cust1 router to display PPP and PPPoE negotiation.

```
Cust1# debug ppp authentication
Cust1# debug pppoe events
```

e. Enable the G0/1 interface on the Cust1 router and observe the debug output as the PPPoE dialer session is established and CHAP authentication takes place.

```
*Jul 30 19:28:42.427: %LINK-3-UPDOWN: Interface GigabitEthernet0/1, changed
state to down
*Jul 30 19:28:46.175: %LINK-3-UPDOWN: Interface GigabitEthernet0/1, changed
state to up
*Jul 30 19:28:47.175: %LINEPROTO-5-UPDOWN: Line protocol on Interface
GigabitEthernet0/1, changed state to up
*Jul 30 19:29:03.839:   padi timer expired
*Jul 30 19:29:03.839:   Sending PADI: Interface = GigabitEthernet0/1
*Jul 30 19:29:03.839: PPPoE 0: I PADO  R:30f7.0da3.0b01 L:30f7.0da3.0bc1 Gi0/1
*Jul 30 19:29:05.887:   PPPOE: we've got our pado and the pado timer went off
```

```
*Jul 30 19:29:05.887: OUT PADR from PPPoE Session
*Jul 30 19:29:05.895: PPPoE 1: I PADS  R:30f7.0da3.0b01 L:30f7.0da3.0bc1 Gi0/1
*Jul 30 19:29:05.895: IN PADS from PPPoE Session
*Jul 30 19:29:05.899: %DIALER-6-BIND: Interface Vi2 bound to profile Di1
*Jul 30 19:29:05.899: PPPoE: Virtual Access interface obtained.
*Jul 30 19:29:05.899: PPPoE : encap string prepared
*Jul 30 19:29:05.899: [0]PPPoE 1: data path set to PPPoE Client
*Jul 30 19:29:05.903: %LINK-3-UPDOWN: Interface Virtual-Access2, changed state
to up
*Jul 30 19:29:05.911: Vi2 PPP: Using dialer call direction
*Jul 30 19:29:05.911: Vi2 PPP: Treating connection as a callout
*Jul 30 19:29:05.911: Vi2 PPP: Session handle[C6000001] Session id[1]
*Jul 30 19:29:05.919: Vi2 PPP: No authorization without authentication
*Jul 30 19:29:05.939: Vi2 CHAP: I CHALLENGE id 1 len 24 from "ISP"
*Jul 30 19:29:05.939: Vi2 PPP: Sent CHAP SENDAUTH Request
*Jul 30 19:29:05.939: Vi2 PPP: Received SENDAUTH Response FAIL
*Jul 30 19:29:05.939: Vi2 CHAP: Using hostname from interface CHAP
*Jul 30 19:29:05.939: Vi2 CHAP: Using password from interface CHAP
*Jul 30 19:29:05.939: Vi2 CHAP: O RESPONSE id 1 len 26 from "Cust1"
*Jul 30 19:29:05.955: Vi2 CHAP: I SUCCESS id 1 len 4
*Jul 30 19:29:05.955: %LINEPROTO-5-UPDOWN: Line protocol on Interface Virtual-
Access2, changed state to up
*Jul 30 19:29:05.983: PPPoE : ipfib_encapstr  prepared
*Jul 30 19:29:05.983: PPPoE : ipfib_encapstr  prepared
```

f. Issue a **show ip interface brief** command on the Cust1 router to display the IP address assigned by the ISP router. Sample output is shown below. By what method was the IP address obtained? _____

```
Cust1# show ip interface brief
Interface                  IP-Address OK? Method Status                Protocol
Embedded-Service-Engine0/0 unassigned YES unset  administratively down down
GigabitEthernet0/0         unassigned YES unset  administratively down down
GigabitEthernet0/1         unassigned YES unset  up                    up
Serial0/0/0                unassigned YES unset  administratively down down
Serial0/0/1                unassigned YES unset  administratively down down
Dialer1                    10.0.0.1   YES IPCP   up                    up
Virtual-Access1            unassigned YES unset  up                    up
Virtual-Access2            unassigned YES unset  up                    up
```

g. Issue a **show ip route** command on the Cust1 router. Sample output is shown below.

```
Cust1# show ip route
Codes: L - local, C - connected, S - static, R - RIP, M - mobile, B - BGP
       D - EIGRP, EX - EIGRP external, O - OSPF, IA - OSPF inter area
       N1 - OSPF NSSA external type 1, N2 - OSPF NSSA external type 2
       E1 - OSPF external type 1, E2 - OSPF external type 2
       i - IS-IS, su - IS-IS summary, L1 - IS-IS level-1, L2 - IS-IS level-2
       ia - IS-IS inter area, * - candidate default, U - per-user static route
       o - ODR, P - periodic downloaded static route, H - NHRP, l - LISP
       + - replicated route, % - next hop override


Gateway of last resort is 0.0.0.0 to network 0.0.0.0
```

```
S*      0.0.0.0/0 is directly connected, Dialer1
        10.0.0.0/32 is subnetted, 2 subnets
C          10.0.0.1 is directly connected, Dialer1
C          10.0.0.254 is directly connected, Dialer1
```

   h. Issue a **show pppoe session** on Cust1 router. Sample output is shown below.

```
Cust1# show pppoe session
    1 client session

Uniq ID  PPPoE  RemMAC          Port                   VT  VA        State
         SID    LocMAC                                      VA-st     Type
    N/A    1    30f7.0da3.0b01  Gi0/1                  Di1 Vi2       UP
                30f7.0da3.0bc1                              UP
```

   i. Issue a ping to 10.0.0.254 from the Cust1 router. The ping should be successful. If not, troubleshoot until you have connectivity.

```
Cust1# ping 10.0.0.254
Type escape sequence to abort.
Sending 5, 100-byte ICMP Echos to 10.0.0.254, timeout is 2 seconds:
!!!!!
Success rate is 100 percent (5/5), round-trip min/avg/max = 1/1/4 ms
```

Reflection

Why do ISPs who use DSL primarily use PPPoE with their customers?

_____

_____

Router Interface Summary Table

Router Interface Summary				
Router Model	Ethernet Interface #1	Ethernet Interface #2	Serial Interface #1	Serial Interface #2
1800	Fast Ethernet 0/0 (F0/0)	Fast Ethernet 0/1 (F0/1)	Serial 0/0/0 (S0/0/0)	Serial 0/0/1 (S0/0/1)
1900	Gigabit Ethernet 0/0 (G0/0)	Gigabit Ethernet 0/1 (G0/1)	Serial 0/0/0 (S0/0/0)	Serial 0/0/1 (S0/0/1)
2801	Fast Ethernet 0/0 (F0/0)	Fast Ethernet 0/1 (F0/1)	Serial 0/1/0 (S0/1/0)	Serial 0/1/1 (S0/1/1)
2811	Fast Ethernet 0/0 (F0/0)	Fast Ethernet 0/1 (F0/1)	Serial 0/0/0 (S0/0/0)	Serial 0/0/1 (S0/0/1)
2900	Gigabit Ethernet 0/0 (G0/0)	Gigabit Ethernet 0/1 (G0/1)	Serial 0/0/0 (S0/0/0)	Serial 0/0/1 (S0/0/1)

Note: To find out how the router is configured, look at the interfaces to identify the type of router and how many interfaces the router has. There is no way to effectively list all the combinations of configurations for each router class. This table includes identifiers for the possible combinations of Ethernet and Serial interfaces in the device. The table does not include any other type of interface, even though a specific router may contain one. An example of this might be an ISDN BRI interface. The string in parentheses is the legal abbreviation that can be used in Cisco IOS commands to represent the interface.

3.2.2.8 Lab–Troubleshoot PPPoE

Topology

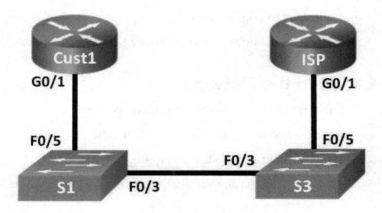

Addressing Table

Device	Interface	IP Address	Subnet Mask	Default Gateway
Cust1	G0/1	Learned via PPP	Learned via PPP	Learned via PPP
ISP	G0/1	N/A	N/A	N/A

Objectives

Part 1: Build the Network

Part 2: Troubleshoot PPPoE on Cust1

Background/Scenario

ISPs sometimes use Point-to-Point Protocol over Ethernet (PPPoE) on DSL links to their customers. PPP supports the assignment of IP address information to a device at the remote end of a PPP link. More importantly, PPP supports CHAP authentication. ISPs can check accounting records to see if a customer's bill has been paid, before letting them connect to the Internet.

In this lab, you will troubleshoot the Cust1 router for PPPoE configuration problems.

Note: The routers used with CCNA hands-on labs are Cisco 1941 Integrated Services Routers (ISRs) with Cisco IOS Release 15.2(4)M3 (universalk9 image). The switches used are Cisco Catalyst 2960s with Cisco IOS Release 15.0(2) (lanbasek9 image). Other routers, switches, and Cisco IOS versions can be used. Depending on the model and Cisco IOS version, the commands available and output produced might vary from what is shown in the labs. Refer to the Router Interface Summary Table at the end of this lab for the correct interface identifiers.

Note: Ensure that the routers and switches have been erased and have no startup configurations. If you are unsure, contact your instructor.

Required Resources

- 2 Routers (Cisco 1941 with Cisco IOS Release 15.2(4)M3 universal image or comparable)
- 2 Switches (Cisco 2960 with Cisco IOS Release 15.0(2) lanbasek9 image or comparable)
- Console cables to configure the Cisco IOS devices via the console ports
- Ethernet cables as shown in the topology

Part 1: Build the Network

Step 1. Cable the network as shown in the topology.

Step 2. Initialize and reload the routers and switches.

Step 3. Copy the configurations on to routers.

a. Copy and paste the Cust1 configuration to the Cust1 router.

```
hostname Cust1
enable secret class
no aaa new-model
no ip domain lookup
interface GigabitEthernet0/1
 no ip address
 duplex auto
 speed auto
 pppoe enable group global
 pppoe-client dial-pool-number 1
 no shut
interface Dialer1
 mtu 1492
 ip address negotiated
 encapsulation ppp
 dialer pool 1
 ppp authentication chap callin
 ppp chap hostname Cust1
 ppp chap password 0 ciscoppp
ip route 0.0.0.0 0.0.0.0 Dialer1
banner motd ^C
Unauthorized Access Prohibited.
^C
line con 0
 password cisco
 logging synchronous
 login
line aux 0
line vty 0 4
 password cisco
 login
end
```

b. Copy and paste the ISP configuration to the ISP router.

```
hostname ISP
enable secret class
username Cust1 password 0 ciscopppoe
bba-group pppoe global
 virtual-template 1
interface GigabitEthernet0/1
 no ip address
 duplex auto
 speed auto
 pppoe enable group global
 no shut
interface Virtual-Template1
 ip address 10.0.0.254 255.255.255.0
 mtu 1492
 peer default ip address pool PPPoEPOOL
 ppp authentication chap callin
ip local pool PPPoEPOOL 10.0.0.1 10.0.0.10
ip forward-protocol nd
banner motd ^C
Unauthorized Access Prohibited.
^C
line con 0
 password cisco
 logging synchronous
 login
line vty 0 4
 password cisco
 login
end
```

Note: Many of the ISP router PPPoE configuration commands are beyond the scope of the course.

c. Save the router configurations.

Part 2: Troubleshoot PPPoE on Cust1

In Part 2, you will troubleshoot PPPoE on the Cust 1 router. The privileged EXEC mode password is **class**, and console and vty passwords are **cisco**. The ISP has provided a username of **Cust1** and a password of **ciscopppoe** for PPPoE CHAP authentication.

The following log messages should be appearing on your console session to Cust1:

```
Cust1#
*Nov  5 22:53:46.999: %DIALER-6-BIND: Interface Vi2 bound to profile Di1
*Nov  5 22:53:47.003: %LINK-3-UPDOWN: Interface Virtual-Access2, changed state to up
*Nov  5 22:53:47.035: %DIALER-6-UNBIND: Interface Vi2 unbound from profile Di1
*Nov  5 22:53:47.039: %LINK-3-UPDOWN: Interface Virtual-Access2, changed state to down
Cust1#
```

Step 1.   Verify that IPv4 Address is assigned to the Cust1 Dialer interface.

The Dialer virtual interface did not receive an IP address.

```
Cust1# show ip interface brief
Interface                    IP-Address   OK? Method Status                 Protocol
Embedded-Service-Engine0/0   unassigned   YES unset  administratively down  down
GigabitEthernet0/0           unassigned   YES unset  administratively down  down
GigabitEthernet0/1           unassigned   YES unset  up                     up
Serial0/0/0                  unassigned   YES unset  administratively down  down
Serial0/0/1                  unassigned   YES unset  administratively down  down
Dialer1                      unassigned   YES manual up                     up
Virtual-Access1              unassigned   YES unset  up                     up
Virtual-Access2              unassigned   YES unset  down                   down
```

Step 2.   Debug PPP to determine if the problem is with authentication.

a.   Turn on debug for PPP authentication.

```
Cust1# debug ppp authentication
PPP authentication debugging is on
Cust1#
*Nov  5 23:09:00.283: %DIALER-6-BIND: Interface Vi2 bound to profile Di1
*Nov  5 23:09:00.287: %LINK-3-UPDOWN: Interface Virtual-Access2, changed state
to up
*Nov  5 23:09:00.287: Vi2 PPP: Using dialer call direction
*Nov  5 23:09:00.287: Vi2 PPP: Treating connection as a callout
*Nov  5 23:09:00.287: Vi2 PPP: Session handle[8A000036] Session id[54]
*Nov  5 23:09:00.315: Vi2 PPP: No authorization without authentication
*Nov  5 23:09:00.315: Vi2 CHAP: I CHALLENGE id 1 len 24 from "ISP"
*Nov  5 23:0
Cust1#9:00.315: Vi2 PPP: Sent CHAP SENDAUTH Request
*Nov  5 23:09:00.315: Vi2 PPP: Received SENDAUTH Response FAIL
*Nov  5 23:09:00.315: Vi2 CHAP: Using hostname from interface CHAP
*Nov  5 23:09:00.315: Vi2 CHAP: Using password from interface CHAP
*Nov  5 23:09:00.315: Vi2 CHAP: O RESPONSE id 1 len 26 from "Cust1"
*Nov  5 23:09:00.315: Vi2 CHAP: I FAILURE id 1 len 25 msg is "Authentication
failed"
*Nov  5 23:09:00.315: %DIALER-6-UNBIND: Interface Vi2 unbound from profile Di1
*Nov  5 23:09:00.319: %LINK-3
Cust1#-UPDOWN: Interface Virtual-Access2, changed state to down
Cust1#
```

b.   End debug mode.

```
Cust1# u all
All possible debugging has been turned off
Cust1#
```

Step 3.   Verify that the PPPoE username and password matches what was given by the ISP.

a.   Display the running configuration; apply a filter to display only the Dialer section. Verify that the username and password matches what was provided by the ISP.

```
Cust1# show run | section Dialer
interface Dialer1
 mtu 1492
 ip address negotiated
```

```
    encapsulation ppp
    dialer pool 1
    ppp authentication chap callin
    ppp chap hostname Cust1
    ppp chap password 0 ciscoppp
ip route 0.0.0.0 0.0.0.0 Dialer1
```

b. The problem appears to be with the password. Enter global configuration mode and fix the ppp password.

```
Cust1# conf t
Enter configuration commands, one per line.  End with CNTL/Z.
Cust1(config)# interface Dialer1
Cust1(config-if)# ppp chap password ciscopppoe
Cust1(config-if)# end
Cust1#
*Nov  5 23:42:07.343: %SYS-5-CONFIG_I: Configured from console by console
Cust1#
*Nov  5 23:42:25.039: %DIALER-6-BIND: Interface Vi2 bound to profile Di1
*Nov  5 23:42:25.043: %LINK-3-UPDOWN: Interface Virtual-Access2, changed state
to up
Cust1#
*Nov  5 23:42:25.063: %LINEPROTO-5-UPDOWN: Line protocol on Interface Virtual-
Access2, changed state to up
```

Step 4.   Verify PPPoE connectivity.

a. Verify that this change resolved the problem and that an IP address has been assigned to the Dialer1 interface.

```
Cust1# show ip interface brief
Interface                  IP-Address OK? Method Status                Protocol
Embedded-Service-Engine0/0 unassigned YES unset  administratively down down
GigabitEthernet0/0         unassigned YES unset  administratively down down
GigabitEthernet0/1         unassigned YES unset  up                    up
Serial0/0/0                unassigned YES unset  administratively down down
Serial0/0/1                unassigned YES unset  administratively down down
Dialer1                    10.0.0.1   YES IPCP   up                    up
Virtual-Access1            unassigned YES unset  up                    up
Virtual-Access2            unassigned YES unset  up                    up
```

b. Display the routing table to verify a route to the ISP router.

```
Cust1# show ip route
Codes: L - local, C - connected, S - static, R - RIP, M - mobile, B - BGP
       D - EIGRP, EX - EIGRP external, O - OSPF, IA - OSPF inter area
       N1 - OSPF NSSA external type 1, N2 - OSPF NSSA external type 2
       E1 - OSPF external type 1, E2 - OSPF external type 2
       i - IS-IS, su - IS-IS summary, L1 - IS-IS level-1, L2 - IS-IS level-2
       ia - IS-IS inter area, * - candidate default, U - per-user static route
       o - ODR, P - periodic downloaded static route, H - NHRP, l - LISP
       a - application route
       + - replicated route, % - next hop override

Gateway of last resort is 0.0.0.0 to network 0.0.0.0
```

```
S*      0.0.0.0/0 is directly connected, Dialer1
        10.0.0.0/32 is subnetted, 2 subnets
C          10.0.0.1 is directly connected, Dialer1
C          10.0.0.254 is directly connected, Dialer1
```

c. Display information about the active PPPoE sessions.

```
Cust1# show pppoe session
    1 client session
```

Uniq ID	PPPoE SID	RemMAC LocMAC	Port	VT	VA VA-st	State Type
N/A	1	30f7.0da3.1641 30f7.0da3.0da1	Gi0/1	Di1	Vi2 UP	UP

Step 5. Adjust the maximum segment size on the physical interface.

The PPPoE header adds an additional 8 bytes to each segment. To prevent TCP sessions from being dropped, the maximum segment size (MSS) needs to be adjusted to its optimum value on the physical interface.

a. Display G0/1s configuration setting to see if the MSS has been adjusted.

```
Cust1# show run interface g0/1
Building configuration...

Current configuration : 136 bytes
!
interface GigabitEthernet0/1
 no ip address
 duplex auto
 speed auto
 pppoe enable group global
 pppoe-client dial-pool-number 1
end
```

b. Adjust the MSS to its optimum value of 1452 bytes.

```
Cust1(config)# interface g0/1
Cust1(config-if)# ip tcp adjust-mss 1452
Cust1(config-if)# end
```

Reflection

Explain why the TCP segment size needs to be adjusted for PPPoE.

_____

_____

_____

_____

Router Interface Summary Table

	Router Interface Summary			
Router Model	**Ethernet Interface #1**	**Ethernet Interface #2**	**Serial Interface #1**	**Serial Interface #2**
1800	Fast Ethernet 0/0 (F0/0)	Fast Ethernet 0/1 (F0/1)	Serial 0/0/0 (S0/0/0)	Serial 0/0/1 (S0/0/1)
1900	Gigabit Ethernet 0/0 (G0/0)	Gigabit Ethernet 0/1 (G0/1)	Serial 0/0/0 (S0/0/0)	Serial 0/0/1 (S0/0/1)
2801	Fast Ethernet 0/0 (F0/0)	Fast Ethernet 0/1 (F0/1)	Serial 0/1/0 (S0/1/0)	Serial 0/1/1 (S0/1/1)
2811	Fast Ethernet 0/0 (F0/0)	Fast Ethernet 0/1 (F0/1)	Serial 0/0/0 (S0/0/0)	Serial 0/0/1 (S0/0/1)
2900	Gigabit Ethernet 0/0 (G0/0)	Gigabit Ethernet 0/1 (G0/1)	Serial 0/0/0 (S0/0/0)	Serial 0/0/1 (S0/0/1)

Note: To find out how the router is configured, look at the interfaces to identify the type of router and how many interfaces the router has. There is no way to effectively list all the combinations of configurations for each router class. This table includes identifiers for the possible combinations of Ethernet and Serial interfaces in the device. The table does not include any other type of interface, even though a specific router may contain one. An example of this might be an ISDN BRI interface. The string in parentheses is the legal abbreviation that can be used in Cisco IOS commands to represent the interface.

Packet Tracer
☐ Activity

3.4.2.4 Packet Tracer–Configuring GRE

Topology

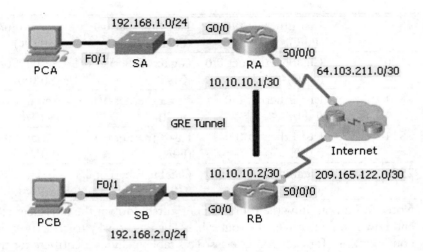

Addressing Table

Device	Interface	IP Address	Subnet Mask	Default Gateway
RA	G0/0	192.168.1.1	255.255.255.0	N/A
	S0/0/0	64.103.211.2	255.255.255.252	N/A
	Tunnel 0	10.10.10.1	255.255.255.252	N/A
RB	G0/0	192.168.2.1	255.255.255.0	N/A
	S0/0/0	209.165.122.2	255.255.255.252	N/A
	Tunnel 0	10.10.10.2	255.255.255.252	N/A
PC-A	NIC	192.168.1.2	255.255.255.0	192.168.1.1
PC-C	NIC	192.168.2.2	255.255.255.0	192.168.2.1

Objectives

Part 1: Verify Router Connectivity

Part 2: Configure GRE Tunnels

Part 3: Verify PC Connectivity

Scenario

You are the network administrator for a company that wants to set up a GRE tunnel to a remote office. Both networks are locally configured, and need only the tunnel configured.

Part 1: Verify Router Connectivity

Step 1.   Ping **RA** from **RB**.

    a.   Use the **show ip interface brief** command on **RA** to determine the IP address of the S0/0/0 port.

    b.   From **RB** ping the IP S0/0/0 address of **RA**.

Step 2.   Ping **PCA** from **PCB**.

Attempt to ping the IP address of **PCA** from **PCB**. We will repeat this test after configuring the GRE tunnel. What were the ping results? Why?

_____

Part 2: Configure GRE Tunnels

Step 1.   Configure the Tunnel 0 interface of **RA**.

    a.   Enter into the configuration mode for **RA** Tunnel 0.

```
RA(config)# interface tunnel 0
```

    b.   Set the IP address as indicated in the Addressing Table.

```
RA(config-if)# ip address 10.10.10.1 255.255.255.252
```

    c.   Set the source and destination for the endpoints of Tunnel 0.

```
RA(config-if)# tunnel source s0/0/0
RA(config-if)# tunnel destination 209.165.122.2
```

    d.   Configure Tunnel 0 to convey IP traffic over GRE.

```
RA(config-if)# tunnel mode gre ip
```

    e.   The Tunnel 0 interface should already be active. In the event that it is not, treat it like any other interface.

```
RA(config-if)# no shutdown
```

Step 2.   Configure the Tunnel 0 interface of **RB**.

Repeat Steps 1 a – e with **RB**. Be sure to change the IP addressing as appropriate.

_____

_____

_____

_____

_____

Step 3.   Configure a route for private IP traffic.

Establish a route between the 192.168.X.X networks using the 10.10.10.0/30 network as the destination.

```
RA(config)# ip route 192.168.2.0 255.255.255.0 10.10.10.2
RB(config)# ip route 192.168.1.0 255.255.255.0 10.10.10.1
```

Part 3: Verify Router Connectivity

Step 1.   Ping **PCA** from **PCB**.

Attempt to ping the IP address of **PCA** from **PCB**. The ping should be successful.

Step 2.   Trace the path from **PCA** to **PCB**.

Attempt to trace the path from **PCA** to **PCB**. Note the lack of public IP addresses in the output.

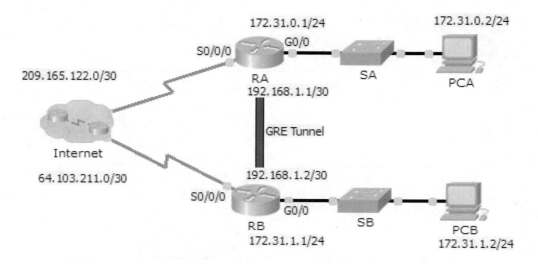

3.4.2.5 Packet Tracer–Troubleshooting GRE

Topology

Addressing Table

Device	Interface	IP Address	Subnet Mask	Default Gateway
RA	G0/0	172.31.0.1	255.255.255.0	N/A
	S0/0/0	209.165.122.2	255.255.255.252	N/A
	Tunnel 0	192.168.1.1	255.255.255.252	N/A
RB	G0/0	172.31.1.1	255.255.255.0	N/A
	S0/0/0	64.103.211.2	255.255.255.252	N/A
	Tunnel 0	192.168.1.2	255.255.255.252	N/A
PC-A	NIC	172.31.0.2	255.255.255.0	172.31.0.1
PC-C	NIC	172.31.1.2	255.255.255.0	172.31.1.1

Objectives

- Find and Correct All Network Errors
- Verify Connectivity

Scenario

A junior network administrator was hired to set up a GRE tunnel between two sites and was unable to complete the task. You have been asked to correct configuration errors in the company network.

Part 1: Find and Correct All Network Errors

Device	Error	Correction

Part 2: Verify Connectivity

Step 1.   Ping **PCA** from **PCB**.

Attempt to ping the IP address of **PCA** from **PCB**. The ping should be successful.

Step 2.   Trace the path from **PCA** to **PCB**.

Attempt to trace the path from **PCA** to **PCB**. Note the lack of public IP addresses in the output.

3.4.2.6 Lab–Configuring a Point-to-Point GRE VPN Tunnel

Topology

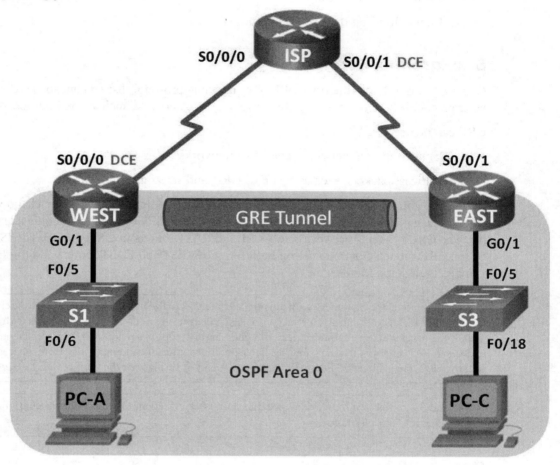

Addressing Table

Device	Interface	IP Address	Subnet Mask	Default Gateway
WEST	G0/1	172.16.1.1	255.255.255.0	N/A
	S0/0/0 (DCE)	10.1.1.1	255.255.255.252	N/A
	Tunnel0	172.16.12.1	255.255.255.252	N/A
ISP	S0/0/0	10.1.1.2	255.255.255.252	N/A
	S0/0/1 (DCE)	10.2.2.2	255.255.255.252	N/A
EAST	G0/1	172.16.2.1	255.255.255.0	N/A
	S0/0/1	10.2.2.1	255.255.255.252	N/A
	Tunnel0	172.16.12.2	255.255.255.252	N/A
PC-A	NIC	172.16.1.3	255.255.255.0	172.16.1.1
PC-C	NIC	172.16.2.3	255.255.255.0	172.16.2.1

Objectives

Part 1: Configure Basic Device Settings

Part 2: Configure a GRE Tunnel

Part 3: Enable Routing over the GRE Tunnel

Background/Scenario

Generic Routing Encapsulation (GRE) is a tunneling protocol that can encapsulate a variety of network layer protocols between two locations over a public network, such as the Internet.

GRE can be used with:

- Connecting IPv6 networks over IPv4 networks
- Multicast packets, such as OSPF, EIGRP, and streaming applications

In this lab, you will configure an unencrypted point-to-point GRE VPN tunnel and verify that network traffic is using the tunnel. You will also configure the OSPF routing protocol inside the GRE VPN tunnel. The GRE tunnel is between the WEST and EAST routers in OSPF area 0. The ISP has no knowledge of the GRE tunnel. Communication between the WEST and EAST routers and the ISP is accomplished using default static routes.

Note: The routers used with CCNA hands-on labs are Cisco 1941 Integrated Services Routers (ISRs) with Cisco IOS Release 15.2(4)M3 (universalk9 image). The switches used are Cisco Catalyst 2960s with Cisco IOS Release 15.0(2) (lanbasek9 image). Other routers, switches, and Cisco IOS versions can be used. Depending on the model and Cisco IOS version, the commands available and output produced might vary from what is shown in the labs. Refer to the Router Interface Summary Table at the end of this lab for the correct interface identifiers.

Note: Make sure that the routers and switches have been erased and have no startup configurations. If you are unsure, contact your instructor.

Required Resources

- 3 Routers (Cisco 1941 with Cisco IOS Release 15.2(4)M3 universal image or comparable)
- 2 Switches (Cisco 2960 with Cisco IOS Release 15.0(2) lanbasek9 image or comparable)
- 2 PCs (Windows with terminal emulation program, such as Tera Term)
- Console cables to configure the Cisco IOS devices via the console ports
- Ethernet and serial cables as shown in the topology

Part 1: Configure Basic Device Settings

In Part 1, you will set up the network topology and configure basic router settings, such as the interface IP addresses, routing, device access, and passwords.

Step 1.   Cable the network as shown in the topology.

Step 2.   Initialize and reload the routers and switches.

Step 3.   Configure basic settings for each router.

   a.   Disable DNS lookup.

   b.   Configure the device names.

   c.   Encrypt plain text passwords.

   d.   Create a message of the day (MOTD) banner warning users that unauthorized access is prohibited.

   e.   Assign **class** as the encrypted privileged EXEC mode password.

   f.   Assign **cisco** as the console and vty password and enable login.

   g.   Set console logging to synchronous mode.

   h.   Apply IP addresses to Serial and Gigabit Ethernet interfaces according to the Addressing Table and activate the physical interfaces. Do NOT configure the Tunnel0 interfaces at this time.

   i.   Set the clock rate to **128000** for DCE serial interfaces.

Step 4.   Configure default routes to the ISP router.

```
WEST(config)# ip route 0.0.0.0 0.0.0.0 10.1.1.2

EAST(config)# ip route 0.0.0.0 0.0.0.0 10.2.2.2
```

Step 5.   Configure the PCs.

Assign IP addresses and default gateways to the PCs according to the Addressing Table.

Step 6.   Verify connectivity.

At this point, the PCs are unable to ping each other. Each PC should be able to ping its default gateway. The routers are able to ping the serial interfaces of the other routers in the topology. If not, troubleshoot until you can verify connectivity.

Step 7.   Save your running configuration.

Part 2: Configure a GRE Tunnel

In Part 2, you will configure a GRE tunnel between the WEST and EAST routers.

Step 1.   Configure the GRE tunnel interface.

   a.   Configure the tunnel interface on the WEST router. Use S0/0/0 on WEST as the tunnel source interface and 10.2.2.1 as the tunnel destination on the EAST router.

```
WEST(config)# interface tunnel 0
WEST(config-if)# ip address 172.16.12.1 255.255.255.252
WEST(config-if)# tunnel source s0/0/0
WEST(config-if)# tunnel destination 10.2.2.1
```

   b.   Configure the tunnel interface on the EAST router. Use S0/0/1 on EAST as the tunnel source interface and 10.1.1.1 as the tunnel destination on the WEST router.

```
EAST(config)# interface tunnel 0
EAST(config-if)# ip address 172.16.12.2 255.255.255.252
```

```
EAST(config-if)# tunnel source 10.2.2.1
EAST(config-if)# tunnel destination 10.1.1.1
```

Note: For the **tunnel source** command, either the interface name or the IP address can be used as the source.

Step 2.   Verify that the GRE tunnel is functional.

   a.   Verify the status of the tunnel interface on the WEST and EAST routers.

```
WEST# show ip interface brief
Interface                    IP-Address    OK? Method Status
Protocol
Embedded-Service-Engine0/0   unassigned    YES unset  administratively down down
GigabitEthernet0/0           unassigned    YES unset  administratively down down
GigabitEthernet0/1           172.16.1.1    YES manual up                      up
Serial0/0/0                  10.1.1.1      YES manual up                      up
Serial0/0/1                  unassigned    YES unset  administratively down down
Tunnel0                      172.16.12.1   YES manual up                      up


EAST# show ip interface brief
Interface                    IP-Address    OK? Method Status               Protocol
Embedded-Service-Engine0/0   unassigned    YES unset  administratively down down
GigabitEthernet0/0           unassigned    YES unset  administratively down down
GigabitEthernet0/1           172.16.2.1    YES manual up                   up
Serial0/0/0                  unassigned    YES unset  administratively down down
Serial0/0/1                  10.2.2.1      YES manual up                   up
Tunnel0                      172.16.12.2   YES manual up                   up
```

   b.   Issue the **show interfaces tunnel 0** command to verify the tunneling protocol, tunnel source, and tunnel destination used in this tunnel.

   What is the tunneling protocol used? What are the tunnel source and destination IP addresses associated with GRE tunnel on each router?

   _____

   _____

   c.   Ping across the tunnel from the WEST router to the EAST router using the IP address of the tunnel interface.

```
WEST# ping 172.16.12.2
Type escape sequence to abort.
Sending 5, 100-byte ICMP Echos to 172.16.12.2, timeout is 2 seconds:
!!!!!
Success rate is 100 percent (5/5), round-trip min/avg/max = 32/34/36 ms
```

   d.   Use the **traceroute** command on the WEST to determine the path to the tunnel interface on the EAST router. What is the path to the EAST router? _____

   _____

   e.   Ping and trace the route across the tunnel from the EAST router to the WEST router using the IP address of the tunnel interface.

   What is the path to the WEST router from the EAST router? _____

   _____

With which interfaces are these IP addresses associated? Explain.

_____

_____

    f. The **ping** and **traceroute** commands should be successful. If not, troubleshoot before continuing to the next part.

Part 3: Enable Routing over the GRE Tunnel

In Part 3, you will configure OSPF routing so that the LANs on the WEST and EAST routers can communicate using the GRE tunnel.

After the GRE tunnel is set up, the routing protocol can be implemented. For GRE tunneling, a network statement will include the IP network of the tunnel, instead of the network associated with the serial interface. just like you would with other interfaces, such as Serial and Ethernet. Remember that the ISP router is not participating in this routing process.

Step 1.   Configure OSPF routing for area 0 over the tunnel.

    a. Configure OSPF process ID 1 using area 0 on the WEST router for the 172.16.1.0/24 and 172.16.12.0/24 networks.

```
WEST(config)# router ospf 1
WEST(config-router)# network 172.16.1.0 0.0.0.255 area 0
WEST(config-router)# network 172.16.12.0 0.0.0.3 area 0
```

    b. Configure OSPF process ID 1 using area 0 on the EAST router for the 172.16.2.0/24 and 172.16.12.0/24 networks.

```
EAST(config)# router ospf 1
EAST(config-router)# network 172.16.2.0 0.0.0.255 area 0
EAST(config-router)# network 172.16.12.0 0.0.0.3 area 0
```

Step 2.   Verify OSPF routing.

    a. From the WEST router, issue the **show ip route** command to verify the route to 172.16.2.0/24 LAN on the EAST router.

```
WEST# show ip route
Codes: L - local, C - connected, S - static, R - RIP, M - mobile, B - BGP
       D - EIGRP, EX - EIGRP external, O - OSPF, IA - OSPF inter area
       N1 - OSPF NSSA external type 1, N2 - OSPF NSSA external type 2
       E1 - OSPF external type 1, E2 - OSPF external type 2
       i - IS-IS, su - IS-IS summary, L1 - IS-IS level-1, L2 - IS-IS level-2
       ia - IS-IS inter area, * - candidate default, U - per-user static route
       o - ODR, P - periodic downloaded static route, H - NHRP, l - LISP
       + - replicated route, % - next hop override

Gateway of last resort is 10.1.1.2 to network 0.0.0.0

S*     0.0.0.0/0 [1/0] via 10.1.1.2
       10.0.0.0/8 is variably subnetted, 2 subnets, 2 masks
C         10.1.1.0/30 is directly connected, Serial0/0/0
L         10.1.1.1/32 is directly connected, Serial0/0/0
       172.16.0.0/16 is variably subnetted, 5 subnets, 3 masks
C         172.16.1.0/24 is directly connected, GigabitEthernet0/1
```

```
L          172.16.1.1/32 is directly connected, GigabitEthernet0/1
O          172.16.2.0/24 [110/1001] via 172.16.12.2, 00:00:07, Tunnel0
C          172.16.12.0/30 is directly connected, Tunnel0
L          172.16.12.1/32 is directly connected, Tunnel0
```

What is the exit interface and IP address to reach the 172.16.2.0/24 network?

_____

b. From the EAST router issue the command to verify the route to 172.16.1.0/24 LAN on the WEST router.

What is the exit interface and IP address to reach the 172.16.1.0/24 network?

_____

Step 3. Verify end-to-end connectivity.

a. Ping from PC-A to PC-C. It should be successful. If not, troubleshoot until you have end-to-end connectivity.

Note: It may be necessary to disable the PC firewall to ping between PCs.

b. Traceroute from PC-A to PC-C. What is the path from PC-A to PC-C?

_____

Reflection

1. What other configurations are needed to create a secured GRE tunnel?

_____

2. If you added more LANs to the WEST or EAST router, what would you need to do so that the network will use the GRE tunnel for traffic?

_____

Router Interface Summary Table

Router Interface Summary				
Router Model	Ethernet Interface #1	Ethernet Interface #2	Serial Interface #1	Serial Interface #2
1800	Fast Ethernet 0/0 (F0/0)	Fast Ethernet 0/1 (F0/1)	Serial 0/0/0 (S0/0/0)	Serial 0/0/1 (S0/0/1)
1900	Gigabit Ethernet 0/0 (G0/0)	Gigabit Ethernet 0/1 (G0/1)	Serial 0/0/0 (S0/0/0)	Serial 0/0/1 (S0/0/1)
2801	Fast Ethernet 0/0 (F0/0)	Fast Ethernet 0/1 (F0/1)	Serial 0/1/0 (S0/1/0)	Serial 0/1/1 (S0/1/1)
2811	Fast Ethernet 0/0 (F0/0)	Fast Ethernet 0/1 (F0/1)	Serial 0/0/0 (S0/0/0)	Serial 0/0/1 (S0/0/1)
2900	Gigabit Ethernet 0/0 (G0/0)	Gigabit Ethernet 0/1 (G0/1)	Serial 0/0/0 (S0/0/0)	Serial 0/0/1 (S0/0/1)

Note: To find out how the router is configured, look at the interfaces to identify the type of router and how many interfaces the router has. There is no way to effectively list all the combinations of configurations for each router class. This table includes identifiers for the possible combinations of Ethernet and Serial interfaces in the device. The table does not include any other type of interface, even though a specific router may contain one. An example of this might be an ISDN BRI interface. The string in parentheses is the legal abbreviation that can be used in Cisco IOS commands to represent the interface.

3.5.3.5 Packet Tracer–Configure and Verify eBGP

Topology

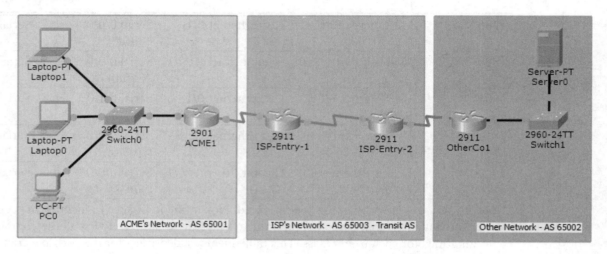

Objectives

Configure and verify eBGP between two autonomous systems.

Background/Scenario

In this activity, you will configure and verify the operation of eBGP between autonomous systems 65001 and 65002. ACME Inc. is a company that has a partnership with Other Company and must exchange routes. Both companies have their own autonomous systems and will use ISP as the transit AS to reach each other.

Note: Only companies with very large networks can afford their own autonomous system.

Address Table

Device	Interface	IPv4 Address	Subnet Mask	Default Gateway
ACME1	G0/0	192.168.0.1	255.255.255.0	N/A
	S0/0/0	1.1.1.2	255.255.255.252	N/A
OtherCo1	G/0/0	172.16.10.1	255.255.255.0	N/A
	S0/0/0	1.1.1.10	255.255.255.252	N/A
ISP1	S0/0/0	1.1.1.1	255.255.255.252	
	S0/0/1	1.1.1.5	255.255.255.252	
ISP2	S0/0/0	1.1.1.9	255.255.255.252	
	S0/0/1	1.1.1.6	255.255.255.252	
PC0	NIC		DHCP	192.168.0.1
Laptop0	NIC		DHCP	192.168.0.1
Laptop1	NIC		DHCP	192.168.0.1
Server	NIC	172.16.10.2	255.255.255.0	172.16.10.1

Step 1.   Configure eBGP in ACME Inc.

ACME Inc. hired an ISP to connect to a partner company called Other Company. The ISP has established network reachability within its network and to Other Company. You must connect ACME to the ISP so that ACME and Other Company can communicate. Because ISP is using BGP as the routing protocol, you must configure ACME1, ACME's border router, to establish a BGP neighbor connection with ISP1, the ISP border router that faces ACME.

   a.   Verify that the ISP has provided IP reachability through its network by pinging 1.1.1.9, the IP address assigned to ISP2's Serial 0/0/0.

   b.   From any device inside ACME's network, ping the Other Company's server 172.16.10.2. The pings should fail as no BGP routing is configured at this time.

   c.   Configure ACME1 to become an eBGP peer with ISP1. ACME's AS number is 65001, while the ISP is using AS number 65003. Use 1.1.1.1 as the neighbor IP address and make sure to add ACME's internal network 192.168.0.0/24 to BGP.

   _____

   _____

   _____

From any device inside ACME's network, ping the Other Company internal server again. Does it work?

_____

Step 2.   Configure eBGP in Other Company Inc.

The network administrator at Other Company is not familiar with BGP and could not configure their side of the link. You must also configure their end of the connection.

Configure OtherCo1 to form an eBGP adjacency with ISP2, the ISP border router facing OtherCo1. Other Company is under AS 65002 while ISP is under AS 65003. Use 1.1.1.9 as the neighbor IP address of ISP2 and make sure to add Other Company's internal network 172.16.10.0/24 to BGP.

   _____

   _____

   _____

Step 3.   eBGP Verification

   a.   Verify that ACME1 has properly formed an eBGP adjacency with ISP1. The **show ip bgp summary** command is very useful here.

   b.   Use the **show ip bgp summary** command to verify all the routes ACME1 has learned via eBGP and their status.

   c.   Look at the routing tables on ACME1 and OtherCo1. ACME1 should have routes learned about Other Company's route 172.16.10.0/24. Similarly, OtherCo1 should now know about ACME's route 192.168.0.0/24.

   d.   Open a web browser in any ACME Inc. end devices and navigate to Other Company's server by entering its IP address 172.16.10.2

   e.   From any ACME Inc. device, ping the Other Company's server at 172.16.10.2.

3.5.3.5 Lab–Configure and Verify eBGP

Topology

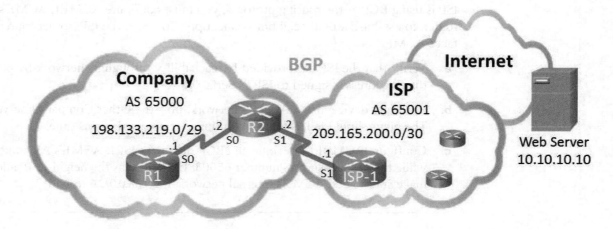

Addressing Table

Device	Interface	IP Address	Subnet Mask
R1	S0/0/0 (DCE)	198.133.219.1	255.255.255.248
R2	S0/0/0	198.133.219.2	255.255.255.248
	S0/0/1 (DCE)	209.165.200.2	255.255.255.252
ISP-1	S0/0/1	209.165.200.1	255.255.255.252
Web Server		10.10.10.10	255.255.255.255

Objectives

Part 1: Build the Network and Configure Basic Device Settings

Part 2: Configure eBGP on R1

Part 3: Verify eBGP Configuration

Background/Scenario

In this lab you will configure eBGP for the Company. The ISP will provide the default route to the Internet. Once configuration is complete you will use various **show** commands to verify that the eBGP configuration is working as expected.

Required Resources

- 3 Routers (Cisco 1941 with Cisco IOS Release 15.2(4)M3 universal image or comparable)
- Console cables to configure the Cisco IOS devices via the console ports
- Serial cables as shown in the topology

Part 1: Build the Network and Configure Basic Device Settings

In Part 1, you will set up the network topology and configure basic settings on R1 and R2 routers. You will also copy the provided configuration for ISP-1 on to that router.

Step 1.   Cable the network as shown in the topology.

Step 2.   Initialize and reload the network devices as necessary.

Step 3.   Configure basic settings on R1 and R2.

    a.   Disable DNS lookup to prevent the routers from attempting to translate incorrectly entered commands as though they were host names.

    b.   Configure the hostnames according to the topology.

    c.   Configure interfaces according to the Addressing Table.

    d.   Save the running configuration to the startup configuration file.

Step 4.   Copy configuration to ISP-1.

Copy and paste the following configuration to ISP-1.

```
hostname ISP-1
no ip domain-lookup
interface Loopback0
 ip address 10.10.10.10 255.255.255.255
interface Serial0/0/1
 ip address 209.165.200.1 255.255.255.252
 no shut
ip route 0.0.0.0 0.0.0.0 lo0
router bgp 65001
 bgp log-neighbor-changes
 network 0.0.0.0
 neighbor 209.165.200.2 remote-as 65000
end
```

Part 2: Configure eBGP on R2

Configure R2 to become an eBGP peer with ISP-1. Refer to the Topology for BGP AS number information.

Step 1.   Enable BGP and identify the AS number for the Company.

```
R2(config)# router bgp 65000
```

Step 2.   Use the neighbor command to identify ISP-1 as the BGP peer.

```
R2(config-router)# neighbor 209.165.200.1 remote-as 65001
```

Step 3.   Add the Company's network to the BGP table so it is advertised to ISP-1.

```
R2(config-router)# network 198.133.219.0 mask 255.255.255.248
```

Part 3: Verify eBGP Configuration

In Part 3, use the BGP verification commands to verify that the BGP configuration is working as expected.

Step 1.   Display the IPv4 routing table on R2.

```
R2# show ip route
Codes: L - local, C - connected, S - static, R - RIP, M - mobile, B - BGP
       D - EIGRP, EX - EIGRP external, O - OSPF, IA - OSPF inter area
       N1 - OSPF NSSA external type 1, N2 - OSPF NSSA external type 2
       E1 - OSPF external type 1, E2 - OSPF external type 2
       i - IS-IS, su - IS-IS summary, L1 - IS-IS level-1, L2 - IS-IS level-2
       ia - IS-IS inter area, * - candidate default, U - per-user static route
       o - ODR, P - periodic downloaded static route, H - NHRP, l - LISP
       a - application route
       + - replicated route, % - next hop override

Gateway of last resort is 209.165.200.1 to network 0.0.0.0

B*     0.0.0.0/0 [20/0] via 209.165.200.1, 00:00:07
       198.133.219.0/24 is variably subnetted, 2 subnets, 2 masks
C         198.133.219.0/29 is directly connected, Serial0/0/0
L         198.133.219.2/32 is directly connected, Serial0/0/0
       209.165.200.0/24 is variably subnetted, 2 subnets, 2 masks
C         209.165.200.0/30 is directly connected, Serial0/0/1
L         209.165.200.2/32 is directly connected, Serial0/0/1
```

Step 2.   Display the BGP table on R2.

```
R2# show ip bgp
BGP table version is 4, local router ID is 209.165.200.2
Status codes: s suppressed, d damped, h history, * valid, > best, i - internal,
              r RIB-failure, S Stale, m multipath, b backup-path, f RT-Filter,
              x best-external, a additional-path, c RIB-compressed,
Origin codes: i - IGP, e - EGP, ? - incomplete
RPKI validation codes: V valid, I invalid, N Not found

     Network          Next Hop         Metric LocPrf Weight Path
 *>  0.0.0.0          209.165.200.1         0             0 65001 i
 *>  198.133.219.0/29 0.0.0.0               0         32768 i
```

Step 3.   Display the BGP connection status on R2.

```
R2# show ip bgp summary
BGP router identifier 209.165.200.2, local AS number 65000
BGP table version is 4, main routing table version 4
2 network entries using 288 bytes of memory
2 path entries using 160 bytes of memory
2/2 BGP path/bestpath attribute entries using 320 bytes of memory
1 BGP AS-PATH entries using 24 bytes of memory
0 BGP route-map cache entries using 0 bytes of memory
0 BGP filter-list cache entries using 0 bytes of memory
```

```
BGP using 792 total bytes of memory
BGP activity 2/0 prefixes, 2/0 paths, scan interval 60 secs

Neighbor          V        AS MsgRcvd MsgSent    TblVer  InQ OutQ Up/Down   State/PfxRcd
209.165.200.1    4     65001       12       11         4    0    0 00:06:56            1
```

Step 4. Display the IPv4 routing table on ISP-1.

Verify that the 198.133.218.0/29 network is being advertised to the ISP-1 router.

```
ISP-1# show ip route
Codes: L - local, C - connected, S - static, R - RIP, M - mobile, B - BGP
       D - EIGRP, EX - EIGRP external, O - OSPF, IA - OSPF inter area
       N1 - OSPF NSSA external type 1, N2 - OSPF NSSA external type 2
       E1 - OSPF external type 1, E2 - OSPF external type 2
       i - IS-IS, su - IS-IS summary, L1 - IS-IS level-1, L2 - IS-IS level-2
       ia - IS-IS inter area, * - candidate default, U - per-user static route
       o - ODR, P - periodic downloaded static route, H - NHRP, l - LISP
       a - application route
       + - replicated route, % - next hop override

Gateway of last resort is 0.0.0.0 to network 0.0.0.0

S*     0.0.0.0/0 is directly connected, Loopback0
       10.0.0.0/32 is subnetted, 1 subnets
C         10.10.10.10 is directly connected, Loopback0
       198.133.219.0/29 is subnetted, 1 subnets
B         198.133.219.0 [20/0] via 209.165.200.2, 00:00:25
       209.165.200.0/24 is variably subnetted, 2 subnets, 2 masks
C         209.165.200.0/30 is directly connected, Serial0/0/1
L         209.165.200.1/32 is directly connected, Serial0/0/1
```

Ping the Web Server from R1. Were the pings successful?

_____

Reflection

The topology used in this lab was created to demonstrate how to configure the BGP routing protocol. However, the BGP protocol would not normally be configured for a topology like this in the real world. Explain.

_____

_____

_____

_____

Router Interface Summary Table

Router Interface Summary				
Router Model	Ethernet Interface #1	Ethernet Interface #2	Serial Interface #1	Serial Interface #2
1800	Fast Ethernet 0/0 (F0/0)	Fast Ethernet 0/1 (F0/1)	Serial 0/0/0 (S0/0/0)	Serial 0/0/1 (S0/0/1)
1900	Gigabit Ethernet 0/0 (G0/0)	Gigabit Ethernet 0/1 (G0/1)	Serial 0/0/0 (S0/0/0)	Serial 0/0/1 (S0/0/1)
2801	Fast Ethernet 0/0 (F0/0)	Fast Ethernet 0/1 (F0/1)	Serial 0/1/0 (S0/1/0)	Serial 0/1/1 (S0/1/1)
2811	Fast Ethernet 0/0 (F0/0)	Fast Ethernet 0/1 (F0/1)	Serial 0/0/0 (S0/0/0)	Serial 0/0/1 (S0/0/1)
2900	Gigabit Ethernet 0/0 (G0/0)	Gigabit Ethernet 0/1 (G0/1)	Serial 0/0/0 (S0/0/0)	Serial 0/0/1 (S0/0/1)

Note: To find out how the router is configured, look at the interfaces to identify the type of router and how many interfaces the router has. There is no way to effectively list all the combinations of configurations for each router class. This table includes identifiers for the possible combinations of Ethernet and Serial interfaces in the device. The table does not include any other type of interface, even though a specific router may contain one. An example of this might be an ISDN BRI interface. The string in parentheses is the legal abbreviation that can be used in Cisco IOS commands to represent the interface.

3.6.1.1 Class Activity–VPN Planning Design

Objective

Explain the use of VPNs in securing site-to-site connectivity in a small- to medium-sized business network.

Scenario

Your small- to medium-sized business has received quite a few new contracts lately. This has increased the need for teleworkers and workload outsourcing. The new contract vendors and clients will also need access to your network as the projects progress.

As network administrator for the business, you recognize that VPNs must be incorporated as a part of your network strategy to support secure access by the teleworkers, employees, and vendors or clients.

To prepare for implementation of VPNs on the network, you devise a planning checklist to bring to the next department meeting for discussion.

Resources

- World Wide Web access
- Packet Tracer software
- Word processing software

Step 1. Visit the VPN Discovery Tool, http://help.mysonicwall.com/sw/eng/4201/ui2/23600/VPN/VPN_Policy.htm, or any other Internet site with VPN-implementation or planning checklist examples.

Step 2. Use Packet Tracer to draw the current topology for your network; no device configurations are necessary. Include:

- Two branch offices: the Internet cloud and one headquarters location
- Current network devices: servers, switches, routers/core routers, broadband ISR devices, and local user workstations

Step 3. On the Packet Tracer topology, indicate:

    a. Where would you implement VPNs?

    b. What types of VPNs would be needed?

        1) Site to site

        2) Remote access

Step 4. Using a word processing software program, create a small VPN planning checklist based on your research from Step 1.

Step 5. Share your work with the class, another group, or your instructor.

3.6.1.2 Packet Tracer–Skills Integration Challenge

Topology

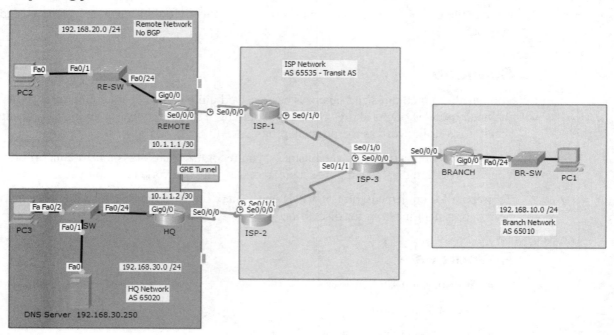

Addressing Table

Device	Interface	IP Address	Subnet Mask	Default Gateway
ISP-1	S0/0/0	209.165.201.1	255.255.255.252	N/A
	S0/1/0	209.165.201.9	255.255.255.252	N/A
ISP-2	S0/0/0	209.165.201.17	255.255.255.252	N/A
	S0/1/1	209.165.201.13	255.255.255.252	N/A
ISP-3	S0/0/0	209.165.201.21	255.255.255.252	N/A
	S0/1/0	209.165.201.10	255.255.255.252	N/A
	S0/1/1	209.165.201.14	255.255.255.252	N/A
REMOTE	S0/0/0	209.165.201.2	255.255.255.252	N/A
	G0/0	192.168.20.1	255.255.255.0	N/A
	Tunnel 10	10.1.1.1	255.255.255.252	N/A
HQ	S0/0/0	209.165.201.18	255.255.255.252	N/A
	G0/0	192.168.30.1	255.255.255.0	N/A
	Tunnel 10	10.1.1.2	255.255.255.252	N/A
BRANCH	S0/0/0	209.165.201.22	255.255.255.252	N/A
	G0/0	192.168.10.1	255.255.255.0	N/A
PC1	NIC	DHCP		192.168.10.1
PC2	NIC	192.168.20.10	255.255.255.0	192.168.20.1
PC3	NIC	DHCP		192.168.30.1
DNS Server	NIC	192.168.30.250	255.255.255.0	192.168.30.1

Background/Scenario

In this skills integration challenge, the XYZ Corporation uses a combination of eBGP, PPP, and GRE WAN connections. Other technologies include DHCP, default routing, OSPF for IPv4, and SSH configurations.

Requirements

Note: The user EXEC password is **cisco** and the privileged EXEC password is **class**.

Interface Addressing

- Configure interface addressing as needed on appropriate devices.
    - Use the topology table to implement addressing on routers REMOTE, HQ, and BRANCH.
    - Configure **PC1** and **PC3** to use DHCP.

SSH

- Configure **HQ** to use SSH for remote access.
    - Set the modulus to **2048**. The domain name is **CISCO.com**.
    - The username is **admin** and the password is **secureaccess**.
    - Only SSH should be allowed on the VTY lines.
    - Modify the SSH defaults: version 2; 60-second timeout; two retries.

PPP

- Configure the WAN link from **BRANCH** to the **ISP-3** router using PPP encapsulation and CHAP authentication.
    - Create a user **ISP-3** with the password of **cisco**.
- Configure the WAN link from **HQ** to the **ISP-2** router using PPP encapsulation and CHAP authentication.
    - Create a user **ISP-2** with the password of **cisco**.

DHCP

- On **BRANCH**, configure a DHCP pool for the BRANCH LAN using the following requirements:
    - Exclude the first 5 IP addresses in the range.
    - The case-sensitive pool name is **LAN**.
    - Include the DNS server attached to the **HQ** LAN as part of the DHCP configuration.
- Configure PC1 to use DHCP.
- On **HQ**, configure a DHCP pool for the HQ LAN using the following requirements:
    - Exclude the first 10 IP addresses in the range.
    - The case-sensitive pool name is **LAN**.
    - Include the DNS server attached to the **HQ** LAN as part of the DHCP configuration.
- Configure PC3 to use DHCP.

Default Routing

- Configure **REMOTE** with a default route to the **ISP-1** router. Use the Next-Hop IP as an argument.

eBGP Routing

- Configure **BRANCH** with eBGP routing.

  - Configure **BRANCH** to peer with **ISP-3**.

  - Add **BRANCH's** internal network to BGP.

- Configure **HQ** with eBGP routing.

  - Configure **HQ** to peer with **ISP-2**.

  - Add **HQ's** internal network to BGP.

GRE Tunneling

- Configure **REMOTE** with a tunnel interface to send IP traffic over GRE to **HQ**.

  - Configure **Tunnel 10** with appropriate addressing information.

  - Configure the tunnel source with the local exit interface.

  - Configure the tunnel destination with the appropriate endpoint IP address.

- Configure **HQ** with a tunnel interface to send IP traffic over GRE to **REMOTE**.

  - Configure **Tunnel 10** with appropriate addressing information.

  - Configure the tunnel source with the local exit interface.

  - Configure the tunnel destination with the appropriate endpoint IP address.

OSPF Routing

- Because the **REMOTE** LAN should have connectivity to the **HQ** LAN, configure OSPF across the GRE tunnel.

  - Configure OSPF process 100 on the **REMOTE** router.

  - **REMOTE** should advertise the LAN network via OSPF.

  - **REMOTE** should be configured to form an adjacency with **HQ** over the GRE tunnel.

  - Disable OSPF updates on appropriate interfaces.

- Because the **HQ** LAN should have connectivity to the **REMOTE** LAN, configure OSPF across the GRE tunnel.

  - Configure OSPF process 100 on the **HQ** router.

  - **HQ** should advertise the LAN network via OSPF.

  - **HQ** should be configured to form an adjacency with **REMOTE** over the GRE tunnel.

  - Disable OSPF updates on appropriate interfaces.

Connectivity

- Verify full connectivity from **PC2** to the **DNS Server**.

- Verify full connectivity from **PC1** to the **DNS Server**.

3.6.1.3 Lab–Configure a Branch Connection

Topology

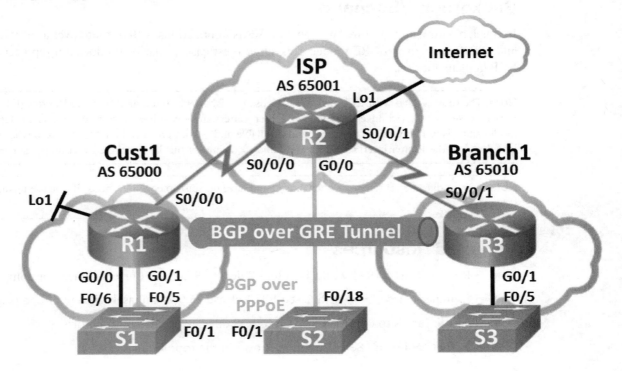

Addressing Table

Device	Interface	IP Address	Subnet Mask
R1	G0/0	192.168.1.1	255.255.255.0
	G0/1	PPPoE Client	
	Lo1	209.165.200.49	255.255.255.240
	S0/0/0 (DCE)	209.165.200.81	255.255.255.252
R2	G0/0	PPPoE Provider	
	Lo1	209.165.200.65	255.255.255.240
	S0/0/0	209.165.200.82	255.255.255.252
	S0/0/1 (DCE)	209.165.200.85	255.255.255.252
R3	G0/1	192.168.3.1	255.255.255.0
	S0/0/1 (DCE)	209.165.200.86	255.255.255.252

Objectives

Part 1: Build the Network and Load Device Configurations

Part 2: Configure a PPPoE Client Connection

Part 3: Configure a GRE Tunnel

Part 4: Configure BGP over PPPoE and BGP over a GRE Tunnel

Background/Scenario

In this lab, you will configure two separate WAN connections, a BGP route over a PPPoE connection, and a BGP route over a GRE tunnel. This lab is a test case scenario and does not represent a realistic BGP implementation.

Note: The routers used with CCNA hands-on labs are Cisco 1941 Integrated Services Routers (ISRs) with Cisco IOS, Release 15.2(4)M3 (universalk9 image). Other routers and Cisco IOS versions can be used. Depending on the model and Cisco IOS version, the commands available and output produced might vary from what is shown in the labs. Refer to the Router Interface Summary Table at the end of this lab for the correct interface identifiers.

Note: Ensure that the routers have been erased and have no startup configurations. If you are unsure, contact your instructor.

Required Resources

- 3 Routers (Cisco 1941 with Cisco IOS Release 15.2(4)M3 universal image or comparable)
- 3 Switches (Cisco 2960 with Cisco IOS Release 15.0(2) lanbasek9 image or comparable)
- Console cables to configure the Cisco IOS devices via the console ports
- Ethernet cables and Serial cables as shown in the topology

Part 1: Build the Network and Load Device Configurations

Step 1. Cable the network as shown in the topology.

Step 2. Load router configurations.

Copy and paste the following configurations into the appropriate routers and switch.

Cust 1 (R1) Configuration:

```
conf t
hostname Cust1
no cdp run
interface Loopback1
 ip address 209.165.200.49 255.255.255.240
interface GigabitEthernet0/0
 ip address 192.168.1.1 255.255.255.0
 no shut
interface Serial0/0/0
 ip address 209.165.200.81 255.255.255.252
 no shut
ip route 0.0.0.0 0.0.0.0 s0/0/0 25
end
```

Note: In the Cust1 configuration above, CDP is disabled with the **no cdp run** command. The static default route with an administrative distance is manually configured to 25 instead of the default 1. The significance of these configurations will be explained later in the lab.

ISP (R2) Configuration:

```
conf t
hostname ISP
username Cust1 password 0 ciscopppoe
bba-group pppoe global
 virtual-template 1
interface Loopback 1
 ip address 209.165.200.65 255.255.255.240
interface GigabitEthernet0/0
 ip tcp adjust-mss 1452
 pppoe enable group global
 no shut
interface Serial0/0/0
 ip address 209.165.200.82 255.255.255.252
 no shut
interface Serial0/0/1
 ip address 209.165.200.85 255.255.255.252
 no shut
interface Virtual-Template1
 mtu 1492
 ip address 209.165.200.30 255.255.255.224
 peer default ip address pool PPPoEPOOL
 ppp authentication chap callin
router bgp 65001
 network 0.0.0.0
 neighbor 209.165.200.1 remote-as 65000
ip local pool PPPoEPOOL 209.165.200.1 209.165.200.20
ip route 0.0.0.0 0.0.0.0 Loopback1
end
```

Branch1 (R3) Configuration:

```
conf t
hostname Branch1
interface GigabitEthernet0/1
 ip address 192.168.3.1 255.255.255.0
 no shut
interface Serial0/0/1
 ip address 209.165.200.86 255.255.255.252
 no shut
ip route 0.0.0.0 0.0.0.0 Serial0/0/1
end
```

S1 Configuration:

```
conf t
hostname S1
vlan 111
interface f0/6
```

```
        switchport mode access
        switchport access vlan 111
            end
```

Note: Because S1 connects to two separate networks, G0/0 and G0/1 on Cust1, it is necessary to segment the switch into two separate VLANs, in this case VLAN111 and VLAN1.

Step 3. Save the configuration on all configured routers and switches.

Part 2: Configure a PPPoE Client Connection

In Part 2, following the PPPoE requirements listed below, you will configure Cust1 as the PPPoE client. The ISP router configuration is already complete.

PPPoE requirements for the Cust1 router:

- Configure an **interface Dialer1** with the following settings:
  - **a negotiated ip address**
  - **mtu 1492**
  - **ppp encapsulation**
  - **dialer pool 1**
  - **ppp chap callin authentication**
  - **ppp chap hostname Cust1**
  - **ppp chap password ciscopppoe (unencrypted)**
- Configure **G0/1** with the following settings:
  - **enable global pppoe**
  - **adjust the TCP maximum segment size to 1452**
  - **set the pppoe-client to dialer pool 1**

List the commands used to configure Cust1 as the PPPoE Client:

_____

_____

_____

_____

_____

_____

_____

_____

_____

_____

_____

If the Cust1 router is configured correctly, it should receive an IP address from the ISP router. What IP address did Cust1 receive and on what interface? What command did you use to check for the IP address and interface?

_____

_____

Note: If Cust1 had CDP running on interface dialer1, it could produce the following repeating log message: *PPP: Outbound cdp packet dropped, NCP not negotiated*. To prevent this, CDP was globally turned off.

Part 3: Configure a GRE Tunnel

In Part 3, following the GRE requirements listed below, you will configure a GRE tunnel between Cust1 and Branch1.

GRE tunnel requirements:

- On Cust1 and Branch1, configure **interface Tunnel 0** with the following settings:
  - **IP address 192.168.2.1/24 and 192.168.2.2/24 respectively**
  - **Tunnel mode GRE over IP**
  - **Tunnel source interface and destination address using serial interfaces**

List the commands used to configure a GRE tunnel between Cust1 and Branch1:

_____

_____

_____

_____

_____

_____

_____

_____

_____

How can you tell if the tunnel was created successfully? What command could you use to test the tunnel?

_____

_____

What would happen if Cust1 did not have a static default route? Test it by removing the static default route. What was the result? Make sure to replace the static default route, as shown in the Cust1 configuration in Part 1 Step 2, before moving on.

_____

_____

Part 4: Configure BGP over PPPoE and BGP over a GRE Tunnel

In Part 4, following the BGP requirements listed below, you will configure BGP on Cust1 and Branch1. The ISP router configuration is already complete.

BGP requirements:

- On Cust1:
    - **Create a BGP routing process AS 65000**
    - **Advertise networks attached to Loopback 1 and G0/0**
    - **Configure BGP neighbors to the ISP and Branch1 routers**
- On Branch1:
    - **Create a BGP routing process AS 65010**
    - **Advertise the network attached to G0/1**
    - **Configure BGP neighbor to Cust1 only**

List the commands used to configure BGP on Cust1 and Branch1:

_____

_____

_____

_____

_____

_____

_____

On Cust1, did you receive console messages regarding BGP neighbor relationships to ISP and Branch1?

_____

On Cust1, can you ping the ISP at 209.165.200.30 over PPPoE? Can you ping the Branch1 local network at 192.168.3.1?

_____

Check the routing table of Cust1. What routes were learned by BGP? There should be a route learned from both ISP and Branch1.

_____

_____

Examine the two routes learned by BGP in the Cust1 routing table. What do they show about routes in the network now?

_____

_____

_____

_____

Router Interface Summary Table

Router Interface Summary				
Router Model	Ethernet Interface #1	Ethernet Interface #2	Serial Interface #1	Serial Interface #2
1800	Fast Ethernet 0/0 (F0/0)	Fast Ethernet 0/1 (F0/1)	Serial 0/0/0 (S0/0/0)	Serial 0/0/1 (S0/0/1)
1900	Gigabit Ethernet 0/0 (G0/0)	Gigabit Ethernet 0/1 (G0/1)	Serial 0/0/0 (S0/0/0)	Serial 0/0/1 (S0/0/1)
2801	Fast Ethernet 0/0 (F0/0)	Fast Ethernet 0/1 (F0/1)	Serial 0/1/0 (S0/1/0)	Serial 0/1/1 (S0/1/1)
2811	Fast Ethernet 0/0 (F0/0)	Fast Ethernet 0/1 (F0/1)	Serial 0/0/0 (S0/0/0)	Serial 0/0/1 (S0/0/1)
2900	Gigabit Ethernet 0/0 (G0/0)	Gigabit Ethernet 0/1 (G0/1)	Serial 0/0/0 (S0/0/0)	Serial 0/0/1 (S0/0/1)

Note: To find out how the router is configured, look at the interfaces to identify the type of router and how many interfaces the router has. There is no way to effectively list all the combinations of configurations for each router class. This table includes identifiers for the possible combinations of Ethernet and Serial interfaces in the device. The table does not include any other type of interface, even though a specific router may contain one. An example of this might be an ISDN BRI interface. The string in parentheses is the legal abbreviation that can be used in Cisco IOS commands to represent the interface.

CHAPTER 4

Access Control Lists

One of the most important skills a network administrator needs is mastery of access control lists (ACLs). An ACL is a sequential list of permit or deny statements that apply to addresses or upper-layer protocols. ACLs provide a powerful way to control traffic into and out of a network. ACLs can be configured for all routed network protocols. In this chapter, you learn how to use standard and extended IPv4 ACLs and IPv6 ACLs on a Cisco router as part of a security solution.

ACL Operation

An ACL is a series of IOS commands that control whether a router forwards or drops packets based on information found in the packet header. ACLs are among the most commonly used features of Cisco IOS software.

Guidelines for ACL Creation

Complete the ACL Operation sentences on the left using words from the Word Bank on the right. Not all words are used.

ACL Operation

a. An access control list (ACL) controls whether the router will _____ or _____ packet traffic based on packet header criteria.

b. A router with three interfaces and two network protocols (IPv4 and IPv6) can have as many as _____ active ACLs.

c. ACLs are often used in routers between internal and external networks to provide a _____.

d. For inbound ACLs, incoming packets are processed _____ they are sent to the outbound interface.

e. For outbound ACLs, incoming packets are processed _____ they are sent to the outbound interface.

f. For every ACL, there is an implied deny statement; if a packet does not match any of the ACL criteria, it will be _____.

g. ACLs can filter data traffic per protocol, per direction, and per _____.

h. ACLs can filter traffic based on source/destination address, _____, and port numbers.

Word Bank

Discarded

Four

Firewall

Interface

Pathway

Deny

After

Processing

6

Protocol

12

Forwarded

Permit

Switch

Before

Calculating Wildcard Masks

A wildcard mask is a string of 32 binary digits used by the router to determine which bits of the address to examine for a match before permitting or denying the packet.

As with subnet masks, the numbers 1 and 0 in the wildcard mask identify how to treat the corresponding IP address bits. However, in a wildcard mask, these bits are used for different purposes and follow different rules. Subnet masks use binary 1s and 0s to identify the network, subnet, and host portion of an IP address. Wildcard masks use binary 1s and 0s to filter individual IP addresses or groups of IP addresses to permit or deny access to resources.

When filtering traffic for a network, the *wildcard-mask* argument is simply the inverse of the subnet mask. For example, the bit pattern for 11110000 (240) becomes 00001111 (15).

For the ACL statements in Table 4-1, record the wildcard mask used to filter the specified IPv4 address or network.

Table 4-1   Determine the Correct Wildcard Mask

ACL Statement	Wildcard Mask
Permit all hosts from the 192.168.1.0/25 network	
Permit all hosts from the 10.0.0.0/16 network	
Deny all hosts from the 10.10.100.0/24 network	
Deny all hosts from the 10.20.30.128/26 network	
Permit all hosts from the 172.18.0.0/23 network	
Permit all hosts from the 192.168.5.0/27 network	
Deny host 172.18.33.1	
Deny all hosts from the 172.16.1.192/29 network	
Permit all hosts from the 172.31.64.0/18 network	
Permit host 10.10.10.1	
Deny all hosts from the 172.25.250.160/28 network	
Deny all hosts from the 172.30.128.0/20 network	
Deny all hosts from 10.10.128.0/19 network	
Permit all hosts from the 172.18.0.0/16 network	
Permit all hosts from the 192.168.200.0/30 network	

Wildcard Mask in Operation

In Table 4-2, for each of the ACL statements and corresponding source addresses, choose whether the router will either permit or deny the packet.

Table 4-2   Determine the Permit or Deny

ACL Statement	Source Address	Permit or Deny
access-list 33 permit 198.168.100.0 0.0.0.63	198.168.100.3	
access-list 20 permit 192.168.223.64 0.0.0.15	192.168.223.72	
access-list 21 permit 192.0.2.11 0.0.0.15	192.0.2.17	
access-list 39 permit 198.168.100.64 0.0.0.63	192.168.22.100.40	
access-list 66 permit 172.16.0.0 0.0.255.255	172.17.0.5	
access-list 65 permit 172.16.1.1 0.0.0.0	172.16.1.1	
access-list 16 permit 10.10.10.0 0.0.0.255	10.10.10.33	
access-list 60 permit 10.10.0.0 0.0.255.255	10.10.33.33	
access-list 50 permit 192.168.122.128 0.0.0.63	192.168.122.195	
access-list 55 permit 192.168.15.0 0.0.0.3	192.168.15.5	
access-list 30 permit 192.168.223.32 0.0.0.31	192.168.223.60	
access-list 1 permit 192.168.155.0 0.0.0.255	192.168.155.245	
access-list 25 permit 172.18.5.0 0.0.0.255	172.18.6.20	
access-list 50 permit 192.168.155.0 0.0.0.255	192.168.156.245	
access-list 18 permit 10.10.10.0 0.0.0.63	10.10.10.50	

Standard Versus Extended IPv4 ACLs

In Table 4-3, indicate whether the description applies to standard, extended, or named ACLs.

Table 4-3   Standard, Extended, and Named ACLs

ACL Type Descriptions	Standard	Extended	Named
Uses ACL numbers 100–199.			
Uses ACL numbers 1300–1999.			
Uses ACL numbers 1–99.			
Entries can be added or deleted within the ACL.			
Simplest type of ACL; used for smaller networks.			
Filters traffic solely based on source address.			
Uses a numeric identifier and filters on protocol numbers.			
Should be typed with ALL CAPITAL LETTERS.			
Starts with a number and filters by destination address.			
Can be used inclusively for ACL numbers 1–199.			

Guidelines for ACL Placement

Every ACL should be placed where it has the greatest impact on efficiency. The basic rules are as follows:

- Locate _____ ACLs as close to the destination as possible because these ACLs do not specify destination addresses.

- Locate _____ ACLs as close as possible to the source of the traffic to be filtered because these ACLs specify the source and the destination.

Use the information shown in Figure 4-1 to determine the router, interface, and direction for each scenario in Table 4-4.

Figure 4-1   ACL Placement Topology

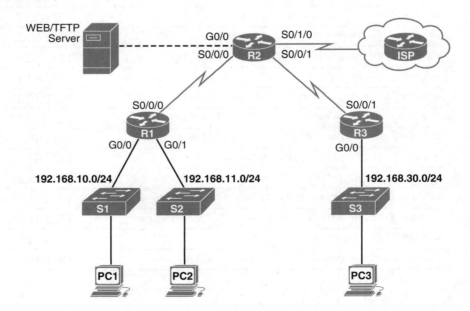

Table 4-4   ACL Placement Scenarios

Scenario	Router	Interface	Direction
Use a standard ACL to stop the 192.168.10.0/24 network from accessing the Internet through the ISP.			
Use a standard ACL to stop the 192.168.11.0/24 network from accessing the 192.168.10.0/24 network.			
Use an extended ACL to allow only TFTP and web traffic to access the WEB/TFTP server.			
Use an extended ACL to stop the 192.168.30.0/24 network from accessing the web/TFTP server.			

Standard IPv4 ACLs

To use numbered or named standard ACLs on a Cisco router, you must first create the standard ACL. Then you must apply the ACL to one of the router's processes such as an interface or Telnet lines.

Configuring Standard IPv4 ACLs

The full command syntax to configure a standard ACL is as follows:

```
Router(config)# access-list access-list-number { deny | permit | remark } source [ source-wildcard ][ log ]
```

The following ACL statement would first add a remark and then permit traffic from the 172.16.0.0/16 network:

```
Router(config)# access-list 1 remark Permit traffic from HR LAN, 172.16.0.0/16
```

```
Router(config)# access-list 1 permit 172.16.0.0 0.0.255.255
```

In this case, the remark is not that helpful. However, in more complex configuration scenarios, the remark option can help to quickly communicate the purpose of an ACL statement.

If the policy calls for filtering traffic for a specific host, you can use the host address and 0.0.0.0 as the wildcard mask. But if you do, the IOS will drop the 0.0.0.0 and just use the host address as shown in Example 4-1.

Note: Older IOS versions convert 0.0.0.0 to the keyword **host** and prepend it before the IP address, such as **host 172.16.1.10**.

Example 4-1   Filtering One IP Address

```
R1(config)# access-list 1 deny 172.16.1.10 0.0.0.0
R1(config)# do show access-lists
Standard IP access list 1
    10 deny   172.16.1.10
R1(config)#
```

If the policy calls for filtering traffic for all sources, you can configure 0.0.0.0 255.255.255.255 as the source address and wildcard mask. The IOS will convert it to the keyword **any**, as shown in Example 4-2.

Example 4-2   Filtering All Addresses

```
R1(config)# access-list 1 deny 172.16.1.10 0.0.0.0

R1(config)# access-list 1 permit 0.0.0.0 255.255.255.255

R1(config)# do show access-lists

Standard IP access list 1

    10 deny  172.16.1.10

    20 permit any

R1(config)#
```

Note: The sequence numbers before each statement can be used to edit the statement, as discussed later.

An ACL has no impact unless it is applied to some process. To filter inbound or outbound traffic, an ACL must be applied to an interface and the direction of traffic specified. The command syntax to apply an ACL to an interface is as follows:

```
Router(config-if)# ip access-group { access-list-number | access-list-name } { in | out }
```

Naming an ACL makes it easier to understand its function. For example, an ACL configured to deny FTP could be called NO_FTP. The command syntax to enter named ACL configuration mode is as follows:

```
Router(config)# ip access-list [ standard | extended ] name
```

The *name* can be any alphanumeric string that does not begin with a number. Once in named ACL configuration mode, the router prompt changes depending on whether you chose standard or extended. The syntax for named standard ACL configuration mode is as follows:

```
Router(config-std-nacl)# [ permit | deny | remark ] { source [source-wildcard] } [log}
```

So, to reconfigure Example 4-2 with a named standard ACL and a remark, we could do something like Example 4-3.

Example 4-3   Standard Named ACL

```
R1(config)# ip access-list standard NOT_BOB

R1(config-std-nacl)# remark Stop Bob

R1(config-std-nacl)# deny host 172.16.1.10

R1(config-std-nacl)# permit any

R1(config-std-nacl)# exit

R1(config)# interface g0/0

R1(config-if)# ip access-group NOT_BOB in

R1(config-if)# do show access-lists

Standard IP access list NOT_BOB

    10 deny host 172.16.1.10

    20 permit any

R1(config-if)#
```

Use the information in Figure 4-2 to write ACL statements for the following three scenarios. Include the router prompt in your configurations.

Figure 4-2   Topology for Standard ACL Configuration Scenarios

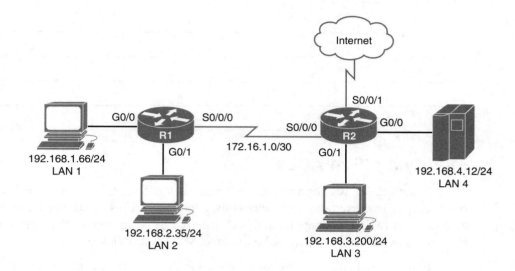

Standard ACL Scenario 1

Record the commands to configure and apply a standard ACL that will filter traffic into the 192.168.1.0 LAN. The 192.168.3.77 host should not be able to access this LAN, but all other hosts on the 192.168.3.0 and 192.168.4.0 networks should be permitted. All other traffic should be blocked.

_____

_____

_____

_____

_____

_____

Standard ACL Scenario 2

Record the commands to configure and apply a standard ACL that will filter traffic to host 192.168.4.12. Both the 192.168.1.66 host and all hosts in the 192.168.2.0 LAN should be permitted access to this host. All other networks should not be able to access the 192.168.4.12 host.

_____

_____

_____

_____

_____

Standard ACL Scenario 3

LAN 1, 2, and 3 should not be accessible from the Internet. Record the commands to configure and apply a standard ACL that will block traffic to LANs. Internet traffic should only be allowed to access the 192.168.4.12 server.

_____

_____

_____

_____

_____

Modifying IPv4 ACLs

The IOS automatically adds a sequence number before the ACL statement, as you can see in the previous examples that used the **show access-lists** command. These sequence numbers can be used to delete an erroneous ACL statement and add back a correct ACL statement. The rules for using sequence numbers to edit a standard or extended numbered ACL are as follows:

1. Enter named ACL configuration mode for the ACL even if it is a numbered ACL.

2. Delete the sequence number that is in error.

3. Use the deleted sequence number to add in the correct ACL statement.

Note: For standard and extended numbered ACLs, you cannot add a new sequence number statement in the middle of the ACL.

In Example 4-4, the wrong address is currently being denied. Enter the commands to delete the erroneous statement and add back a statement to deny 192.168.1.66.

Example 4-4   Standard Numbered ACL with Error

```
R1(config)# access-list 1 deny 192.168.1.65
R1(config)# access-list 1 permit any
R1(config)# do show access-lists
Standard IP access list 1
    10 deny   192.168.1.65
    20 permit any
R1(config)# ip access-list standard 1
```

_____

_____

_____

_____

_____

_____

_____

Extended IPv4 ACLs

For more precise traffic-filtering control, extended IPv4 ACLs can be created. Extended ACLs are numbered 100 to 199 and 2000 to 2699, providing a total of 799 possible extended numbered ACLs. Extended ACLs can also be named.

Configuring Extended IPv4 ACL Statements

The procedural steps for configuring extended ACLs are the same as for standard ACLs. The extended ACL is first configured, and then it is activated on an interface. However, the command syntax and parameters are more complex to support the additional features provided by extended ACLs. The command syntax for an extended ACL with some of the available options is as follows:

```
Router(config)# access-list access-list-number { deny | permit | remark } protocol source
[source-wildcard] destination [destination-wildcard] [operand] [port-number or name]
[established]
```

Use the operand to compare source or destination ports. Possible operands are **lt** (less than), **gt** (greater than), **eq** (equal), **neq** (not equal), and **range**.

For example, to allow host 172.16.1.11 web access to 10.10.10.10, you might use the following ACL statement:

```
R1(config)# access-list 100 permit tcp host 172.16.1.11 host 10.10.10.10 eq 80
```

Note: You must either use the **host** keyword or **0.0.0.0** for the wildcard mask when configuring an extended ACL to filter one IP address.

The steps for configuring, applying, and editing named and numbered extended ACLs is the same as standard ACLs.

Extended ACL Configuration Scenarios

Refer to the topology in Figure 4-3. Then use the bank of ACL statement components to construct an ACL statement for the following scenarios. Some components may be equivalent. Some components will not be used.

Figure 4-3   Topology for Extended ACL Configuration Scenarios

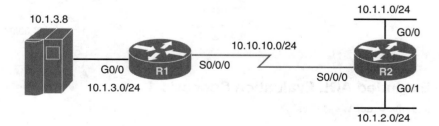

ACL Components

10.1.3.0	50	udp	10.1.2.0	99	any
eq 21	0.0.0.0	eq 53	deny	host	10.1.3.8
101	150	ip	10.1.1.0	122	10.10.10.0
permit	eq 80	access-list	0.0.0.255	10.1.2.9	tcp

Extended ACL Scenario 1

Record the command to configure a numbered ACL statement that will only allow users on the 10.1.1.0/24 network to have HTTP access to the Web Server on the 10.1.3.0/24 network. The ACL is applied to R2 G0/0 inbound.

Extended ACL Scenario 2

Record the command to configure a numbered ACL statement that will block host 10.1.2.9 from having FTP access to the 10.1.1.0/24 network. The ACL is applied to R2 G0/1 inbound.

Extended ACL Scenario 3

Record the command to configure a numbered ACL statement that will allow only host 10.1.3.8 on the 10.1.3.0/24 network to reach destinations beyond that network. The ACL is applied to R1 G0/0 inbound.

Evaluating Extended IPv4 ACL Statements

Refer to the topology in Figure 4-4. Each of the following scenarios applies an extended ACL to R1 G0/0 for inbound traffic. Evaluate the scenarios to determine whether the packets listed in the scenario's table will be permitted or denied. Each scenario is independent of the other two scenarios.

Figure 4-4   Evaluating an Extended ACL

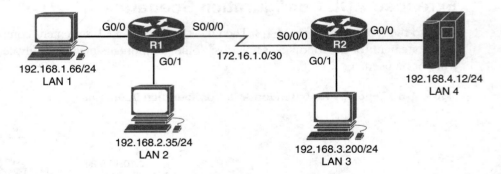

Extended ACL Evaluation Scenario 1

```
R1# show access-lists
Extended IP access list 103
    permit ip host 192.168.1.66 host 192.168.4.12
    permit ip host 192.168.1.77 host 192.168.4.12
    deny ip 192.168.1.0 0.0.0.255 192.168.4.0 0.0.0.255
    permit ip 192.168.1.0 0.0.0.255 192.168.2.0 0.0.0.255
```

Inbound Packets for Scenario 1

Source	Destination	Permit	Deny
192.168.1.66	192.168.3.51		
192.168.1.33	192.168.2.34		
192.168.1.88	192.168.4.39		
192.168.1.77	192.168.3.75		
192.168.1.88	192.168.2.51		
192.168.1.66	192.168.3.75		

Extended ACL Evaluation Scenario 2

```
R1# show access-lists
Extended IP access list 104
    deny tcp host 192.168.1.66 host 192.168.4.12 eq www
    permit tcp host 192.168.1.77 host 192.168.3.75 eq 22
    deny ip 192.168.1.0 0.0.0.255 192.168.3.0 0.0.0.255
    permit ip 192.168.1.0 0.0.0.255 192.168.4.0 0.0.0.255
```

Inbound Packets for Scenario 2

Source	Destination	Protocol	Permit	Deny
192.168.1.66	192.168.3.200	http		
192.168.1.88	192.168.2.75	http		
192.168.1.77	192.168.3.75	ssh		
192.168.1.77	192.168.3.75	http		
192.168.1.66	192.168.4.92	http		
192.168.1.66	192.168.4.75	ssh		

Extended ACL Evaluation Scenario 3

```
R1# show access-lists
Extended IP access list 105
    permit tcp 192.168.1.0 0.0.0.255 host 192.168.3.200 eq www
    permit ip host 192.168.1.66 host 192.168.3.200
    permit tcp 192.168.1.0 0.0.0.255 host 192.168.4.12 eq 22
    permit tcp host 192.168.1.66 192.168.2.0 0.0.0.255 eq telnet
```

Inbound Packets for Scenario 3

Source	Destination	Protocol	Permit	Deny
192.168.1.77	192.168.2.75	Telnet		
192.168.1.67	192.168.2.88	http		
192.168.1.66	192.168.3.200	Telnet		
192.168.1.66	192.168.2.75	Telnet		
192.168.1.77	192.168.3.75	http		
192.168.1.66	192.168.4.12	ssh		

Extended ACL Quiz

Refer to the topology in Figure 4-5 and the following scenario to answer the five questions.

Figure 4-5   Extended ACL Quiz Topology

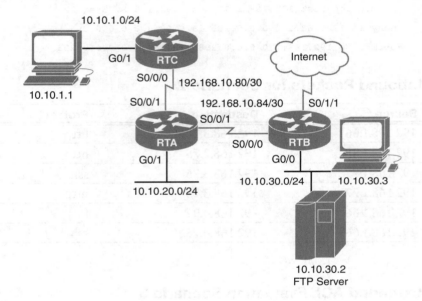

Scenario

A single access list needs to be created to deny the 10.10.1.0 /24 network and the 10.10.20.0 /24 network from reaching the 10.10.30.0 /24 network. The host 10.10.1.1 should have access to the FTP server only. The rest of the 10.0.0.0 network should have access to the 10.10.30.0 /24 network. All devices should be able to access the Internet.

Question 1

What should be the first line of the new access list in the practice scenario just described?

a. `access-list 101 permit ip 10.10.1.1 0.0.0.0 10.10.30.0 0.0.0.255`

b. `access-list 101 deny ip 10.10.1.0 0.0.0.255 10.10.30.0 0.0.0.255`

c. `access-list 10 deny 10.10.1.0 0.0.0.255`

d. `access-list 101 permit ip host 10.10.1.1 host 10.10.30.2`

Question 2

What should be the second line of the new access list in the practice scenario just described?

    a. `access-list 101 permit ip host 10.10.1.1  host 10.10.30.0 0.0.0.255`

    b. `access-list 101 deny ip 10.10.1.0 0.0.0.255 10.10.30.0 0.0.0.255`

    c. `access-list 101 deny ip 10.10.1.0 0.0.0.255 any`

    d. `access-list 101 permit ip host 10.10.1.1 host 10.10.30.1`

Question 3

What should be the third line of the new access list in the practice scenario just described?

    a. `access-list 101 deny ip 10.10.20.0 0.0.0.255 10.10.30.0 0.0.0.255`

    b. `access-list 101 permit ip host 10.10.1.1 10.10.30.0 0.0.0.255`

    c. `access-list 101 deny ip 10.20.1.0 0.0.0.255 any`

    d. `access-list 101 permit ip host 10.10.1.1  host 10.10.30.1 eq ftp`

Question 4

What should be the fourth line of the new access list in the practice scenario just described?

    a. `access-list 10 permit ip host 10.0.0.0 0.0.0.255`

    b. `access-list 101 permit ip 10.0.0.0 0.0.0.0 10.10.30.0 0.0.0.255`

    c. `access-list 101 deny ip 10.10.1.0 0.0.0.255 10.10.30.0 0.0.0.255 eq any`

    d. `access-list 101 permit ip any any`

Question 5

Where should the new access list in the practice scenario just described be placed to ensure its effectiveness?

    a. G 0/0 on RTB as an outbound list

    b. G 0/1 on RTA as an inbound list

    c. S 0/1/1 on RTB as an outbound list

    d. S 0/0/1 on RTA as an outbound list

Answers to Questions 1–5

IPv6 ACLs

IPv6 ACLs are similar to IPv4 ACLs in both operation and configuration. Being familiar with IPv4 access lists makes IPv6 ACLs easy to understand and configure.

Comparing IPv4 and IPv6 ACLs

With IPv6, there is only one type of ACL, which is equivalent to an IPv4 extended named ACL. There are no numbered ACLs in IPv6. To summarize, IPv6 ACLs are

- Named ACLs only
- Equivalent to the functionality of an IPv4 extended ACL

An IPv4 ACL and an IPv6 ACL cannot share the same name.

What are three significant differences between IPv4 and IPv6 ACLs?

_____

_____

_____

_____

_____

_____

_____

_____

Configuring IPv6 ACLs

What is the command syntax to enter IPv6 ACL configuration mode?

_____

What is the command syntax to configure an IPv6 ACL statement?

_____

_____

What is the command syntax to apply an IPv6 ACL to an interface?

_____

Refer to Figure 4-6. Record the commands to configure and apply the IPv6 ACL name NO-RTC that will block the RTC LAN from accessing the RTB LAN using port 80 but will allow all other traffic.

Figure 4-6   Topology for IPv6 ACL Configuration Scenario

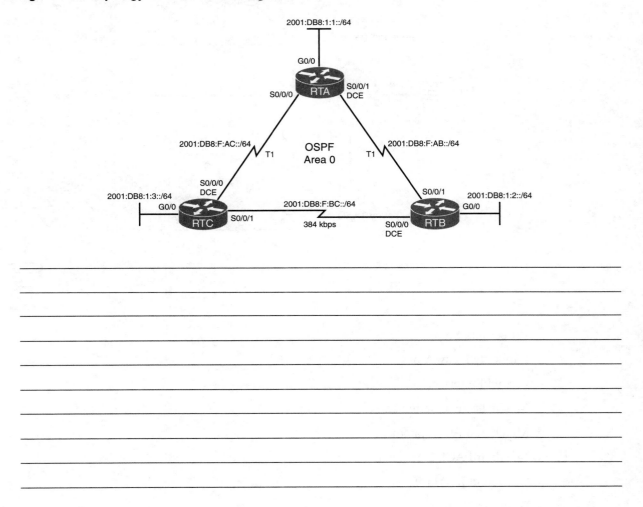

_____

_____

_____

_____

_____

_____

_____

_____

_____

_____

_____

Troubleshoot ACLs

When troubleshooting ACLs, it is important to first understand precisely how the router processes and filters packets. In addition, you should check for several common errors. The most common errors are entering ACLs in the wrong order and not applying adequate criteria to the ACL rules.

When processing packets, a router looks twice to see whether an ACL needs to be evaluated—inbound and outbound. In Figure 4-7, label each stage in the ACL processing flowchart with one of the processing steps. All processing steps are used. Some processing steps are used more than once.

Figure 4-7   Processing Flowchart for an ACL

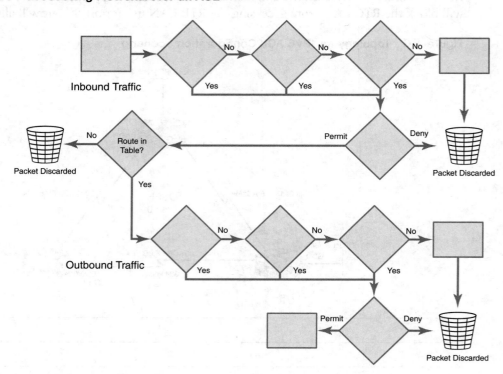

Processing Steps

Implicitly Deny Any

Inbound Interface

Match 1st ACL Statement

Match 2nd ACL Statement

Match 3rd ACL Statement

Outbound Interface

Permit or Deny

Labs and Activities

Command Reference

In Table 4-5, record the command, including the correct router prompt, that fits the description. Fill in any blanks with the appropriate missing information.

Table 4-5   Commands for Chapter 4, Access Control Lists

Command	Description
	Configure the comment for ACL 10 "Allow only 10.1.1.10."
	Configure a standard ACL 10 statement to allow host 10.1.1.10.
	Configure a standard ACL 10 to block 10.1.1.0/24.
	Apply ACL 10 inbound on the interface.
	Configure a standard ACL 10 to block 10.1.1.0/24.
	Apply ACL 10 inbound on the interface.
	Name an extended ACL "NO_WEB."
	Configure an ACL statement for NO_WEB to block 172.16.1.0/24 from using WEB to access 10.1.1.0/24
	List the command, other than **show run**, to view all the IPv4 and IPv6 ACLs configured on the router.
	List the command, other than **show run**, to view the placement of an IPv4 ACL.
	List the command, other than **show run**, to view the placement of an IPv6 ACL.

4.1.3.5 Packet Tracer–Configure Standard IPv4 ACLs

Topology

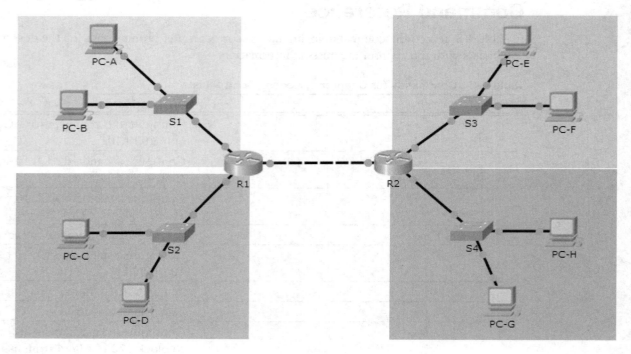

Addressing Table

Device	Interface	IP Address	Subnet Mask	Default Gateway
R1	G0/0	192.168.1.1	255.255.255.0	N/A
	G0/1	192.168.2.1	255.255.255.0	
	G0/2	192.168.250.1	255.255.255.0	
R2	G0/0	172.16.1.1	255.255.255.0	N/A
	G0/1	172.16.2.1	255.255.255.0	
	G0/2	192.168.250.2	255.255.255.0	
PC-A	NIC	192.168.1.100	255.255.255.0	192.168.1.1
PC-B	NIC	192.168.1.150	255.255.255.0	192.168.1.1
PC-C	NIC	192.168.2.50	255.255.255.0	192.168.2.1
PC-D	NIC	192.168.2.112	255.255.255.0	192.168.2.1
PC-E	NIC	172.16.1.10	255.255.255.0	172.16.1.1
PC-F	NIC	172.16.1.20	255.255.255.0	172.16.1.1
PC-G	NIC	172.16.2.100	255.255.255.0	172.16.2.1
PC-H	NIC	172.16.2.200	255.255.255.0	172.16.2.1

Objectives

Restrict traffic on the network by configuring standard IPv4 ACLs.

Background/Scenario

An organization has recently decided to restrict traffic using standard IPv4 ACLs. As the network administrator, it is your job to configure two standard IPv4 ACLs to restrict traffic to the Pink LAN and the Blue LAN (see PT Topology Diagram). You must also configure a named standard IPv4 ACL to restrict remote access to router R1. Router interfaces and default/static routes have already been configured. Remote SSH access has also been enabled on the routers. You will need the following access information for console, VTY, and privileged EXEC mode:

Username: **admin01**

Password: **ciscoPA55**

Enable secret: **secretPA55**

Part 1: Configure a Standard IPv4 ACL to Restrict Access to the Pink LAN

In Part 1, you will configure and apply access list 10 to restrict access to the Pink LAN.

Step 1.   Outline what you wish to accomplish with access list 10.

Access list 10 should have 4 access control entries to do the following:

   1)   Access list 10 should start with the following comment: ACL_TO_PINK_LAN

   2)   Permit PC-C to reach the Pink LAN

   3)   Permit only the first half of hosts on the Yellow LAN, so they can reach the Pink LAN

   4)   Permit all of the hosts on the Blue LAN to reach the Pink LAN

Access list 10 should be configured on the correct router, and applied to the correct interface and in the right direction.

Step 2.   Create, apply, and test access-list 10.

After configuring and applying access list 10, you should be able to execute the following network tests:

   1)   A ping from PC-A to a host in the Pink LAN should be successful, but a ping from PC-B should be denied.

   2)   A ping from PC-C to a host in the Pink LAN should be successful, but a ping from PC-D should be denied.

   3)   Pings from hosts in the Blue LAN to hosts in the Pink LAN should be successful.

What message is sent back to the PCs when a ping is denied due to an ACL?

_____

Which IP addresses on the Yellow LAN are permitted to ping hosts on the Pink LAN?

_____

Part 2: Configure a Standard IPv4 ACL to Restrict Access to the Blue LAN

In Part 2, you will configure and apply access list 20 to restrict access to the Blue LAN.

Step 1. Outline what you wish to accomplish with access list 20.

Access list 20 should have 3 access control entries to do the following:

1) Access list 20 should start with the following comment: ACL_TO_BLUE_LAN

2) Permit PC-A to reach the Blue LAN

3) Deny the Yellow LAN from reaching the Blue LAN

4) Allow all other networks to reach the Blue LAN

Access list 20 should be configured on the correct router, and applied to the correct interface and in the right direction.

Step 2. Create, apply, and test access-list 20.

After configuring and applying access list 20 you should be able to execute the following network tests:

1) Only PC-A on the Yellow LAN can successfully ping the Blue LAN.

2) Pings from hosts in the Yellow LAN to the Blue LAN should fail.

3) Pings from hosts in the Green and Pink LANs to the Blue LAN should be successful.

Step 3. Insert an ACE into access-list 20.

You need to make a change to access list 20. Insert an access control entry into access list 20 to permit PC-A to reach the Blue LAN. Insert the ACE prior to the other access list 20 permit and deny access control entries.

How do you insert or remove an ACE into a specific line of an ACL?

_____

What line did you enter the ACE on?

_____

Part 3: Configure a Named Standard IPv4 ACL

In Part 3, you will configure and apply a named standard IPv4 ACL to restrict remote access to router R1.

Step 1. Outline what you wish to accomplish with named standard ACL.

The named access list should do the following:

1) On R1 create a standard ACL named ADMIN_VTY

2) Permit a single host, PC-C

3) Apply the ACL to the VTY lines

Step 2. Test access list ADMIN_VTY.

After configuring and applying access list ADMIN_VTY, you should be able to execute the following network test:

1) An SSH connection from host PC-C to R1 should be successful.

2) SSH connections from all other hosts should fail.

Reflection

This lab features two standard ACLs to restrict traffic to the Pink and Blue LANs. Could you create two more standard ACLs to restrict traffic to the Yellow and Green ACLs and which router would those ACLs need to be created on?

_____

_____

4.2.2.10 Packet Tracer–Configuring Extended ACLs–Scenario 1

Topology

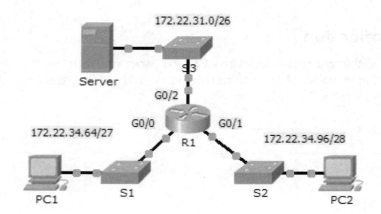

Addressing Table

Device	Interface	IP Address	Subnet Mask	Default Gateway
R1	G0/0	172.22.34.65	255.255.255.224	N/A
	G0/1	172.22.34.97	255.255.255.240	N/A
	G0/2	172.22.34.1	255.255.255.192	N/A
Server	NIC	172.22.34.62	255.255.255.192	172.22.34.1
PC1	NIC	172.22.34.66	255.255.255.224	172.22.34.65
PC2	NIC	172.22.34.98	255.255.255.240	172.22.34.97

Objectives

Part 1: Configure, Apply, and Verify an Extended Numbered ACL

Part 2: Configure, Apply, and Verify an Extended Named ACL

Background/Scenario

Two employees need access to services provided by the server. **PC1** only needs FTP access while **PC2** only needs web access. Both computers are able to ping the server, but not each other.

Part 1: Configure, Apply, and Verify an Extended Numbered ACL

Step 1.   Configure an ACL to permit FTP and ICMP.

   a.   From global configuration mode on **R1**, enter the following command to determine the first valid number for an extended access list.

```
R1(config)# access-list ?
   <1-99>      IP standard access list
   <100-199>  IP extended access list
```

b. Add **100** to the command, followed by a question mark.

```
R1(config)# access-list 100 ?
  deny    Specify packets to reject
  permit  Specify packets to forward
  remark  Access list entry comment
```

c. To permit FTP traffic, enter **permit**, followed by a question mark.

```
R1(config)# access-list 100 permit ?
  ahp    Authentication Header Protocol
  eigrp  Cisco's EIGRP routing protocol
  esp    Encapsulation Security Payload
  gre    Cisco's GRE tunneling
  icmp   Internet Control Message Protocol
  ip     Any Internet Protocol
  ospf   OSPF routing protocol
  tcp    Transmission Control Protocol
  udp    User Datagram Protocol
```

d. This ACL permits FTP and ICMP. ICMP is listed above, but FTP is not, because FTP uses TCP. So you enter TCP. Enter **tcp** to further refine the ACL help.

```
R1(config)# access-list 100 permit tcp ?
  A.B.C.D  Source address
  any      Any source host
  host     A single source host
```

e. Notice that we could filter just for **PC1** by using the **host** keyword or we could allow **any** host. In this case, any device is allowed that has an address belonging to the 172.22.34.64/27 network. Enter the network address, followed by a question mark.

```
R1(config)# access-list 100 permit tcp 172.22.34.64 ?
  A.B.C.D  Source wildcard bits
```

f. Calculate the wildcard mask determining the binary opposite of a subnet mask.

```
11111111.11111111.11111111.11100000 = 255.255.255.224
00000000.00000000.00000000.00011111 = 0.0.0.31
```

g. Enter the wildcard mask, followed by a question mark.

```
R1(config)# access-list 100 permit tcp 172.22.34.64 0.0.0.31 ?
  A.B.C.D  Destination address
  any      Any destination host
  eq       Match only packets on a given port number
  gt       Match only packets with a greater port number
  host     A single destination host
  lt       Match only packets with a lower port number
  neq      Match only packets not on a given port number
  range    Match only packets in the range of port numbers
```

h. Configure the destination address. In this scenario, we are filtering traffic for a single destination, the server. Enter the **host** keyword followed by the server's IP address.

```
R1(config)# access-list 100 permit tcp 172.22.34.64 0.0.0.31 host 172.22.34.62
?
  dscp         Match packets with given dscp value
  eq           Match only packets on a given port number
  established  established
  gt           Match only packets with a greater port number
```

```
lt            Match only packets with a lower port number
neq           Match only packets not on a given port number
precedence    Match packets with given precedence value
range         Match only packets in the range of port numbers
<cr>
```

i. Notice that one of the options is **<cr>** (carriage return). In other words, you can press **Enter** and the statement would permit all TCP traffic. However, we are only permitting FTP traffic; therefore, enter the **eq** keyword, followed by a question mark to display the available options. Then, enter **ftp** and press **Enter**.

```
R1(config)# access-list 100 permit tcp 172.22.34.64 0.0.0.31 host 172.22.34.62
eq ?
  <0-65535>  Port number
  ftp        File Transfer Protocol (21)
  pop3       Post Office Protocol v3 (110)
  smtp       Simple Mail Transport Protocol (25)
  telnet     Telnet (23)
  www        World Wide Web (HTTP, 80)
R1(config)# access-list 100 permit tcp 172.22.34.64 0.0.0.31 host 172.22.34.62
eq ftp
```

j. Create a second access list statement to permit ICMP (ping, etc.) traffic from **PC1** to **Server**. Note that the access list number remains the same and a specific type of ICMP traffic does not need to be specified.

```
R1(config)# access-list 100 permit icmp 172.22.34.64 0.0.0.31 host 172.22.34.62
```

k. All other traffic is denied, by default.

Step 2. Apply the ACL on the correct interface to filter traffic.

From **R1**'s perspective, the traffic that ACL 100 applies to is inbound from the network connected to Gigabit Ethernet 0/0 interface. Enter interface configuration mode and apply the ACL.

```
R1(config)# interface gigabitEthernet 0/0
R1(config-if)# ip access-group 100 in
```

Step 3. Verify the ACL implementation.

a. Ping from **PC1** to **Server**. If the pings are unsuccessful, verify the IP addresses before continuing.

b. FTP from **PC1** to **Server**. The username and password are both **cisco**.

```
PC> ftp 172.22.34.62
```

c. Exit the FTP service of the **Server**.

```
ftp> quit
```

d. Ping from **PC1** to **PC2**. The destination host should be unreachable, because the traffic was not explicitly permitted.

Part 2: Configure, Apply, and Verify an Extended Named ACL

Step 1. Configure an ACL to permit HTTP access and ICMP.

a. Named ACLs start with the **ip** keyword. From global configuration mode of **R1**, enter the following command, followed by a question mark.

```
R1(config)# ip access-list ?
  extended  Extended Access List
  standard  Standard Access List
```

b. You can configure named standard and extended ACLs. This access list filters both source and destination IP addresses; therefore, it must be extended. Enter **HTTP_ONLY** as the name. (For Packet Tracer scoring, the name is case-sensitive.)

```
R1(config)# ip access-list extended HTTP_ONLY
```

c. The prompt changes. You are now in extended named ACL configuration mode. All devices on the **PC2** LAN need TCP access. Enter the network address, followed by a question mark.

```
R1(config-ext-nacl)# permit tcp 172.22.34.96 ?
  A.B.C.D  Source wildcard bits
```

d. An alternative way to calculate a wildcard is to subtract the subnet mask from 255.255.255.255.

```
   255.255.255.255
-  255.255.255.240
   -----------------
=    0.  0.  0. 15
R1(config-ext-nacl)# permit tcp 172.22.34.96 0.0.0.15 ?
```

e. Finish the statement by specifying the server address as you did in Part 1 and filtering **www** traffic.

```
R1(config-ext-nacl)# permit tcp 172.22.34.96 0.0.0.15 host 172.22.34.62 eq www
```

f. Create a second access list statement to permit ICMP (ping, etc.) traffic from **PC2** to **Server**.

Note: The prompt remains the same and a specific type of ICMP traffic does not need to be specified.

```
R1(config-ext-nacl)# permit icmp 172.22.34.96 0.0.0.15 host 172.22.34.62
```

g. All other traffic is denied, by default. Exit out of extended named ACL configuration mode.

Step 2. Apply the ACL on the correct interface to filter traffic.

From **R1**'s perspective, the traffic that access list **HTTP_ONLY** applies to is inbound from the network connected to Gigabit Ethernet 0/1 interface. Enter the interface configuration mode and apply the ACL.

```
R1(config)# interface gigabitEthernet 0/1
R1(config-if)# ip access-group HTTP_ONLY in
```

Step 3. Verify the ACL implementation.

a. Ping from **PC2** to **Server**. If the pings unsuccessful, verify the IP addresses before continuing.

b. FTP from **PC2** to **Server**. The connection should fail.

c. Open the web browser on **PC2** and enter the IP address of **Server** as the URL. The connection should be successful.

4.2.2.11 Packet Tracer–Configuring Extended ACLs– Scenario 2

Topology

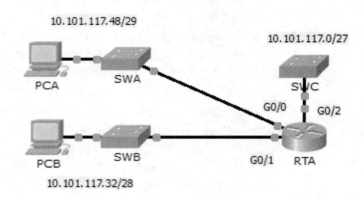

Addressing Table

Device	Interface	IP Address	Subnet Mask	Default Gateway
RTA	G0/0	10.101.117.49	255.255.255.248	N/A
	G0/1	10.101.117.33	255.255.255.240	N/A
	G0/2	10.101.117.1	255.255.255.224	N/A
PCA	NIC	10.101.117.51	255.255.255.248	10.101.117.49
PCB	NIC	10.101.117.35	255.255.255.240	10.101.117.33
SWC	VLAN1	10.101.117.2	255.255.255.224	10.101.117.1

Objectives

Part 1: Configure, Apply, and Verify an Extended Numbered ACL

Part 2: Reflection Questions

Background/Scenario

In this scenario, devices on one LAN are allowed to remotely access devices in another LAN using the Telnet protocol. Besides ICMP, all traffic from other networks is denied.

Part 1: Configure, Apply, and Verify an Extended Numbered ACL

Configure, apply, and verify an ACL to satisfy the following policy:

- Telnet traffic from devices on the 10.101.117.32/28 network is allowed to devices on the 10.101.117.0/27 networks.

- ICMP traffic is allowed from any source to any destination.

- All other traffic to 10.101.117.0/27 is blocked.

Step 1. Configure the extended ACL.

    a. From the appropriate configuration mode on **RTA**, use the last valid extended access list number to configure the ACL. Use the following steps to construct the first ACL statement:

        1) The last extended list number is 199.

        2) The protocol is TCP.

        3) The source network is 10.101.117.32.

        4) The wildcard can be determined by subtracting 255.255.255.240 from 255.255.255.255.

        5) The destination network is 10.101.117.0.

        6) The wildcard can be determined by subtracting 255.255.255.224 from 255.255.255.255.

        7) The protocol is Telnet.

    What is the first ACL statement?

    _____

    _____

    b. ICMP is allowed, and a second ACL statement is needed. Use the same access list number to permit all ICMP traffic, regardless of the source or destination address. What is the second ACL statement? (Hint: Use the any keywords)

    _____

    c. All other IP traffic is denied, by default.

Step 2. Apply the extended ACL.

The general rule is to place extended ACLs close to the source. However, since access list 199 affects traffic originating from both networks 10.101.117.48/29 and 10.101.117.32/28, the best placement for this ACL might be on interface Gigabit Ethernet 0/2 in the outbound direction. What is the command to apply ACL 199 to the Gigabit Ethernet 0/2 interface?

_____

Step 3. Verify the extended ACL implementation.

    a. Ping from **PCB** to all of the other IP addresses in the network. If the pings are unsuccessful, verify the IP addresses before continuing.

    b. Telnet from **PCB** to **SWC**. The password is **cisco**.

    c. Exit the Telnet service of the **SWC**.

    d. Ping from **PCA** to all of the other IP addresses in the network. If the pings are unsuccessful, verify the IP addresses before continuing.

    e. Telnet from **PCA** to **SWC**. The access list causes the router to reject the connection.

f.   Telnet from **PCA** to **SWB**. The access list is placed on **G0/2** and does not affect this connection.

g.   After logging into **SWB**, do not log out. Telnet to **SWC**.

Part 2: Reflection Questions

1.   How was PCA able to bypass access list 199 and Telnet to SWC?

_____

2.   What could have been done to prevent PCA from accessing SWC indirectly, while allowing PCB Telnet access to SWC?

_____

_____

Suggested Scoring Rubric

Activity Section	Question Location	Possible Points	Earned Points
Part 1: Configure, Apply, and Verify an Extended Numbered ACL	Step 1a	4	
	Step 1b	4	
	Step 2	4	
	Part 1 Total	**12**	
Part 2: Reflection Questions	Question 1	4	
	Question 2	4	
	Part 2 Total	**8**	
	Packet Tracer Score	80	
	Total Score	**100**	

4.2.2.12 Packet Tracer–Configuring Extended ACLs– Scenario 3

Topology

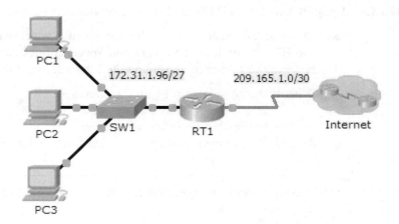

Addressing Table

Device	Interface	IP Address	Subnet Mask	Default Gateway
RT1	G0/0	172.31.1.126	255.255.255.224	N/A
	S0/0/0	209.165.1.2	255.255.255.252	N/A
PC1	NIC	172.31.1.101	255.255.255.224	172.31.1.126
PC2	NIC	172.31.1.102	255.255.255.224	172.31.1.126
PC3	NIC	172.31.1.103	255.255.255.224	172.31.1.126
Server1	NIC	64.101.255.254		
Server2	NIC	64.103.255.254		

Objectives

Part 1: Configure a Named Extended ACL

Part 2: Apply and Verify the Extended ACL

Background/Scenario

In this scenario, specific devices on the LAN are allowed to various services on servers located on the Internet.

Part 1: Configure a Named Extended ACL

Use one named ACL to implement the following policy:

- Block HTTP and HTTPS access from **PC1** to **Server1** and **Server2**. The servers are inside the cloud and you only know their IP addresses.

- Block FTP access from **PC2** to **Server1** and **Server2**.

- Block ICMP access from **PC3** to **Server1** and **Server2**.

Note: For scoring purposes, you must configure the statements in the order specified in the following steps.

Step 1.   Deny PC1 to access HTTP and HTTPS services on Server1 and Server2.

a.   Create an extended IP access list named ACL which will deny **PC1** access to the HTTP and HTTPS services of **Server1** and **Server2**. Because it is impossible to directly observe the subnet of servers on the Internet, four rules are required.

What is the command to begin the named ACL?

_____

b.   Record the statement that denies access from **PC1** to **Server1**, only for HTTP (port 80).

_____

c.   Record the statement that denies access from **PC1** to **Server1**, only for HTTPS (port 443).

_____

d.   Record the statement that denies access from **PC1** to **Server2**, only for HTTP.

_____

e.   Record the statement that denies access from **PC1** to **Server2**, only for HTTPS.

_____

Step 2.   Deny PC2 to access FTP services on Server1 and Server2.

a.   Record the statement that denies access from **PC2** to **Server1**, only for FTP (port 21 only).

_____

b.   Record the statement that denies access from **PC2** to **Server2**, only for FTP (port 21 only).

_____

Step 3.   Deny PC3 to ping Server1 and Server2.

a.   Record the statement that denies ICMP access from **PC3** to **Server1**.

_____

b.   Record the statement that denies ICMP access from **PC3** to **Server2**.

_____

Step 4.   Permit all other IP traffic.

By default, an access list denies all traffic that does not match any rule in the list. What command permits all other traffic?

_____

Part 2: Apply and Verify the Extended ACL

The traffic to be filtered is coming from the 172.31.1.96/27 network and is destined for remote networks. Appropriate ACL placement also depends on the relationship of the traffic with respect to **RT1**.

Step 1.   Apply the ACL to the correct interface and in the correct direction.

    a.   What are the commands you need to apply the ACL to the correct interface and in the correct direction?

        _____

        _____

Step 2.   Test access for each PC.

    a.   Access the websites of **Server1** and **Server2** using the Web Browser of **PC1** and using both HTTP and HTTPS protocols.

    b.   Access FTP of **Server1** and **Server2** using **PC1**. The username and password is "**cisco**".

    c.   Ping **Server1** and **Server2** from **PC1**.

    d.   Repeat Step 2a to Step 2c with **PC2** and **PC3** to verify proper access list operation.

4.2.2.13 Lab–Configuring and Verifying Extended ACLs

Topology

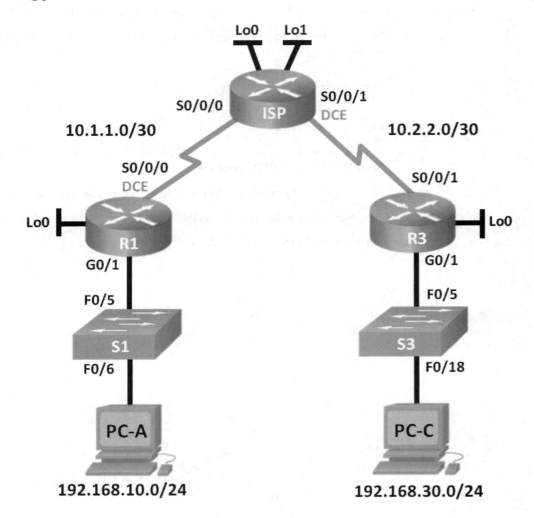

Addressing Table

Device	Interface	IP Address	Subnet Mask	Default Gateway
R1	G0/1	192.168.10.1	255.255.255.0	N/A
	Lo0	192.168.20.1	255.255.255.0	N/A
	S0/0/0 (DCE)	10.1.1.1	255.255.255.252	N/A
ISP	S0/0/0	10.1.1.2	255.255.255.252	N/A
	S0/0/1 (DCE)	10.2.2.2	255.255.255.252	N/A
	Lo0	209.165.200.225	255.255.255.224	N/A
	Lo1	209.165.201.1	255.255.255.224	N/A
R3	G0/1	192.168.30.1	255.255.255.0	N/A
	Lo0	192.168.40.1	255.255.255.0	N/A
	S0/0/1	10.2.2.1	255.255.255.252	N/A

Device	Interface	IP Address	Subnet Mask	Default Gateway
S1	VLAN 1	192.168.10.11	255.255.255.0	192.168.10.1
S3	VLAN 1	192.168.30.11	255.255.255.0	192.168.30.1
PC-A	NIC	192.168.10.3	255.255.255.0	192.168.10.1
PC-C	NIC	192.168.30.3	255.255.255.0	192.168.30.1

Objectives

Part 1: Set Up the Topology and Initialize Devices

Part 2: Configure Devices and Verify Connectivity

- Configure basic settings on PCs, routers, and switches.

- Configure OSPF routing on R1, ISP, and R3.

Part 3: Configure and Verify Extended Numbered and Named ACLs

- Configure, apply, and verify a numbered extended ACL.

- Configure, apply, and verify a named extended ACL.

Part 4: Modify and Verify Extended ACLs

Background/Scenario

Extended access control lists (ACLs) are extremely powerful. They offer a much greater degree of control than standard ACLs as to the types of traffic that can be filtered, as well as where the traffic originated and where it is going.

In this lab, you will set up filtering rules for two offices represented by R1 and R3. Management has established some access policies between the LANs located at R1 and R3, which you must implement. The ISP router between R1 and R3 does not have any ACLs placed on it. You would not be allowed any administrative access to an ISP router as you can only control and manage your own equipment.

Note: The routers used with CCNA hands-on labs are Cisco 1941 Integrated Services Routers (ISRs) with Cisco IOS Release 15.2(4)M3 (universalk9 image). The switches used are Cisco Catalyst 2960s with Cisco IOS Release 15.0(2) (lanbasek9 image). Other routers, switches, and Cisco IOS versions can be used. Depending on the model and Cisco IOS version, the commands available and output produced might vary from what is shown in the labs. Refer to the Router Interface Summary Table at the end of the lab for the correct interface identifiers.

Note: Make sure that the routers and switches have been erased and have no startup configurations. If you are unsure, contact your instructor.

Required Resources

- 3 Routers (Cisco 1941 with Cisco IOS Release 15.2(4)M3 universal image or comparable)

- 2 Switches (Cisco 2960 with Cisco IOS Release 15.0(2) lanbasek9 image or comparable)

- 2 PCs (Windows 7, Vista, or XP with terminal emulation program, such as Tera Term)

- Console cables to configure the Cisco IOS devices via the console ports

- Ethernet and serial cables as shown in the topology

Part 1: Set Up the Topology and Initialize Devices

In Part 1, you will set up the network topology and clear any configurations if necessary.

Step 1.   Cable the network as shown in the topology.

Step 2.   Initialize and reload the routers and switches.

Part 2: Configure Devices and Verify Connectivity

In Part 2, you will configure basic settings on the routers, switches, and PCs. Refer to the Topology and Addressing Table for device names and address information.

Step 1.   Configure IP addresses on PC-A and PC-C.

Step 2.   Configure basic settings on R1.

    a.   Disable DNS lookup.

    b.   Configure the device name as shown in the topology.

    c.   Create a loopback interface on R1.

    d.   Configure interface IP addresses as shown in the Topology and Addressing Table.

    e.   Configure a privileged EXEC mode password of **class**.

    f.   Assign a clock rate of **128000** to the S0/0/0 interface.

    g.   Assign **cisco** as the console and vty password and enable Telnet access. Configure **logging synchronous** for both the console and vty lines.

    h.   Enable web access on R1 to simulate a Web Server with local authentication for user **admin**.

```
R1(config)# ip http server
R1(config)# ip http authentication local
R1(config)# username admin privilege 15 secret class
```

Step 3.   Configure basic settings on ISP.

    a.   Configure the device name as shown in the topology.

    b.   Create the loopback interfaces on ISP.

    c.   Configure interface IP addresses as shown in the Topology and Addressing Table.

    d.   Disable DNS lookup.

    e.   Assign **class** as the privileged EXEC mode password.

    f.   Assign a clock rate of **128000** to the S0/0/1 interface.

    g.   Assign **cisco** as the console and vty password and enable Telnet access. Configure **logging synchronous** for both console and vty lines.

    h.   Enable web access on the ISP. Use the same parameters as in Step 2h.

Step 4.   Configure basic settings on R3.

    a.   Configure the device name as shown in the topology.

    b.   Create a loopback interface on R3.

    c.   Configure interface IP addresses as shown in the Topology and Addressing Table.

    d. Disable DNS lookup.

    e. Assign **class** as the privileged EXEC mode password.

    f. Assign **cisco** as the console password and configure **logging synchronous** on the console line.

    g. Enable SSH on R3.

```
R3(config)# ip domain-name cisco.com
R3(config)# crypto key generate rsa modulus 1024
R3(config)# line vty 0 4
R3(config-line)# login local
R3(config-line)# transport input ssh
```

    h. Enable web access on R3. Use the same parameters as in Step 2h.

Step 5. (Optional) Configure basic settings on S1 and S3.

    a. Configure the hostnames as shown in the topology.

    b. Configure the management interface IP addresses as shown in the Topology and Addressing Table.

    c. Disable DNS lookup.

    d. Configure a privileged EXEC mode password of **class**.

    e. Configure a default gateway address.

Step 6. Configure OSPF routing on R1, ISP, and R3.

    a. Assign 1 as the OSPF process ID and advertise all networks on R1, ISP, and R3. The OSPF configuration for R1 is included for reference.

```
R1(config)# router ospf 1
R1(config-router)# network 192.168.10.0 0.0.0.255 area 0
R1(config-router)# network 192.168.20.0 0.0.0.255 area 0
R1(config-router)# network 10.1.1.0 0.0.0.3 area 0
```

_____

_____

_____

_____

_____

_____

_____

_____

_____

    b. After configuring OSPF on R1, ISP, and R3, verify that all routers have complete routing tables listing all networks. Troubleshoot if this is not the case.

Step 7. Verify connectivity between devices.

> **Note:** It is very important to verify connectivity **before** you configure and apply ACLs! Ensure that your network is properly functioning before you start to filter out traffic.

    a. From PC-A, ping PC-C and the loopback and serial interfaces on R3.

        Were your pings successful? _____

    b. From R1, ping PC-C and the loopback and serial interface on R3.

        Were your pings successful? _____

    c. From PC-C, ping PC-A and the loopback and serial interface on R1.

        Were your pings successful? _____

    d. From R3, ping PC-A and the loopback and serial interface on R1.

        Were your pings successful? _____

    e. From PC-A, ping the loopback interfaces on the ISP router.

        Were your pings successful? _____

    f. From PC-C, ping the loopback interfaces on the ISP router.

        Were your pings successful? _____

    g. Open a web browser on PC-A and go to http://209.165.200.225 on ISP. You will be prompted for a username and password. Use **admin** for the username and **class** for the password. If you are prompted to accept a signature, accept it. The router will load the Cisco Configuration Professional (CCP) Express in a separate window. You may be prompted for a username and password. Use **admin** for the username and **class** for the password.

    h. Open a web browser on PC-C and go to http://10.1.1.1 on R1. You will be prompted for a username and password. Use **admin** for username and **class** for the password. If you are prompted to accept a signature, accept it. The router will load CCP Express in a separate window. You may be prompted for a username and password. Use **admin** for the username and **class** for the password.

Part 3: Configure and Verify Extended Numbered and Named ACLs

Extended ACLs can filter traffic in many different ways. Extended ACLs can filter on source IP addresses, source ports, destination IP addresses, destination ports, as well as various protocols and services.

Security policies are as follows:

    1. Allow web traffic originating from the 192.168.10.0/24 network to go to any network.

    2. Allow an SSH connection to the R3 serial interface from PC-A.

    3. Allow users on 192.168.10.0/24 network access to 192.168.20.0/24 network.

    4. Allow web traffic originating from the 192.168.30.0/24 network to access R1 via the web interface and the 209.165.200.224/27 network on ISP. The 192.168.30.0/24 network should NOT be allowed to access any other network via the web.

In looking at the security policies listed above, you will need at least two ACLs to fulfill the security policies. A best practice is to place extended ACLs as close to the source as possible. We will follow this practice for these policies.

Step 1.   Configure a numbered extended ACL on R1 for security policy numbers 1 and 2.

You will use a numbered extended ACL on R1. What are the ranges for extended ACLs?

_____

a. Configure the ACL on R1. Use 100 for the ACL number.

```
R1(config)# access-list 100 remark Allow Web & SSH Access
R1(config)# access-list 100 permit tcp host 192.168.10.3 host 10.2.2.1 eq 22
R1(config)# access-list 100 permit tcp any any eq 80
```

What does the 80 signify in the command output listed above?

_____

To what interface should ACL 100 be applied?

_____

_____

In what direction should ACL 100 be applied?

_____

_____

b. Apply ACL 100 to the S0/0/0 interface.

```
R1(config)# interface s0/0/0
R1(config-if)# ip access-group 100 out
```

c. Verify ACL 100.

1) Open up a web browser on PC-A, and access http://209.165.200.225 (the ISP router). It should be successful; troubleshoot, if not.

2) Establish an SSH connection from PC-A to R3 using 10.2.2.1 for the IP address. Log in with admin and class for your credentials. It should be successful; troubleshoot, if not.

3) From privileged EXEC mode prompt on R1, issue the show access-lists command.

```
R1# show access-lists
Extended IP access list 100
    10 permit tcp host 192.168.10.3 host 10.2.2.1 eq 22 (22 matches)
    20 permit tcp any any eq www (111 matches)
```

4) From the PC-A command prompt, issue a ping to 10.2.2.1. Explain your results.

_____

_____

_____

Step 2.   Configure a named extended ACL on R3 for security policy number 3.

    a.   Configure the policy on R3. Name the ACL WEB-POLICY.

```
R3(config)# ip access-list extended WEB-POLICY
R3(config-ext-nacl)# permit tcp 192.168.30.0 0.0.0.255 host 10.1.1.1 eq 80
R3(config-ext-nacl)# permit tcp 192.168.30.0 0.0.0.255 209.165.200.224 0.0.0.31
eq 80
```

    b.   Apply ACL WEB-POLICY to the S0/0/1 interface.

```
R3(config-ext-nacl)# interface S0/0/1
R3(config-if)# ip access-group WEB-POLICY out
```

    c.   Verify the ACL WEB-POLICY.

        1)   From R3 privileged EXEC mode command prompt, issue the show ip interface s0/0/1 command.

            What, if any, is the name of the ACL? _____

            In what direction is the ACL applied? _____

        2)   Open up a web browser on PC-C and access http://209.165.200.225 (the ISP router). It should be successful; troubleshoot, if not.

        3)   From PC-C, open a web session to http://10.1.1.1 (R1). It should be successful; troubleshoot, if not.

        4)   From PC-C, open a web session to http://209.165.201.1 (ISP router). It should fail; troubleshoot, if not.

        5)   From a PC-C command prompt, ping PC-A. What was your result and why?

        _____

Part 4: Modify and Verify Extended ACLs

Because of the ACLs applied on R1 and R3, no pings or any other kind of traffic is allowed between the LAN networks on R1 and R3. Management has decided that all traffic between the 192.168.10.0/24 and 192.168.30.0/24 networks should be allowed. You must modify both ACLs on R1 and R3.

Step 1.   Modify ACL 100 on R1.

    a.   From R1 privileged EXEC mode, issue the **show access-lists** command.

        How many lines are there in this access list? _____

    b.   Enter global configuration mode and modify the ACL on R1.

```
R1(config)# ip access-list extended 100
R1(config-ext-nacl)# 30 permit ip 192.168.10.0 0.0.0.255 192.168.30.0 0.0.0.255
R1(config-ext-nacl)# end
```

    c.   Issue the **show access-lists** command.

        Where did the new line that you just added appear in ACL 100?

        _____

Step 2.   Modify ACL WEB-POLICY on R3.

    a.   From R3 privileged EXEC mode, issue the **show access-lists** command.

        How many lines are there in this access list? _____

b. Enter global configuration mode and modify the ACL on R3.

```
R3(config)# ip access-list extended WEB-POLICY
R3(config-ext-nacl)# 30 permit ip 192.168.30.0 0.0.0.255 192.168.10.0 0.0.0.255
R3(config-ext-nacl)# end
```

c. Issue the **show access-lists** command to verify that the new line was added at the end of the ACL.

Step 3. Verify modified ACLs.

a. From PC-A, ping the IP address of PC-C. Were the pings successful? _____

b. From PC-C, ping the IP address of PC-A. Were the pings successful? _____

Why did the ACLs work immediately for the pings after you changed them?

_____

Reflection

1. Why is careful planning and testing of ACLs required?

_____

_____

2. Which type of ACL is better: standard or extended?

_____

_____

_____

_____

3. Why are OSPF hello packets and routing updates not blocked by the implicit deny any access control entry (ACE) or ACL statement of the ACLs applied to R1 and R3?

_____

_____

_____

_____

Router Interface Summary Table

Router Interface Summary				
Router Model	Ethernet Interface #1	Ethernet Interface #2	Serial Interface #1	Serial Interface #2
1800	Fast Ethernet 0/0 (F0/0)	Fast Ethernet 0/1 (F0/1)	Serial 0/0/0 (S0/0/0)	Serial 0/0/1 (S0/0/1)
1900	Gigabit Ethernet 0/0 (G0/0)	Gigabit Ethernet 0/1 (G0/1)	Serial 0/0/0 (S0/0/0)	Serial 0/0/1 (S0/0/1)
2801	Fast Ethernet 0/0 (F0/0)	Fast Ethernet 0/1 (F0/1)	Serial 0/1/0 (S0/1/0)	Serial 0/1/1 (S0/1/1)
2811	Fast Ethernet 0/0 (F0/0)	Fast Ethernet 0/1 (F0/1)	Serial 0/0/0 (S0/0/0)	Serial 0/0/1 (S0/0/1)
2900	Gigabit Ethernet 0/0 (G0/0)	Gigabit Ethernet 0/1 (G0/1)	Serial 0/0/0 (S0/0/0)	Serial 0/0/1 (S0/0/1)

Note: To find out how the router is configured, look at the interfaces to identify the type of router and how many interfaces the router has. There is no way to effectively list all the combinations of configurations for each router class. This table includes identifiers for the possible combinations of Ethernet and Serial interfaces in the device. The table does not include any other type of interface, even though a specific router may contain one. An example of this might be an ISDN BRI interface. The string in parentheses is the legal abbreviation that can be used in Cisco IOS commands to represent the interface.

4.3.2.6 Packet Tracer–Configuring IPv6 ACLs

Topology

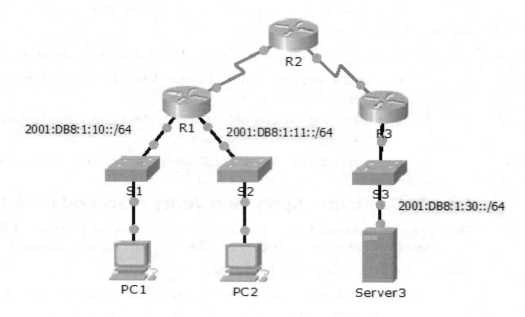

Addressing Table

Device	Interface	IPv6 Address/Prefix	Default Gateway
Server3	NIC	2001:DB8:1:30::30/64	FE80::30

Objectives

Part 1: Configure, Apply, and Verify an IPv6 ACL

Part 2: Configure, Apply, and Verify a Second IPv6 ACL

Part 1: Configure, Apply, and Verify an IPv6 ACL

Logs indicate that a computer on the 2001:DB8:1:11::0/64 network is repeatedly refreshing their web page causing a Denial-of-Service (DoS) attack against **Server3**. Until the client can be identified and cleaned, you must block HTTP and HTTPS access to that network with an access list.

Step 1.   Configure an ACL that will block HTTP and HTTPS access.

Configure an ACL named **BLOCK_HTTP** on **R1** with the following statements.

a.   Block HTTP and HTTPS traffic from reaching **Server3**.

```
R1(config)# deny tcp any host 2001:DB8:1:30::30 eq www
R1(config)# deny tcp any host 2001:DB8:1:30::30 eq 443
```

b.   Allow all other IPv6 traffic to pass.

Step 2.   Apply the ACL to the correct interface.

Apply the ACL on the interface closest the source of the traffic to be blocked.

```
R1(config-if)# ipv6 traffic-filter BLOCK_HTTP in
```

Step 3.   Verify the ACL implementation.

Verify the ACL is operating as intended by conducting the following tests:

- Open the **web browser** of **PC1** to http://2001:DB8:1:30::30 or https://2001:DB8:1:30::30. The website should appear.

- Open the **web browser** of **PC2** to http://2001:DB8:1:30::30 or https://2001:DB8:1:30::30. The website should be blocked

- Ping from **PC2** to 2001:DB8:1:30::30. The ping should be successful.

Part 2: Configure, Apply, and Verify a Second IPv6 ACL

The logs now indicate that your server is receiving pings from many different IPv6 addresses in a Distributed Denial of Service (DDoS) attack. You must filter ICMP ping requests to your server.

Step 1.   Create an access list to block ICMP.

Configure an ACL named **BLOCK_ICMP** on **R3** with the following statements:

a.   Block all ICMP traffic from any hosts to any destination.

_____

b.   Allow all other IPv6 traffic to pass.

_____

Step 2.   Apply the ACL to the correct interface.

In this case, ICMP traffic can come from any source. To ensure that ICMP traffic is blocked regardless of its source or changes that occur to the network topology, apply the ACL closest to the destination.

_____

_____

Step 3.   Verify that the proper access list functions.

a.   Ping from **PC2** to 2001:DB8:1:30::30. The ping should fail.

b.   Ping from **PC1** to 2001:DB8:1:30::30. The ping should fail.

Open the web browser of PC1 to http://2001:DB8:1:30::30 or https://2001:DB8:1:30::30. The website should display.

4.3.2.7 Lab—Configuring and Verifying IPv6 ACLs

Topology

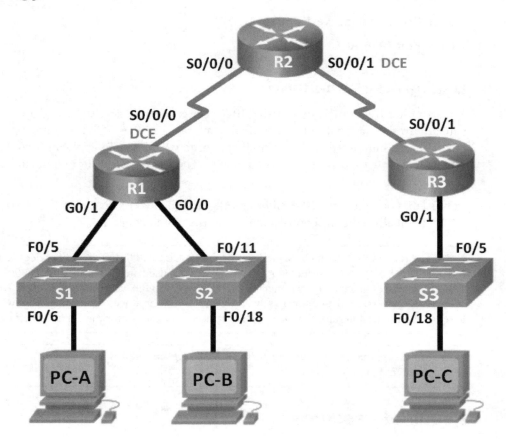

Addressing Table

Device	Interface	IP Address	Default Gateway
R1	G0/0	2001:DB8:ACAD:B::1/64	N/A
	G0/1	2001:DB8:ACAD:A::1/64	N/A
	S0/0/0 (DCE)	2001:DB8:AAAA:1::1/64	N/A
R2	S0/0/0	2001:DB8:AAAA:1::2/64	N/A
	S0/0/1 (DCE)	2001:DB8:AAAA:2::2/64	N/A
R3	G0/1	2001:DB8:CAFE:C::1/64	N/A
	S0/0/1	2001:DB8:AAAA:2::1/64	N/A
S1	VLAN1	2001:DB8:ACAD:A::A/64	N/A
S2	VLAN1	2001:DB8:ACAD:B::A/64	N/A
S3	VLAN1	2001:DB8:CAFE:C::A/64	N/A
PC-A	NIC	2001:DB8:ACAD:A::3/64	FE80::1
PC-B	NIC	2001:DB8:ACAD:B::3/64	FE80::1
PC-C	NIC	2001:DB8:CAFE:C::3/64	FE80::1

Objectives

Part 1: Set Up the Topology and Initialize Devices

Part 2: Configure Devices and Verify Connectivity

Part 3: Configure and Verify IPv6 ACLs

Part 4: Edit IPv6 ACLs

Background/Scenario

You can filter IPv6 traffic by creating IPv6 access control lists (ACLs) and applying them to interfaces similarly to the way that you create IPv4 named ACLs. IPv6 ACL types are extended and named. Standard and numbered ACLs are no longer used with IPv6. To apply an IPv6 ACL to a vty interface, you use the new **ipv6 access-class** command. The **ipv6 traffic-filter** command is still used to apply an IPv6 ACL to interfaces.

In this lab, you will apply IPv6 filtering rules and then verify that they are restricting access as expected. You will also edit an IPv6 ACL and clear the match counters.

Note: The routers used with CCNA hands-on labs are Cisco 1941 Integrated Services Routers (ISRs) with Cisco IOS Release 15.2(4)M3 (universalk9 image). The switches used are Cisco Catalyst 2960s with Cisco IOS Release 15.0(2) (lanbasek9 image). Other routers, switches and Cisco IOS versions can be used. Depending on the model and Cisco IOS version, the commands available and output produced might vary from what is shown in the labs. Refer to the Router Interface Summary Table at the end of the lab for the correct interface identifiers.

Note: Make sure that the routers and switches have been erased and have no startup configurations. If you are unsure, contact your instructor.

Required Resources

- 3 Routers (Cisco 1941 with Cisco IOS Release 15.2(4)M3 universal image or comparable)
- 3 Switches (Cisco 2960 with Cisco IOS Release 15.0(2) lanbasek9 image or comparable)
- 3 PCs (Windows 7, Vista, or XP with terminal emulation program, such as Tera Term)
- Console cables to configure the Cisco IOS devices via the console ports
- Ethernet and serial cables as shown in the topology

Part 1: Set Up the Topology and Initialize Devices

In Part 1, you set up the network topology and clear any configurations if necessary.

Step 1.   Cable the network as shown in the topology.

Step 2.   Initialize and reload the routers and switches.

Part 2: Configure Devices and Verify Connectivity

In Part 2, you configure basic settings on the routers, switches, and PCs. Refer to the Topology and Addressing Table at the beginning of this lab for device names and address information.

Step 1.   Configure IPv6 addresses on all PCs.

Configure IPv6 global unicast addresses according to the Addressing Table. Use the link-local address of **FE80::1** for the default-gateway on all PCs.

Step 2.   Configure the switches.

    a.   Disable DNS lookup.

    b.   Assign the hostname.

    c.   Assign a domain-name of **ccna-lab.com**.

    d.   Encrypt plain text passwords.

    e.   Create a MOTD banner warning users that unauthorized access is prohibited.

    f.   Create a local user database with a username of **admin** and password as **classadm**.

    g.   Assign **class** as the privileged EXEC encrypted password.

    h.   Assign **cisco** as the console password and enable login.

    i.   Enable login on the VTY lines using the local database.

    j.   Generate a crypto rsa key for ssh using a modulus size of 1024 bits.

    k.   Change the transport input VTY lines to all for SSH and Telnet only.

    l.   Assign an IPv6 address to VLAN 1 according to the Addressing Table.

    m.   Administratively disable all inactive interfaces.

Step 3.   Configure basic settings on all routers.

    a.   Disable DNS lookup.

    b.   Assign the hostname.

    c.   Assign a domain-name of **ccna-lab.com**.

    d.   Encrypt plain text passwords.

    e.   Create a MOTD banner warning users that unauthorized access is prohibited.

    f.   Create a local user database with a username of **admin** and password as **classadm**.

    g.   Assign **class** as the privileged EXEC encrypted password.

    h.   Assign **cisco** as the console password and enable login.

    i.   Enable login on the VTY lines using the local database.

    j.   Generate a crypto rsa key for ssh using a modulus size of 1024 bits.

    k.   Change the transport input VTY lines to all for SSH and Telnet only.

Step 4.   Configure IPv6 settings on R1.

    a.   Configure the IPv6 unicast address on interface G0/0, G0/1, and S0/0/0.

    b.   Configure the IPv6 link-local address on interface G0/0, G0/1, and S0/0/0. Use **FE80::1** for the link-local address on all three interfaces.

    c.   Set the clock rate on S0/0/0 to 128000.

    d.   Enable the interfaces.

e.   Enable IPv6 unicast routing.

f.   Configure an IPv6 default route to use interface S0/0/0.

```
R1(config)# ipv6 route ::/0 s0/0/0
```

Step 5.   Configure IPv6 settings on R2.

a.   Configure the IPv6 unicast address on interface S0/0/0 and S0/0/1.

b.   Configure the IPv6 link-local address on interface S0/0/0 and S0/0/1. Use **FE80::2** for the link-local address on both interfaces.

c.   Set the clock rate on S0/0/1 to 128000.

d.   Enable the interfaces.

e.   Enable IPv6 unicast routing.

f.   Configure static IPv6 routes for traffic handling of R1 and R3 LAN subnets.

```
R2(config)# ipv6 route 2001:db8:acad::/48 s0/0/0
R2(config)# ipv6 route 2001:db8:cafe:c::/64 s0/0/1
```

Step 6.   Configure IPv6 settings on R3.

a.   Configure the IPv6 unicast address on interface G0/1 and S0/0/1.

b.   Configure the IPv6 link-local address on interface G0/1 and S0/0/1. Use **FE80::1** for the link-local address on both interfaces.

c.   Enable the interfaces.

d.   Enable IPv6 unicast routing.

e.   Configure an IPv6 default route to use interface S0/0/1.

```
R3(config)# ipv6 route ::/0 s0/0/1
```

Step 7.   Verify connectivity.

a.   Each PC should be able to ping the other PCs in the topology.

b.   Telnet to R1 from all PCs in the Topology.

c.   SSH to R1 from all PCs in the Topology.

d.   Telnet to S1 from all PCs in the Topology.

e.   SSH to S1 from all PCs in the Topology.

f.   Troubleshoot connectivity issues now because the ACLs that you create in Part 3 of this lab will restrict access to some areas of the network.

Note: Tera Term requires the target IPv6 address to be enclosed in brackets. Enter the IPv6 address as shown, click **OK** and then click **Continue** to accept the security warning and connect to the router.

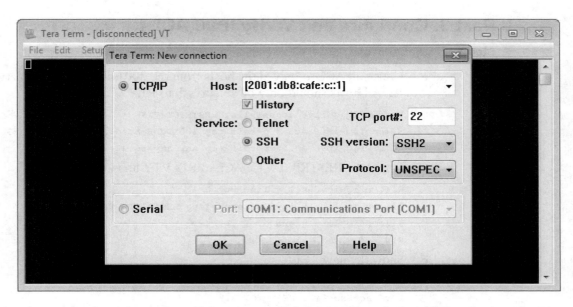

Input the user credentials configured (username **admin** and password **classadm**) and select the **Use plain password to log in** in the SSH Authentication dialog box. Click **OK** to continue.

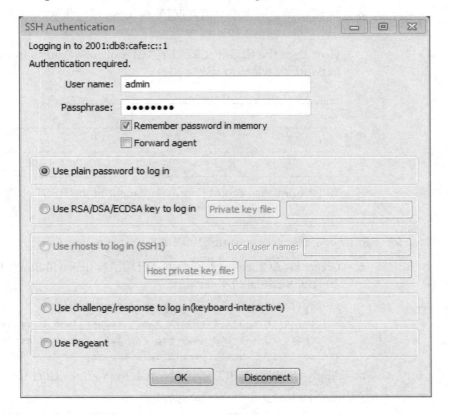

Part 3: Configure and Verify IPv6 ACLs

Step 1.   Configure and verify VTY restrictions on R1.

a.   Create an ACL to only allow hosts from the 2001:db8:acad:a::/64 network to telnet to R1. All hosts should only be able to ssh to R1.

```
R1(config)# ipv6 access-list RESTRICT-VTY
R1(config-ipv6-acl)# permit tcp 2001:db8:acad:a::/64 any eq 23
R1(config-ipv6-acl)# permit tcp any any eq 22
```

b.   Apply the RESTRICT-VTY ACL to R1's VTY lines.

```
R1(config-ipv6-acl)# line vty 0 4
R1(config-line)# ipv6 access-class RESTRICT-VTY in
R1(config-line)# end
R1#
```

c.   Show the new ACL.

```
R1# show access-lists
IPv6 access list RESTRICT-VTY
    permit tcp 2001:DB8:ACAD:A::/64 any sequence 10
    permit tcp any any eq 22 sequence 20
```

d.   Verify that the RESTRICT-VTY ACL is only allowing Telnet traffic from the 2001:db8:acad:a::/64 network.

How does the RESTRICT-VTY ACL only allow hosts from the 2001:db8:acad:a::/64 network to telnet to R1?

_____

_____

_____

_____

What does the second permit statement in the RESTRICT-VTY ACL do?

_____

Step 2.   Restrict Telnet access to the 2001:db8:acad:a::/64 network.

a.   Create an ACL called RESTRICTED-LAN that will block Telnet access to the 2001:db8:acad:a::/64 network.

```
R1(config)# ipv6 access-list RESTRICTED-LAN
R1(config-ipv6-acl)# remark Block Telnet from outside
R1(config-ipv6-acl)# deny tcp any 2001:db8:acad:a::/64 eq telnet
R1(config-ipv6-acl)# permit ipv6 any any
```

b.   Apply the RESTRICTED-LAN ACL to interface G0/1 for all outbound traffic.

```
R1(config-ipv6-acl)# int g0/1
R1(config-if)# ipv6 traffic-filter RESTRICTED-LAN out
R1(config-if)# end
```

c.   Telnet to S1 from PC-B and PC-C to verify that Telnet has been restricted. SSH to S1 from PC-B to verify that it can still be reached using SSH. Troubleshoot if necessary.

d. Use the **show ipv6 access-list** command to view the RESTRICTED-LAN ACL.

```
R1# show ipv6 access-lists RESTRICTED-LAN
IPv6 access list RESTRICTED-LAN
    deny tcp any 2001:DB8:ACAD:A::/64 eq telnet (6 matches) sequence 20
    permit ipv6 any any (45 matches) sequence 30
```

Notice that each statement identifies the number of hits or matches that have occurred since the ACL was applied to the interface.

e. Use the **clear ipv6 access-list** to reset the match counters for the RESRICTED-LAN ACL.

```
R1# clear ipv6 access-list RESTRICTED-LAN
```

f. Redisplay the ACL with the **show access-lists** command to confirm that the counters were cleared.

```
R1# show access-lists RESTRICTED-LAN
IPv6 access list RESTRICTED-LAN
    deny tcp any 2001:DB8:ACAD:A::/64 eq telnet sequence 20
    permit ipv6 any any sequence 30
```

Part 4: Edit IPv6 ACLs

In Part 4, you will edit the RESTRICTED-LAN ACL that you created in Part 3. It is always a good idea to remove the ACL from the interface to which it is applied before editing it. After you complete your edits, then reapply the ACL to the interface.

Note: Many network administrators will make a copy of the ACL and edit the copy. When editing is complete, the administrator will remove the old ACL and apply the newly edited ACL to the interface. This method keeps the ACL in place until you are ready to apply the edited copy of the ACL.

Step 1. Remove the ACL from the interface.

```
R1(config)# int g0/1
R1(config-if)# no ipv6 traffic-filter RESTRICTED-LAN out
R1(config-if)# end
```

Step 2. Use the show access-lists command to view the ACL.

```
R1# show access-lists
IPv6 access list RESTRICT-VTY
    permit tcp 2001:DB8:ACAD:A::/64 any (4 matches) sequence 10
    permit tcp any any eq 22 (6 matches) sequence 20
IPv6 access list RESTRICTED-LAN
    deny tcp any 2001:DB8:ACAD:A::/64 eq telnet sequence 20
    permit ipv6 any any (36 matches) sequence 30
```

Step 3. Insert a new ACL statement using sequence numbering.

```
R1(config)# ipv6 access-list RESTRICTED-LAN
R1(config-ipv6-acl)# permit tcp 2001:db8:acad:b::/64 host 2001:db8:acad:a::a eq 23
sequence 15
```

What does this new permit statement do?

Step 4. Insert a new ACL statement at the end of the ACL.

```
R1(config-ipv6-acl)# permit tcp any host 2001:db8:acad:a::3 eq www
```

Note: This permit statement is only used to show how to add a statement to the end of an ACL. This ACL line would never be matched because the previous permit statement is matching on everything.

Step 5. Use the **do show access-list** command to view the ACL change.

```
R1(config-ipv6-acl)# do show access-list
IPv6 access list RESTRICT-VTY
    permit tcp 2001:DB8:ACAD:A::/64 any (2 matches) sequence 10
    permit tcp any any eq 22 (6 matches) sequence 20
IPv6 access list RESTRICTED-LAN
    permit tcp 2001:DB8:ACAD:B::/64 host 2001:DB8:ACAD:A::A eq telnet sequence 15
    deny tcp any 2001:DB8:ACAD:A::/64 eq telnet sequence 20
    permit ipv6 any any (124 matches) sequence 30
    permit tcp any host 2001:DB8:ACAD:A::3 eq www sequence 40
```

Note: The **do** command can be used to execute any privileged EXEC command while in global configuration mode or a submode.

Step 6. Delete an ACL statement.

Use the **no** command to delete the permit statement that you just added.

```
R1(config-ipv6-acl)# no permit tcp any host 2001:DB8:ACAD:A::3 eq www
```

Step 7. Use the do show access-list RESTRICTED-LAN command to view the ACL.

```
R1(config-ipv6-acl)# do show access-list RESTRICTED-LAN
IPv6 access list RESTRICTED-LAN
    permit tcp 2001:DB8:ACAD:B::/64 host 2001:DB8:ACAD:A::A eq telnet sequence 15
    deny tcp any 2001:DB8:ACAD:A::/64 eq telnet sequence 20
    permit ipv6 any any (214 matches) sequence 30
```

Step 8. Re-apply the RESTRICTED-LAN ACL to the interface G0/1.

```
R1(config-ipv6-acl)# int g0/1
R1(config-if)# ipv6 traffic-filter RESTRICTED-LAN out
R1(config-if)# end
```

Step 9. Test ACL changes.

Telnet to S1 from PC-B. Troubleshoot if necessary.

Reflection

1. What is causing the match count on the RESTRICTED-LAN permit ipv6 any any statement to continue to increase?

_____

_____

_____

_____

2. What command would you use to reset the counters for the ACL on the VTY lines?

_____

Router Interface Summary Table

Router Interface Summary				
Router Model	Ethernet Interface #1	Ethernet Interface #2	Serial Interface #1	Serial Interface #2
1800	Fast Ethernet 0/0 (F0/0)	Fast Ethernet 0/1 (F0/1)	Serial 0/0/0 (S0/0/0)	Serial 0/0/1 (S0/0/1)
1900	Gigabit Ethernet 0/0 (G0/0)	Gigabit Ethernet 0/1 (G0/1)	Serial 0/0/0 (S0/0/0)	Serial 0/0/1 (S0/0/1)
2801	Fast Ethernet 0/0 (F0/0)	Fast Ethernet 0/1 (F0/1)	Serial 0/1/0 (S0/1/0)	Serial 0/1/1 (S0/1/1)
2811	Fast Ethernet 0/0 (F0/0)	Fast Ethernet 0/1 (F0/1)	Serial 0/0/0 (S0/0/0)	Serial 0/0/1 (S0/0/1)
2900	Gigabit Ethernet 0/0 (G0/0)	Gigabit Ethernet 0/1 (G0/1)	Serial 0/0/0 (S0/0/0)	Serial 0/0/1 (S0/0/1)

Note: To find out how the router is configured, look at the interfaces to identify the type of router and how many interfaces the router has. There is no way to effectively list all the combinations of configurations for each router class. This table includes identifiers for the possible combinations of Ethernet and Serial interfaces in the device. The table does not include any other type of interface, even though a specific router may contain one. An example of this might be an ISDN BRI interface. The string in parentheses is the legal abbreviation that can be used in Cisco IOS commands to represent the interface.

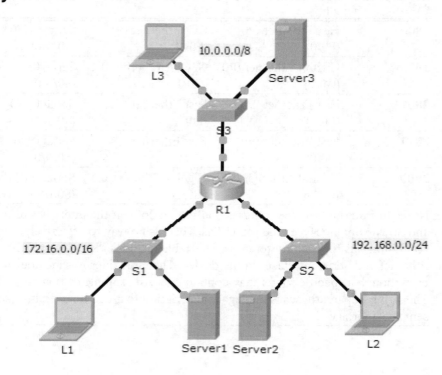

Packet Tracer
☐ Activity

4.4.2.9 Packet Tracer–Troubleshooting IPv4 ACLs

Topology

Addressing Table

Device	Interface	IP Address	Subnet Mask	Default Gateway
R1	G0/0	10.0.0.1	255.0.0.0	N/A
	G0/1	172.16.0.1	255.255.0.0	N/A
	G0/2	192.168.0.1	255.255.255.0	N/A
Server1	NIC	172.16.255.254	255.255.0.0	172.16.0.1
Server2	NIC	192.168.0.254	255.255.255.0	192.168.0.1
Server3	NIC	10.255.255.254	255.0.0.0	10.0.0.1
L1	NIC	172.16.0.2	255.255.0.0	172.16.0.1
L2	NIC	192.168.0.2	255.255.255.0	192.168.0.1
L3	NIC	10.0.0.2	255.0.0.0	10.0.0.1

Objectives

Part 1: Troubleshoot ACL Issue 1

Part 2: Troubleshoot ACL Issue 2

Part 3: Troubleshoot ACL Issue 3

Scenario

This network is meant to have the following three policies implemented:

- Hosts from the 192.168.0.0/24 network are unable to access any TCP service of **Server3**.

- Hosts from the 10.0.0.0/8 network are unable to access the HTTP service of **Server1**.

- Hosts from the 172.16.0.0/16 network are unable to access the FTP service of **Server2**.

Note: All FTP usernames and passwords are "cisco".

No other restrictions should be in place. Unfortunately, the rules that have been implemented are not working correctly. Your task is to find and fix the errors related to the access lists on **R1**.

Part 1: Troubleshoot ACL Issue 1

Hosts from the 192.168.0.0/24 network are intentionally unable to access any TCP service of **Server3**, but should not be otherwise restricted.

Step 1.   Determine the ACL problem.

As you perform the following tasks, compare the results to what you would expect from the ACL.

    a.   Using **L2**, attempt to access FTP and HTTP services of **Server1**, **Server2**, and **Server3**.

    b.   Using **L2**, ping **Server1**, **Server2**, and **Server3**.

    c.   Using **L2**, ping **G0/2** of **R1**.

    d.   View the running configuration on **R1**. Examine access list **192_to_10** and its placement on the interfaces. Is the access list placed on the correct interface and in the correct direction? Is there any statement in the list that permits or denies traffic to other networks? Are the statements in the correct order?

    e.   Perform other tests, as necessary.

Step 2.   Implement a solution.

Make an adjustment to access list **192_to_10** to fix the problem.

Step 3.   Verify that the problem is resolved and document the solution.

If the problem is resolved, document the solution: otherwise return to Step 1.

Part 2: Troubleshoot ACL Issue 2

Hosts from the 10.0.0.0/8 network are intentionally unable to access the HTTP service of **Server1**, but should not be otherwise restricted.

Step 1.   Determine the ACL problem.

As you perform the following tasks, compare the results to what you would expect from the ACL.

    a.   Using **L3**, attempt to access FTP and HTTP services of **Server1**, **Server2**, and **Server3**.

    b.   Using **L3**, ping **Server1**, **Server2**, and **Server3**.

   c. View the running configuration on **R1**. Examine access list **10_to_172** and its placement on the interfaces. Is the access list placed on the correct interface and in the correct direction? Is there any statement in the list that permits or denies traffic to other networks? Are the statements in the correct order?

   d. Run other tests as necessary.

Step 2.   Implement a solution.

   Make an adjustment to access list **10_to_172** to fix the problem.

Step 3.   Verify the problem is resolved and document the solution.

   If the problem is resolved, document the solution; otherwise return to Step 1.

_____

_____

Part 3: Troubleshoot ACL Issue 3

Hosts from the 172.16.0.0/16 network are intentionally unable to access the FTP service of **Server2**, but should not be otherwise restricted.

Step 1.   Determine the ACL problem.

   As you perform the following tasks, compare the results to the expectations of the ACL.

   a. Using **L1**, attempt to access FTP and HTTP services of **Server1**, **Server2**, and **Server3**.

   b. Using **L1**, ping **Server1**, **Server2**, and **Server3**.

   c. View the running configuration on **R1**. Examine access list **172_to_192** and its placement on the interfaces. Is the access list placed on the correct port in the correct direction? Is there any statement in the list that permits or denies traffic to other networks? Are the statements in the correct order?

   d. Run other tests as necessary.

Step 2.   Implement a solution.

   Make an adjustment to access list **172_to_192** to fix the problem.

Step 3.   Verify the problem is resolved and document the solution.

   If the problem is resolved, document the solution; otherwise return to Step 1.

_____

_____

Suggested Scoring Rubric

Question Location	Possible Points	Earned Points
Documentation Score	10	
Packet Tracer Score	90	
Total Score	100	

4.4.2.10 Packet Tracer–Troubleshooting IPv6 ACLs

Topology

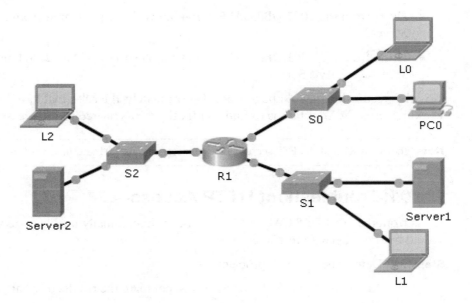

Addressing Table

Device	Interface	IPv6 Address / Prefix	Default Gateway
R1	G0/0	2001:DB8:CAFE::1/64	N/A
	G0/1	2001:DB8:CAFE:1::1/64	N/A
	G0/2	2001:DB8:CAFE:2::1/64	N/A
PC0	NIC	2001:DB8:CAFE::2/64	FE80::1
Server1	NIC	2001:DB8:CAFE:1::2/64	FE80::1
Server2	NIC	2001:DB8:CAFE:2::2/64	FE80::1
L0	NIC	2001:DB8:CAFE::3/64	FE80::1
L1	NIC	2001:DB8:CAFE:1::3/64	FE80::1
L2	NIC	2001:DB8:CAFE:2::3/64	FE80::1

Objectives

Part 1: Troubleshoot HTTP Access

Part 2: Troubleshoot FTP Access

Part 3: Troubleshoot SSH Access

Scenario

The following three policies have been implemented on the network:

- Hosts from the 2001:DB8:CAFÉ::/64 network do not have HTTP access to the other networks.

- Hosts from the 2001:DB8:CAFÉ:1::/64 network are prevented from access to the FTP service on Server2.

- Hosts from the 2001:DB8:CAFE:1::/64 and 2001:DB8:CAFE:2::/64 networks are prevented from accessing **R1** via SSH.

No other restrictions should be in place. Unfortunately, the rules that have been implemented are not working correctly. Your task is to find and fix the errors related to the access lists on **R1**.

Note: To access **R1** and the FTP servers, use the username **user01** and password **user01pass**.

Part 1: Troubleshoot HTTP Access

Hosts from the 2001:DB8:CAFE::/64 network are intentionally unable to access the HTTP service, but should not be otherwise restricted.

Step 1. Determine the ACL problem.

As you perform the following tasks, compare the results to what you would expect from the ACL.

- **a.** Using **L0**, **L1**, and **L2**, attempt to access HTTP services of **Server1** and **Server2**.

- **b.** Using **L0**, ping **Server1** and **Server2**.

- **c.** Using **PC0**, access the HTTPS services of **Server1** and **Server2**.

- **d.** View the running configuration on **R1**. Examine access list **G0-ACCESS** and its placement on the interfaces. Is the access list placed on the correct interface and in the correct direction? Is there any statement in the list that permits or denies traffic to other networks? Are the statements in the correct order?

- **e.** Run other tests as necessary.

Step 2. Implement a solution.

Make adjustments to access lists to fix the problem.

_____

_____

Step 3. Verify the problem is resolved and document the solution.

If the problem is resolved, document the solution; otherwise return to Step 1.

_____

_____

Part 2: Troubleshoot FTP Access

Hosts from the 2001:DB8:CAFE:1::/64 network are prevented from accessing the FTP service of **Server2**, but no other restriction should be in place.

Step 1.   Determine the ACL problem.

As you perform the following tasks, compare the results to the expectations of the ACL.

  a.   Using **L0**, **L1**, and **L2**, attempt to access FTP service of **Server2**.

```
PC> ftp 2001:db8:cafe:2::2
```

  b.   View the running configuration on **R1**. Examine access list **G1-ACCESS** and its placement on the interfaces. Is the access list placed on the correct port in the correct direction? Is there any statement in the list that permits or denies traffic to other networks? Are the statements in the correct order?

  c.   Run other tests as necessary.

Step 2.   Implement a solution.

Make adjustments to access lists to fix the problem.

_____

_____

_____

Step 3.   Verify the problem is resolved and document the solution.

If the problem is resolved, document the solution; otherwise return to Step 1.

_____

_____

Part 3: Troubleshoot SSH Access

Only the hosts from 2001:DB8:CAFE::/64 network are permitted remote access to **R1** via SSH.

Step 1.   Determine the ACL problem.

As you perform the following tasks, compare the results to what you would expect from the ACL.

  a.   From **L0** or **PC0**, verify SSH access to **R1**.

  b.   Using **L1** and **L2**, attempt to access **R1** via SSH.

  c.   View the running configuration on **R1**. Examine access lists and their placements on the interfaces. Is the access list placed on the correct interface and in the correct direction? Is there any statement in the list that permits or denies traffic to other networks? Are the statements in the correct order?

  d.   Perform other tests, as necessary.

Step 2.   Implement a solution.

Make adjustments to access lists to fix the problem.

_____

_____

_____

_____

Step 3.   Verify that the problem is resolved and document the solution.

If the problem is resolved, document the solution: otherwise return to Step 1.

_____

_____

_____

Suggested Scoring Rubric

Question Location	Possible Points	Earned Points
Documentation Score	10	
Packet Tracer Score	90	
Total Score	100	

4.4.2.11 Lab–Troubleshooting ACL Configuration and Placement

Topology

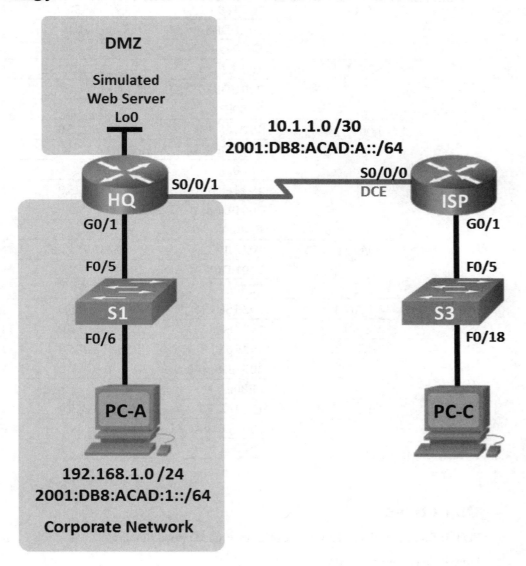

Addressing Table

Device	Interface	IP Address	Subnet Mask	Default Gateway
		IPv6 Address / Prefix		
		Link Local Address		
HQ	G0/1	192.168.1.1	255.255.255.0	N/A
		2001:DB8:ACAD:1::1/64		
		FE80::1		
	S0/0/1	10.1.1.2	255.255.255.252	N/A
		2001:DB8:ACAD:A::2/64		
		FE80::2		
	Lo0	192.168.4.1	255.255.255.0	N/A
		2001:DB8:ACAD:4::1/64		
		FE80::1		
ISP	G0/1	192.168.3.1	255.255.255.0	N/A
		2001:DB8:ACAD:3::1/64		
		FE80::1		
	S0/0/0 (DCE)	10.1.1.1	255.255.255.252	N/A
		2001:DB8:ACAD:A::1/64		
		FE80::1		
S1	VLAN 1	192.168.1.11	255.255.255.0	192.168.1.1
S3	VLAN 1	192.168.3.11	255.255.255.0	192.168.3.1
PC-A	NIC	192.168.1.3	255.255.255.0	192.168.1.1
		2001:DB8:ACAD:1::3/64		FE80::1
		FE80::3		
PC-C	NIC	192.168.3.3	255.255.255.0	192.168.3.1
		2001:DB8:ACAD:3::3/64		FE80::1
		FE80::3		

Objectives

Part 1: Build the Network and Configure Basic Device Settings

Part 2: Troubleshoot Internal Access

Part 3: Troubleshoot Remote Access

Background/Scenario

An access control list (ACL) is a series of IOS commands that provide basic traffic filtering on a Cisco router. ACLs are used to select the types of traffic to be processed.

A single ACL statement is called an access control entry (ACE). The ACEs in the ACL are evaluated from top to bottom with an implicit deny all ACE at the end of the list. ACLs can also control the types of traffic into or out of a network by the source and destination hosts or network. To process the desired traffic correctly, the placement of the ACLs is critical.

In this lab, a small company has just added a Web Server to the network to allow customers to access confidential information. The company IPv4 and IPv6 network is divided into two zones: Corporate network zone and Demilitarized Zone (DMZ). The corporate network zone houses private servers and internal clients. The DMZ houses the externally accessible Web Server (simulated by Lo0 on HQ).

To secure access to the corporate and DMZ networks, several ACLs were configured on the HQ router. However, there are problems with the configured ACLs. In this lab, you will examine what the ACLs are doing and take corrective actions to implement them properly.

When troubleshooting ACLs, it is important that its purpose and desired outcome is well understood. For this reason, the following describes the ACLs configured on HQ:

- **ACL 101** is implemented to limit the traffic leaving the corporate network zone. This zone is often referred to as the private or internal network because it houses the private servers and internal clients. In this topology, this zone is assigned network address 192.168.1.0/24. Therefore, only traffic from that network should be permitted to leave the internal network.

- **ACL 102** is used to limit the traffic into the corporate network. Only responses to requests that originated from within the corporate network are allowed back into that network. This includes TCP-based requests from internal hosts such as Web and FTP. ICMP is allowed into the network for troubleshooting purposes so that incoming ICMP messages generated in response to pings can be received by internal hosts. No other network should be able to access the corporate zone.

- **ACL 121** controls outside traffic to the DMZ and corporate network. Only HTTP traffic is allowed to the DMZ Web Server (simulated by Lo0 on HQ). Other network related traffic, such as EIGRP, is allowed from outside networks. Furthermore, valid internal private addresses, such as 192.168.1.0, loopback address such as 127.0.0.1 and multicast addresses are denied entrance to the corporate network to prevent malicious network attacks from outside users.

- **IPv6 ACL** named NO-ICMP denies ICMP traffic to the DMZ and corporate network originated from the outside. ICMP response is allowed into the network that is responding to the requests from the internet hosts. Other network related traffic, such as EIGRP, is allowed from outside networks. Furthermore, the outside network is allowed to access the DMZ Web Server (simulated by Lo0 on HQ).

Note: The routers used with CCNA hands-on labs are Cisco 1941 Integrated Services Routers (ISRs) with Cisco IOS Release 15.4(3) (universalk9 image). The switches used are Cisco Catalyst 2960s with Cisco IOS Release 15.0(2) (lanbasek9 image). Other routers, switches and Cisco IOS versions can be used. Depending on the model and Cisco IOS version, the commands available and output produced might vary from what is shown in the labs. Refer to the Router Interface Summary Table at the end of the lab for the correct interface identifiers.

Note: Make sure that the routers and switches have been erased and have no startup configurations. If you are unsure, contact your instructor.

Required Resources

- 2 Routers (Cisco 1941 with Cisco IOS Release 15.4(3) universal image or comparable)
- 2 Switches (Cisco 2960 with Cisco IOS Release 15.0(2) lanbasek9 image or comparable)
- 2 PCs (Windows with terminal emulation program, such as Tera Term)
- Console cables to configure the Cisco IOS devices via the console ports
- Ethernet and serial cables as shown in the topology

Part 1: Build the Network and Configure Basic Device Settings

In Part 1, you will set up the network topology and configure the routers and switches with basic settings such as passwords and IP addresses. Preset configurations are also provided for you for the initial router configurations. You will also configure the IP settings for the PCs in the topology.

Step 1.   Cable the network as shown in the topology.

Step 2.   Configure PC hosts according to the Addressing Table.

Step 3.   Initialize and reload the routers and switches as necessary.

Step 4.   (Optional) Configure basic settings for each switch.

    a.   Disable DNS lookup.

    b.   Configure host names as shown in the Topology.

    c.   Configure IP addresses and default gateways as shown in the Addressing Table.

    d.   Assign **cisco** as the console and vty passwords.

    e.   Assign **class** as the privileged EXEC password.

    f.   Configure **logging synchronous** to prevent console messages from interrupting command entry.

Step 5.   Configure basic settings for each router.

    a.   Disable DNS lookup.

    b.   Configure host names as shown in the topology.

    c.   Assign **class** as the privileged EXEC password.

    d.   Assign **cisco** as the console and vty passwords.

    e.   Configure **logging synchronous** to prevent console messages from interrupting command entry.

Step 6.   Configure HTTP access and user credentials on HQ router.

Local user credentials are configured to access the simulated Web Server (192.168.4.1).

```
HQ(config)# ip http server
HQ(config)# username admin privilege 15 secret adminpass
HQ(config)# ip http authentication local
```

Step 7.   Load router configurations.

The configurations for the routers ISP and HQ are provided for you. There are errors within these configurations, and it is your task to correct them.

Router ISP

```
hostname ISP
ipv6 unicast-routing
ipv6 router eigrp 1
 eigrp router-id 10.1.1.1
 no shutdown
interface GigabitEthernet0/1
 ip address 192.168.3.1 255.255.255.0
```

```
    ipv6 address FE80::1 link-local
    ipv6 address 2001:DB8:ACAD:3::1/64
    ipv6 eigrp 1
    no shutdown
interface Serial0/0/0
    ip address 10.1.1.1 255.255.255.252
    clock rate 128000
    ipv6 address FE80::1 link-local
    ipv6 address 2001:DB8:ACAD:A::1/64
    ipv6 eigrp 1
    no shutdown
router eigrp 1
    network 10.1.1.0 0.0.0.3
    network 192.168.3.0
    no auto-summary
end
```

Router HQ

```
hostname HQ
ipv6 unicast-routing
ipv6 router eigrp 1
    eigrp router-id 10.1.1.2
    no shutdown
interface Loopback0
    ip address 192.168.4.1 255.255.255.0
    ipv6 address FE80::1 link-local
    ipv6 address 2001:DB8:ACAD:4::1/64
    ipv6 eigrp 1
interface GigabitEthernet0/1
    ip address 192.168.1.1 255.255.255.0
    ipv6 address FE80::1 link-local
    ipv6 address 2001:DB8:ACAD:1::1/64
    ip access-group 101 out
    ip access-group 102 in
    ipv6 eigrp 1
    no shutdown
interface Serial0/0/1
    ip address 10.1.1.2 255.255.255.252
    ip access-group 121 in
    ipv6 address FE80::2 link-local
    ipv6 address 2001:DB8:ACAD:A::2/64
    ipv6 eigrp 1
    ipv6 traffic-filter NO-ICMP out
    no shutdown
```

```
router eigrp 1
 network 10.1.1.0 0.0.0.3
 network 192.168.1.0
 network 192.168.4.0
 no auto-summary
ip http server
access-list 101 permit ip 192.168.11.0 0.0.0.255 any
access-list 101 deny ip any any
access-list 102 permit tcp any any established
access-list 102 permit icmp any any echo-reply
access-list 102 permit icmp any any unreachable
access-list 102 deny ip any any
access-list 121 permit tcp any host 192.168.4.1 eq 89
access-list 121 deny icmp any host 192.168.4.11
access-list 121 deny ip 192.168.1.0 0.0.0.255 any
access-list 121 deny ip 127.0.0.0 0.255.255.255 any
access-list 121 deny ip 224.0.0.0 31.255.255.255 any
access-list 121 permit ip any any
access-list 121 deny ip any any
ipv6 access-list NO-ICMP
 deny icmp any any echo-request
 permit ipv6 any any
end
```

Part 2: Troubleshoot Internal Access

In Part 2, the ACLs on router HQ are examined to determine if they are configured correctly.

Step 1.   Troubleshoot ACL 101

ACL 101 is implemented to limit the traffic leaving the corporate network zone. This zone houses only internal clients and private servers. Only 192.168.1.0/24 network can exit this corporate network zone.

a.   Can PC-A ping its default gateway? _____

b.   After verifying that PC-A was configured correctly, examine the HQ router to find possible configuration errors by viewing the summary of ACL 101. Enter the command **show access-lists 101.**

```
HQ# show access-lists 101
Extended IP access list 101
    10 permit ip 192.168.11.0 0.0.0.255 any
    20 deny ip any any
```

c.   Are there any problems with ACL 101?

_____

d. Correct ACL 101. Record the commands used to correct the errors.

_____

_____

_____

e. Can PC-A ping its default gateway? _____

f. PC-A still cannot ping its default gateway, therefore verify that ACL 101 is applied in the correct direction on the G0/1 interface. Enter the **show ip interface g0/1** command.

```
HQ# show ip interface g0/1
GigabitEthernet0/1 is up, line protocol is up
  Internet address is 192.168.1.1/24
  Broadcast address is 255.255.255.255
  Address determined by setup command
  MTU is 1500 bytes
  Helper address is not set
  Directed broadcast forwarding is disabled
  Multicast reserved groups joined: 224.0.0.10
  Outgoing access list is 101
  Inbound  access list is 102
```

Is the direction for interface G0/1 configured correctly for ACL 101?

_____

g. Correct the direction of ACL 101 on the G0/1 interface. Record the commands used to correct the errors.

_____

_____

_____

_____

_____

h. Verify the traffic from network 192.168.1.0 /24 can exit the corporate network. PC-A should now be able to ping its default gateway interface.

Step 2. Troubleshoot ACL 102

ACL 102 is implemented to limit traffic going into the corporate network. Traffic originating from the outside network is not allowed onto the corporate network. Remote traffic is allowed into the corporate network if the established traffic originated from the internal network. ICMP reply messages are allowed for troubleshooting purposes.

a. Can PC-A ping PC-C? _____

b. Examine the HQ router to find possible configuration errors by viewing the summary of ACL 102. Enter the command **show access-lists 102**.

```
HQ# show access-lists 102
Extended IP access list 102
    10 permit tcp any any established
    20 permit icmp any any echo-reply
```

```
      30 permit icmp any any unreachable
      40 deny ip any any (57 matches)
```

c.   Are there any problems with ACL 102? _____

d.   Verify that the ACL 102 is applied in the correct direction on G0/1 interface. Enter the **show ip interface g0/1** command.

```
HQ# show ip interface g0/1
GigabitEthernet0/1 is up, line protocol is up
  Internet address is 192.168.1.1/24
  Broadcast address is 255.255.255.255
  Address determined by setup command
  MTU is 1500 bytes
  Helper address is not set
  Directed broadcast forwarding is disabled
  Multicast reserved groups joined: 224.0.0.10
  Outgoing access list is 101
  Inbound  access list is 101
```

e.   Are there any problems with the application of ACL 102 to interface G0/1?

_____

f.   Correct any errors found regarding ACL 102. Record the commands used to correct the errors.

_____

_____

g.   Can PC-A ping PC-C now? _____

Part 3: Troubleshoot Remote Access

In Part 3, ACL 121 is configured to prevent spoofing attacks from the outside networks and allow only remote HTTP access to the Web Server (192.168.4.1) in the DMZ.

a.   Verify ACL 121 has been configured correctly. Enter the **show ip access-list 121** command.

```
HQ# show ip access-lists 121
Extended IP access list 121
      10 permit tcp any host 192.168.4.1 eq 89
      20 deny icmp any host 192.168.4.11
      30 deny ip 192.168.1.0 0.0.0.255 any
      40 deny ip 127.0.0.0 0.255.255.255 any
      50 deny ip 224.0.0.0 31.255.255.255 any
      60 permit ip any any (354 matches)
      70 deny ip any any
```

Are there any problems with this ACL?

_____

_____

b. Make and record the necessary configuration changes to ACL 121.

_____

_____

_____

_____

_____

_____

c. Verify that the ACL 121 is applied in the correct direction on the HQ S0/0/1 interface. Enter the **show ip interface s0/0/1** command.

```
HQ# show ip interface s0/0/1
Serial0/0/1 is up, line protocol is up
  Internet address is 10.1.1.2/30
  Broadcast address is 255.255.255.255
<output omitted>
  Multicast reserved groups joined: 224.0.0.10
  Outgoing access list is not set
  Inbound  access list is 121
```

Are there any problems with the application of this ACL?

_____

_____

d. Verify that PC-C can only access the simulated Web Server on HQ by using the web browser. Provide the username **admin** and password **adminpass** to access the Web Server (192.168.4.1).

Part 4: Troubleshoot IPv6 ACL

In Part 4, an IPv6 ACL named NO-ICMP denies ICMP traffic to the DMZ and corporate network originating from the outside. ICMP response to the internal hosts, EIGRP packets, and network related traffic are allowed from outside networks. Furthermore, the outside network is allowed to access the DMZ Web Server (simulated by Lo0 on HQ).

a. Verify ACL **NO-ICMP** has been configured correctly. Enter the **show ipv6 access-list NO-ICMP** command.

```
HQ# show ipv6 access-list NO-ICMP
IPv6 access list NO-ICMP
    deny icmp any any echo-request sequence 10
permit ipv6 any any sequence 20
```

Are there any problems with this ACL?

_____

_____

b. Verify that the ACL NO-ICMP is applied in the correct direction on the HQ S0/0/1 interface. Enter the **show ipv6 interface s0/0/1** command.

```
HQ# show ipv6 interface s0/0/1
Serial0/0/1 is up, line protocol is up
```

```
          IPv6 is enabled, link-local address is FE80::2
          No Virtual link-local address(es):
          Global unicast address(es):
            2001:DB8:ACAD:A::1, subnet is 2001:DB8:ACAD:A::/64
          Joined group address(es):
            FF02::1
            FF02::2
            FF02::A
            FF02::1:FF00:1
            FF02::1:FF00:2
        MTU is 1500 bytes
        ICMP error messages limited to one every 100 milliseconds
        ICMP redirects are enabled
        ICMP unreachables are sent
        Output features: Access List
        Outgoing access list NO-ICMP
        ND DAD is enabled, number of DAD attempts: 1
        ND reachable time is 30000 milliseconds (using 30000)
        ND RAs are suppressed (periodic)
        Hosts use stateless autoconfig for addresses.
```

Are there any problems with the application of this ACL?

_____

_____

c. Make and record the necessary configuration changes to ACL NO-ICMP.

_____

_____

_____

_____

_____

_____

Reflection

1. How should the ACL statement be ordered? From general to specific or vice versa?

_____

_____

2. If you delete an ACL by using the no access-list command and the ACL is still applied to the interface, what happens? _____

_____

Router Interface Summary Table

Router Interface Summary				
Router Model	Ethernet Interface #1	Ethernet Interface #2	Serial Interface #1	Serial Interface #2
1800	Fast Ethernet 0/0 (F0/0)	Fast Ethernet 0/1 (F0/1)	Serial 0/0/0 (S0/0/0)	Serial 0/0/1 (S0/0/1)
1900	Gigabit Ethernet 0/0 (G0/0)	Gigabit Ethernet 0/1 (G0/1)	Serial 0/0/0 (S0/0/0)	Serial 0/0/1 (S0/0/1)
2801	Fast Ethernet 0/0 (F0/0)	Fast Ethernet 0/1 (F0/1)	Serial 0/1/0 (S0/1/0)	Serial 0/1/1 (S0/1/1)
2811	Fast Ethernet 0/0 (F0/0)	Fast Ethernet 0/1 (F0/1)	Serial 0/0/0 (S0/0/0)	Serial 0/0/1 (S0/0/1)
2900	Gigabit Ethernet 0/0 (G0/0)	Gigabit Ethernet 0/1 (G0/1)	Serial 0/0/0 (S0/0/0)	Serial 0/0/1 (S0/0/1)

Note: To find out how the router is configured, look at the interfaces to identify the type of router and how many interfaces the router has. There is no way to effectively list all the combinations of configurations for each router class. This table includes identifiers for the possible combinations of Ethernet and Serial interfaces in the device. The table does not include any other type of interface, even though a specific router may contain one. An example of this might be an ISDN BRI interface. The string in parentheses is the legal abbreviation that can be used in Cisco IOS commands to represent the interface.

4.5.1.1 Packet Tracer–Skills Integration Challenge

Topology

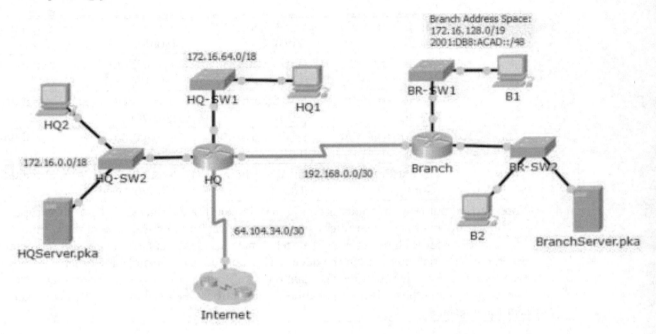

Addressing Table

Device	Interface	IP Address	Subnet Mask	Default Gateway
		IPv6 Address / Prefix		
HQ	G0/0	172.16.127.254	255.255.192.0	N/A
	G0/1	172.16.63.254	255.255.192.0	N/A
	S0/0/0	192.168.0.1	255.255.255.252	N/A
	S0/0/1	64.104.34.2	255.255.255.252	64.104.34.1
Branch	G0/0			N/A
	G0/1			N/A
	S0/0/0	192.168.0.2	255.255.255.252	N/A
HQ1	NIC	172.16.64.1	255.255.192.0	172.16.127.254
HQ2	NIC	172.16.0.2	255.255.192.0	172.16.63.254
HQServer.pka	NIC	172.16.0.1	255.255.192.0	172.16.63.254
B1	NIC			
B2	NIC	172.16.128.2	255.255.240.0	172.16.143.254
BranchServer. pka	NIC	172.16.128.1	255.255.240.0	172.16.143.254
		2001:DB8:ACAD:B2::3/64		2001:DB8:ACAD:B2::1

Scenario

In this challenge activity, you will finish the addressing scheme, configure routing, and implement named access control lists.

Requirements

a. Divide 172.16.128.0/19 into two equal subnets for use on **Branch**.

    1) Assign the last usable IPv4 address of the second subnet to the Gigabit Ethernet 0/0 interface.

    2) Assign the last usable IPv4 address of the first subnet to the Gigabit Ethernet 0/1 interface.

    3) Document the IPv4 addressing in the Addressing Table.

    4) Configure Branch with appropriate IPv4 addressing.

b. Configure **B1** with appropriate IPv4 address using the first available address of the network to which it is attached.

    1) Assign 2001:DB8:ACAD:B1::1/64 and 2001:DB8:ACAD:B2::1/64 to Branch's Gigabit Ethernet 0/0 and Gigabit Ethernet 0/1, respectively.

c. Configure **Branch** with appropriate IPv6 addressing.

d. Configure **B1** and **B2** with appropriate IPv6 addresses using the first available address of the network to which it is attached.

e. Document the addressing in the Addressing Table.

f. Configure **HQ** and **Branch** with OSPFv2 routing for IPv4 according to the following criteria:

    ■ Assign the process ID 1.

    ■ Advertise all attached IPv4 networks. Do not advertise the link to the Internet.

    ■ Configure appropriate interfaces as passive.

g. Set a IPv4 default route on **HQ** that directs traffic to S0/0/1 interface. Redistribute the route to **Branch**.

h. Design an IPv4 named access list **HQServer** to prevent any computers attached to the Gigabit Ethernet 0/0 interface of the **Branch** router from accessing **HQServer.pka**. All other traffic is permitted. Configure the access list on the appropriate router, apply it to the appropriate interface and in the appropriate direction.

i. Design an IPv4 named access list **BranchServer** to prevent any computers attached to the Gigabit Ethernet 0/0 interface of the **HQ** router from accessing the HTTP and HTTPS service of the **Branch** server. All other traffic is permitted. Configure the access list on the appropriate router, apply it to the appropriate interface and in the appropriate direction.

j. Design an IPv6 access-list named **NO-B1** to prevent any IPv6 traffic originating on **B1** to reach the **BranchServer.pka**. No traffic should be permitted from **B1** to **BranchServer.pka**. Apply the IPv6 access to the most appropriated location (interface and direction).

CHAPTER 5

Network Security and Monitoring

Most of your CCNA studies have focused on implementing networking technologies. But what if there is currently no design or implementation to do in your job as network administrator? What if the network is already up and running? Then chances are you will be responsible for monitoring the behavior and security of the network. This chapter focuses on LAN security, Simple Network Management Protocol (SNMP), and Cisco Switch Port Analyzer (SPAN).

LAN Security

In modern networks, security is integral to implementing any device, protocol, or technology. You should already have strong skills in configuring passwords on a switch, configuring Secure Shell (SSH), and configuring port security. The exercise in this section reviews common security attacks.

Common Security Attacks

Match the security attack description on the left with the security attack type on the right.

Security Attack Description

a. Floods the DHCP server with DHCP requests to use all the available addresses (simulates a denial-of-service [DoS] attack on the switch)

b. Uses fake MAC addresses to overflow the MAC address table

c. Allows an attacker to configure a fake DHCP server on the network to issue DHCP addresses to clients

d. Allows the attacker to see surrounding IP addresses, software versions, and native VLAN information to enact a DoS attack

e. Uses a "dictionary" to find common passwords (tries to initiate a Telnet session using what the "dictionary" suggests for the passwords)

Security Attack Type

___ Brute force

___ CDP

___ MAC flooding

___ DHCP starvation

___ DHCP spoofing

LAN Attack Mitigation

Match the LAN attack mitigation tool with its description.

Tool Description

a. Prevents basic VLAN attacks on access ports

b. Authentication protocol that is considered the more secure AAA protocol

c. Prevents MAC and IP address spoofing attacks

d. Authentication protocol that uses the concepts of supplicant, authenticator, and authentication server

e. Authentication protocol that encrypts the password

f. Limits the number of MAC addresses allowed on a port

g. Prevents ARP spoofing and ARP poisoning attacks

h. Uses the concept of trusted and untrusted ports

LAN Attack Mitigation Tool

___ 802.1X

___ TACACS+

___ DHCP snooping

___ RADIUS

___ Disable DTP

___ IP Source Guard

___ DAI

___ Port security

SNMP

SNMP began with a series of three RFCs back in 1988 (1065, 1066, and 1067). The SNMP name is derived from RFC 1067, *A Simple Network Management Protocol*. Since then, SNMP has undergone several revisions.

SNMP Operation

Fill in the missing words and phrases in the following:

SNMP is a/an _____ layer protocol that provides a standardized way of communicating information between SNMP agents and SNMP managers using UDP port _____. The SNMP manager is part of a network management system (NMS). The SNMP manager can collect information from agents using _____ messages. Each agent stores data about the device in the _____ locally so that it is ready to respond to these messages from the NMS. Agents can also be configured to forward directly to the NMS using _____ messages.

In Table 5-1, indicate the SNMP message type for each of the descriptions provided.

Table 5-1   SNMP Message Type

Operation	Description
	Retrieves a value from a specific variable.
	Retrieves a value from a variable within a table. The SNMP manager does not need to know the exact variable name; a sequential search is performed to find the needed variable from within a table.
	Retrieves large blocks of data, such as multiple rows in a table; only works with SNMPv2 or later.
	Replies to messages sent by an NMS.
	Stores a value in a specific variable.
	An unsolicited message sent by an SNMP agent to an SNMP manager when some event has occurred.

Although SNMPv1 is legacy, Cisco IOS supports all three versions. All versions of SNMP use SNMP managers, agents, and MIBs. In today's networks, you will most likely encounter SNMPv3 or SNMPv2c. In Table 5-2, indicate whether the SNMP characteristic applies to SNMPv2c, SNMPv3, or both.

Table 5-2   Comparing SNMPv2c and SNMPv3

Characteristic	SNMPv2c	SNMPv3	Both
Used for interoperability and includes message integrity			
Provides services for security models			
Uses community-based forms of security			
Includes expanded error codes with types			
Provides services for both security models and security levels			
Authenticates the source of management messages			
Cannot provide encrypted management messages			
Supported by Cisco IOS software			

In SNMPv1 and SNMPv2c, access to the MIB is controlled through the use of two types of
_____ :

_____

_____

Why is this type of access no longer considered best practice?

_____

_____

The MIB defines a variable using an MIB object ID. These IDs are derived hierarchically using the
scheme shown in Figure 5-1. Label Figure 5-1 with the most common public variables.

Figure 5-1 Management Information Base Object ID Scheme

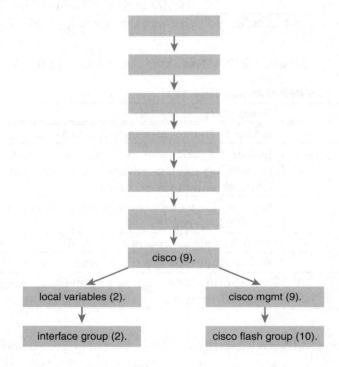

Configuring SNMP v2c

In Figure 5-2, RTA is an SNMP agent and NMS is an SNMP manager. Record the commands to configure SNMPv2 on RTA with the following requirements:

- Use an ACL to allow NMS read-only access to the router using community string **NMS_eyesonly**.

- Location is **Aloha_Net** and the contact is **Bob Metcalfe**.

- Specify that 10.10.10.10 is the recipient of traps and explicitly configure the router to send traps.

Figure 5-2   SNMP Configuration Topology

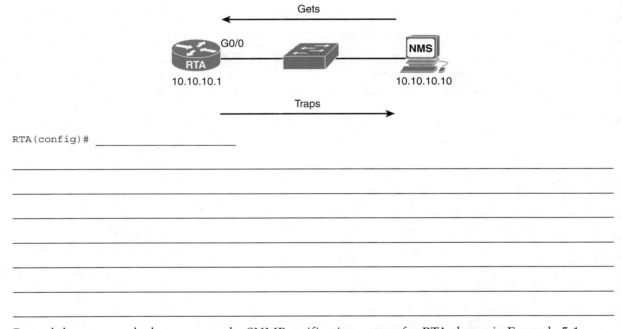

```
RTA(config)# _____
```

_____

_____

_____

_____

_____

_____

_____

Record the commands that generate the SNMP verification output for RTA shown in Example 5-1.

Example 5-1   SNMP Verification Commands

```
RTA# _____
Chassis: FTX163283RZ
Contact: Bob Metcalfe
Location: Aloha_Net
0 SNMP packets input
    0 Bad SNMP version errors
    0 Unknown community name
    0 Illegal operation for community name supplied
    0 Encoding errors
    0 Number of requested variables
    0 Number of altered variables
    0 Get-request PDUs
    0 Get-next PDUs
```

```
         0 Set-request PDUs

         0 Input queue packet drops (Maximum queue size 1000)

 0 SNMP packets output

         0 Too big errors (Maximum packet size 1500)

         0 No such name errors

         0 Bad values errors

         0 General errors

         0 Response PDUs

         0 Trap PDUs

 SNMP Dispatcher:

    queue 0/75 (current/max), 0 dropped

 SNMP Engine:

    queue 0/1000 (current/max), 0 dropped


 SNMP logging: enabled

      Logging to 10.10.10.10.162, 0/10, 0 sent, 0 dropped.


 RTA# _____


 Community name: ILMI

 Community Index: cisco0

 Community SecurityName: ILMI

 storage-type: read-only        active



 Community name: NMS_eyesonly

 Community Index: cisco1

 Community SecurityName: NMS_eyesonly

 storage-type: nonvolatile      active access-list: SNMP



 Community name: NMS_eyesonly@1

 Community Index: cisco2

 Community SecurityName: NMS_eyesonly@1

 storage-type: nonvolatile      active access-list: SNMP
```

Configuring SNMP v3

Now configure RTA in Figure 5-2 to use SNMPv3. Complete the configuration using the following steps and requirements:

Step 1.   Configure a standard ACL named **SNMP3** to permit the NMS.

Step 2.   Configure an SNMP view **SNMP-ALL** to include all the OIDs in the MIB tree.

Step 3. Configure an SNMP v3 group **NMS** that is read-only access for the SNMP view. Use the ACL to filter which devices belong to the group.

Step 4. Configure an SNMP v3 user **PatrickG** as part of the group. Authentication uses SHA with password **C1$c0-snmp** and AES 128 encryption with key **v3-54321**.

```
RTA(config)# _____
```

_____

_____

_____

_____

_____

Cisco Switch Port Analyzer

SPAN is Cisco's port mirroring technology that a network administrator can use to copy unicast traffic between source and destination ports and send that traffic to a packet analyzer, such as Wireshark, or Intrusion Prevention System (IPS). This section reviews the concepts and configurations of SPAN.

SPAN Terminology

Match the SPAN term with its definition.

Definition

a. A feature that allows a switch to make a copy of Ethernet frames, and then send it out a port with a packet analyzer attached for capture.

b. Traffic that leaves the switch.

c. Traffic that enters the switch.

d. A feature on Cisco switches that sends copies of frames entering a port out another port on the same switch to be analyzed.

e. The SPAN port where a packet analyzer or IPS is connected.

f. Detect network attacks as they happen.

g. Allows source and destination ports to be in different switches.

h. The port that is monitored by SPAN.

i. An association of a destination port with one or more source ports.

j. Capture traffic for troubleshooting purposes.

Term

___ SPAN session

___ Local SPAN

___ IPS

___ Source port

___ RSPAN

___ Packet analyzer

___ Ingress traffic

___ Egress traffic

___ Port mirroring

___ Destination port

SPAN Configuration

Refer to the topology in Figure 5-3. Using session number 10, enter the SPAN commands to capture traffic being sent from and to PC1. The captured traffic should be sent to the Packet Analyzer workstation.

Figure 5-3   SPAN Configuration Topology

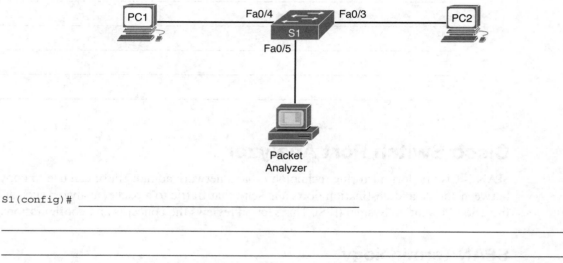

```
S1(config)# _____
```

_____

_____

_____

Answer the following questions about the output in Example 5-2.

What command was entered to generate the output?

_____

What does "Both" mean?

_____

What does "Disabled" mean?

_____

Example 5-2   SPAN Verification Commands

```
S1# _____

Session 10
----------
Type                    : Local Session
Source Ports            :
    Both                : Fa0/4
Destination Ports       : Fa0/5
    Encapsulation       : Native
        Ingress         : Disabled
S1#
```

Labs and Activities

Command Reference

In Table 5-3, record the command, including the correct router or switch prompt, that fits the description. Fill in any blanks with the appropriate missing information.

Table 5-3   Commands for Chapter 5, Network Security and Monitoring

Command	Description
	Configure a named standard ACL HOST-50.
	Configure a statement in a standard named ACL to permit the NMS at 172.16.1.50.
	Configure an SNMP v2c community ADMIN for read-write access. Filter allowed devices with the HOST-50 ACL.
	Enter the command to view the number of SNMP packets sent and received.
	Enter the command to view the SNMP community parameters.
	Configure port Fa0/10 to be the monitored SPAN port in session 20.
	Configure port Fa0/15 to the SPAN port that sends out the copied traffic from the monitored port in session 20.
	Enter the command to verify the SPAN session.

5.0.1.2 Class Activity–Network Maintenance Development

Objective

Describe the different levels of router log messages.

Scenario

Currently, there are no formal policies or procedures for recording problems experienced on your company's network. Furthermore, when network problems occur, you must try many methods to find the causes—and this troubleshooting approach takes time.

You know there must be a better way to resolve these issues. You decide to create a network maintenance plan to keep repair records and pinpoint the causes of errors on the network.

Resources

- Word processing software

Directions

Step 1.   Brainstorm different types of network maintenance records you would like to keep.

Step 2.   Sort the record types into main categories. Suggested categories include:

- Equipment (Routers and Switches)
- Traffic
- Security

Step 3.   Create an outline to guide the network maintenance planning process for the company.

5.2.1.9 Lab–Researching Network Monitoring Software

Objectives

Part 1: Survey Your Understanding of Network Monitoring

Part 2: Research Network Monitoring Tools

Part 3: Select a Network Monitoring Tool

Background/Scenario

Network monitoring is needed for any sized network. Proactively monitoring the network infrastructure can assist network administrators with their day-to-day duties. The wide variety of networking tools available vary in cost, depending on the features, number of network locations, and number of nodes supported.

In this lab, you will conduct research on available network monitoring software. You will gather information on software products and features of those products. You will investigate one product in greater detail and list some of the key features available.

Required Resources

- PC with Internet access

Part 1: Survey Your Understanding of Network Monitoring

Describe network monitoring as you understand it. Give an example of how it might be used in a production network.

_____

_____

_____

_____

_____

_____

Part 2: Research Network Monitoring Tools

Step 1.   Research and find three network monitoring tools.

List the three tools that you found.

_____

_____

_____

Step 2.   Complete the following form for the network monitoring tools selected.

Vendor	Product Name	Features

Part 3: Select a Network Monitoring Tool

Step 1.   Select one or more monitoring tools from your research.

From your research, identify one or more tools you would choose for monitoring your network. List the tools and explain your reasons for choosing them, including specific features that you consider important.

_____

_____

_____

_____

_____

_____

Step 2.   Investigate the PRTG network monitoring tool.

Navigate to www.paessler.com/prtg.

Give examples of some of the features that you found for PRTG in the space provided below.

_____

_____

_____

_____

_____

_____

Reflection

Based on your research, what conclusions have you reached regarding network monitoring software?

_____

_____

_____

_____

5.2.2.6 Lab–Configuring SNMP

Topology

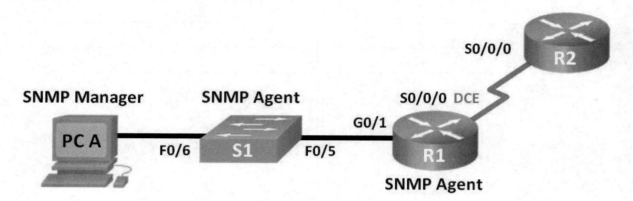

Addressing Table

Device	Interface	IP Address	Subnet Mask	Default Gateway
R1	G0/1	192.168.1.1	255.255.255.0	N/A
	S0/0/0	192.168.2.1	255.255.255.252	N/A
R2	S0/0/0	192.168.2.2	255.255.255.252	N/A
S1	VLAN 1	192.168.1.2	255.255.255.0	N/A
PC-A	NIC	192.168.1.3	255.255.255.0	192.168.1.1

Objectives

Part 1: Build the Network and Configure Basic Device Settings

Part 2: Configure an SNMPv2 Manager and Agent

Part 3: Configure an SNMPv3 Manager and Agent

Background/Scenario

Simple Network Management Protocol (SNMP) is a network management protocol and an IETF standard that can be used to both monitor and control clients on the network. SNMP can be used to get and set variables related to the status and configuration of network hosts like routers and switches, as well as network client computers. The SNMP manager can poll SNMP agents for data, or data can be automatically sent to the SNMP manager by configuring traps on the SNMP agents.

In this lab, you will download, install, and configure SNMP management software on PC-A. You will also configure a Cisco router and Cisco switch as SNMP agents. After capturing SNMP notification messages from the SNMP agent, you will convert the MIB/Object ID codes to learn the details of the messages using the Cisco SNMP Object Navigator.

Note: The routers used with CCNA hands-on labs are Cisco 1941 Integrated Services Routers (ISRs) with Cisco IOS Release 15.4(3) (universalk9 image). The switches used are Cisco Catalyst 2960s with Cisco IOS Release 15.0(2) (lanbasek9 image). Other routers, switches and Cisco IOS versions can be used. Depending on the model and Cisco IOS version, the commands available and output produced might vary from what is shown in the labs. Refer to the Router Interface Summary Table at the end of the lab for the correct interface identifiers.

Note: Make sure that the routers and switches have been erased and have no startup configurations. If you are unsure, contact your instructor.

Note: The **snmp-server** commands in this lab will cause the Cisco 2960 switch to issue a warning message when saving the configuration file to NVRAM. To avoid this warning message verify that the switch is using the **lanbase-routing** template. The IOS template is controlled by the Switch Database Manager (SDM). When changing the preferred template, the new template will be used after reboot even if the configuration is not saved.

```
S1# show sdm prefer
```

Use the following commands to assign the **lanbase-routing** template as the default SDM template.

```
S1# configure terminal
S1(config)# sdm prefer lanbase-routing
S1(config)# end
S1# reload
```

Required Resources

- 2 Routers (Cisco 1941 with Cisco IOS, Release 15.4(3) universal image or comparable)
- 1 Switch (Cisco 2960 with Cisco IOS Release 15.0(2) lanbasek9 image or comparable)
- 1 PC (Windows with terminal emulation program, such as Tera Term, SNMP manager, such as SNMP MIB Browser by ManageEngine, and Wireshark)
- Console cables to configure the Cisco IOS devices via the console ports
- Ethernet and serial cables as shown in the topology
- SNMP Management Software (SNMP MIB Browser by ManageEngine)

Part 1: Build the Network and Configure Basic Device Settings

In Part 1, you will set up the network topology and configure the devices with basic settings.

Step 1. Cable the network as shown in the topology.

Step 2. Configure the PC host.

Step 3. Initialize and reload the switch and routers as necessary.

Step 4. Configure basic settings for the routers and switch.

    a. Disable DNS lookup.

    b. Configure device names as shown in the topology.

    c. Configure IP addresses as shown in the Addressing Table. (Do not configure or enable the VLAN 1 interface on S1 at this time.)

    d. Assign **cisco** as the console and vty password and enable login.

    e. Assign **class** as the encrypted privileged EXEC mode password.

f. Configure **logging synchronous** to prevent console messages from interrupting command entry.

g. Verify successful connectivity between PC-A and R1 and between the routers by issuing the **ping** command.

h. Copy the running configuration to the startup configuration.

Part 2: Configure SNMPv2 Manager and Agent

In Part 2, SNMP management software will be installed and configured on PC-A, and R1 and S1 will be configured as SNMP agents.

Step 1.   Install an SNMP management program.

a. Download and install the SNMP MIB Browser by ManageEngine from the following URL: **https://www.manageengine.com/products/mibbrowser-free-tool/download. html**. You will be asked to provide an email address to download the software.

b. Launch the ManageEngine MibBrowswer program.

1) If you receive an error message regarding the failure to load MIBs, navigate to the MibBrowser Free Tool folder:

    32bit: C:\Program Files (x86)\ManageEngine\MibBrowser Free Tool

    64bit: C:\Program Files\ManageEngine\MibBrowser Free Tool

2) Right-click the mibs folder and select the **Security** tab. Click **Edit**. Select **Users**. Click **Full control**. Click **OK** to change the permission.

3) Repeat the previous step with the **conf** folder.

4) Launch the ManageEngine MibBrowswer program again.

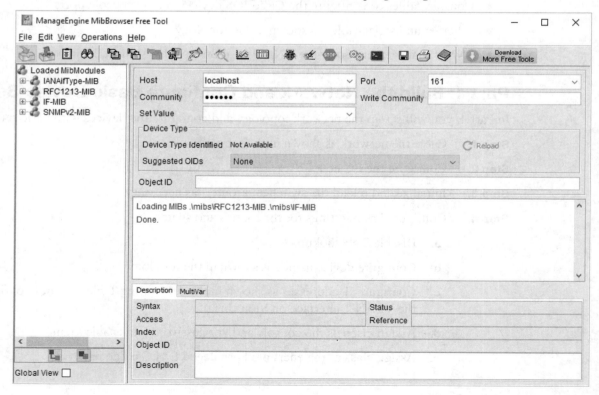

Step 2.   Configure an SNMPv2 agent.

On S1, enter the following commands from the global configuration mode to configure the switch as an SNMP agent. In line 1 below, the SNMP community string is **ciscolab**, with read-only privileges, and the named access list SNMP_ACL defines which hosts are allowed to get SNMP information from S1. In lines 2 and 3, the SNMP manager location and contact commands provide descriptive contact information. Line 4 specifies the IP address of the host that will receive SNMP notifications, the SNMP version, and the community string. Line 5 enables all default SNMP traps, and lines 6 and 7 create the named access list, to control which hosts are permitted to get SNMP information from the switch.

```
S1(config)# snmp-server community ciscolab ro SNMP_ACL
S1(config)# snmp-server location Company_HQ
S1(config)# snmp-server contact admin@company.com
S1(config)# snmp-server host 192.168.1.3 version 2c ciscolab
S1(config)# snmp-server enable traps
S1(config)# ip access-list standard SNMP_ACL
S1(config-std-nacl)# permit 192.168.1.3
```

Step 3.   Verify the SNMPv2 settings.

Use the **show** commands to verify the SNMPv2 settings.

```
S1# show snmp
Chassis: FCQ1628Y5MG
Contact: admin@company.com
Location: Company_HQ
0 SNMP packets input
    0 Bad SNMP version errors
    0 Unknown community name
    0 Illegal operation for community name supplied
    0 Encoding errors
    0 Number of requested variables
    0 Number of altered variables
    0 Get-request PDUs
    0 Get-next PDUs
    0 Set-request PDUs
    0 Input queue packet drops (Maximum queue size 1000)
0 SNMP packets output
    0 Too big errors (Maximum packet size 1500)
    0 No such name errors
    0 Bad values errors
    0 General errors
    0 Response PDUs
    0 Trap PDUs
SNMP global trap: enabled

SNMP logging: enabled
    Logging to 192.168.1.3.162, 0/10, 0 sent, 0 dropped.
SNMP agent enabled

S1# show snmp community

Community name: ciscolab
```

```
Community Index: ciscolab
Community SecurityName: ciscolab
storage-type: nonvolatile          active access-list: SNMP_ACL
<output omitted>
```

What is the configured SNMP community?

_____

Step 4.   Enable SNMP trap.

In this step, you will start the SNMP trap and observe the messages when you configure and enable SVI on VLAN 1 for S1.

a.   In the MibBrowser, click **Edit > Settings**. Verify that v2c is selected as the SNMP Version. Click **OK** to continue.

b.   Click **Trap Viewer UI ( )**.

c.   Verify 162 is the Port number and configure ciscolab as the Community.

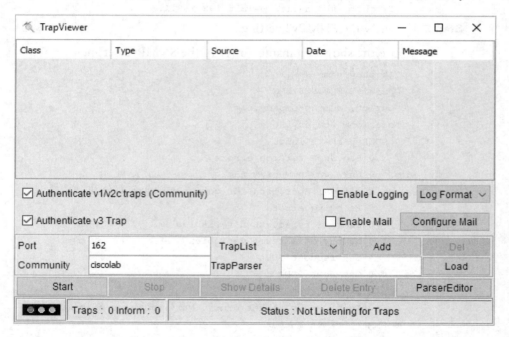

d.   Click **Start** after you have verified the settings. The TrapList field displays **162:ciscolab**.

e.   To generate SNMP messages, configure and enable SVI on S1. Use the IP address **192.168.1.2 /24** for VLAN 1 and disable and enable the interface.

f.   Enter the **show snmp** command to verify the SNMP messages were sent.

```
S1# show snmp
Chassis: FCQ1628Y5MG
Contact: admin@company.com
Location: Company_HQ
0 SNMP packets input
    0 Bad SNMP version errors
    0 Unknown community name
    0 Illegal operation for community name supplied
    0 Encoding errors
    0 Number of requested variables
```

```
    0 Number of altered variables
    0 Get-request PDUs
    0 Get-next PDUs
    0 Set-request PDUs
    0 Input queue packet drops (Maximum queue size 1000)
2 SNMP packets output
    0 Too big errors (Maximum packet size 1500)
    0 No such name errors
    0 Bad values errors
    0 General errors
    0 Response PDUs
    2 Trap PDUs
SNMP global trap: enabled

SNMP logging: enabled
    Logging to 192.168.1.3.162, 0/10, 2 sent, 0 dropped.
SNMP agent enabled
SNMP agent enabled
```

g. Navigate to the TrapViewer. View the messages that have been trapped by MibBrowser. To see the details of each message, click **Show Details**.

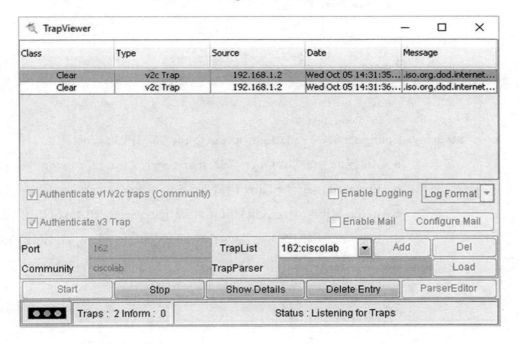

Part 3: Configure SNMPv3 Manager and Agent

Step 1. Configure an SNMPv3 agent on R1.

On R1, enter the following commands from the global configuration mode to configure the router as an SNMP agent. In lines 1 – 3 below, a standard ACL named PERMIT-ADMIN permits only the hosts of the network 192.168.1.0 /24 to access the SNMP agent running on R1. Line 4 configures an SNMP view, SNMP-RO, and it includes the iso tree from the MIB. In line 5, an SNMP group is configured with the name ADMIN, is set to SNMPv3 with authentication and encryption required, and only allows access limit to hosts permitted in the PERMIT-ADMIN ACL. Line 5 defines a user named USER1 with the group ADMIN. Authentication is set to use SHA with the password cisco12345 and encryption is set for AES 128 with cisco54321 as the configured password.

```
R1(config)# ip access-list standard PERMIT-ADMIN
R1(config-std-nacl)# permit 192.168.1.0 0.0.0.255
R1(config-std-nacl)# exit
R1(config)# snmp-server view SNMP-RO iso included
R1(config)# snmp-server group ADMIN v3 priv read SNMP-RO access PERMIT-ADMIN
R1(config)# snmp-server user USER1 ADMIN v3 auth sha cisco12345 pri aes 128
cisco54321
R1(config)#
*Aug  5 02:52:50.715: Configuring snmpv3 USM user, persisting snmpEngineBoots.
Please Wait...
```

Step 2.   Verify the SNMPv3 configuration on R1.

Use the **show** commands to verify the SNMPv3 settings.

```
R1# show run | include snmp
snmp-server group ADMIN v3 priv read SNMP-RO access PERMIT-ADMIN
snmp-server view SNMP-RO iso included


R1# show snmp user


User name: USER1
Engine ID: 800000090300D48CB5CEA0C0
storage-type: nonvolatile        active
Authentication Protocol: SHA
Privacy Protocol: AES128
Group-name: ADMIN
```

Step 3.   Configure SNMP manager access to the SNMPv3 agent.

a. Navigate to PC-A Open **Wireshark**. Start a live capture on the appropriate interface.

b. Enter **snmp** in the Filter field.

c. In the MibBrowser, click **Edit > Settings**. Select **v3** for SNMP Version. Then click **Add**.

d. Enter the SNMPv3 settings that were configured on R1. Click **OK** to continue.

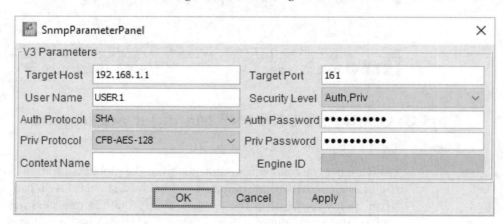

SNMPv3 Parameters	Settings
Target Host	192.168.1.1
User Name	USER1
Auth Protocol	SHA
Priv Protocol	CFB-AES-128
Target Port	161
Security Level	Auth,Priv
Auth Password	cisco12345
Priv Password	cisco54321

e. Click **Edit > Find Node**. Enter **ipAddrTable** in the Find What field and click **Close**. Verify **ipAddrTable** is selected in the left panel and **.iso.org.dod.internet.mgmt.mib-2. ip.ipAddrTable** is listed in the ObjectID field.

f. Click **Operation > GET** to get all the objects under the select MIB object, **ipAddrTable** in this instance.

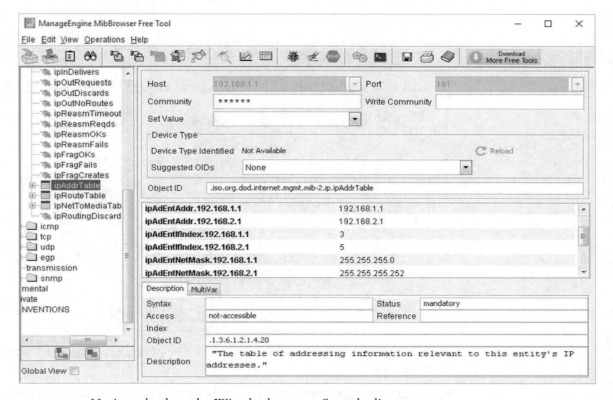

g. Navigate back to the Wireshark screen. Stop the live capture.

h. In the Results panel, right-click one of the results. **Select Protocol Preferences > Simple Network Management Preferences.**

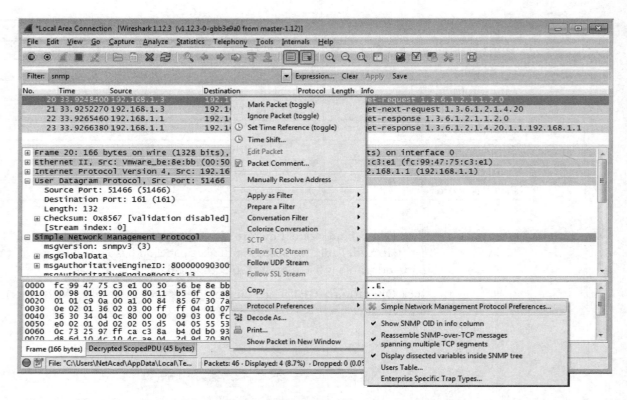

i. Click **Edit** for the Users Table. Click **New** and enter user information in Step 1. Click **OK**.

j. Click **OK** to accept the user information. Click **OK** again to exit the Wireshark Preferences window.

k. Select one of the lines. Expand the SNMP result and view the decrypted messages.

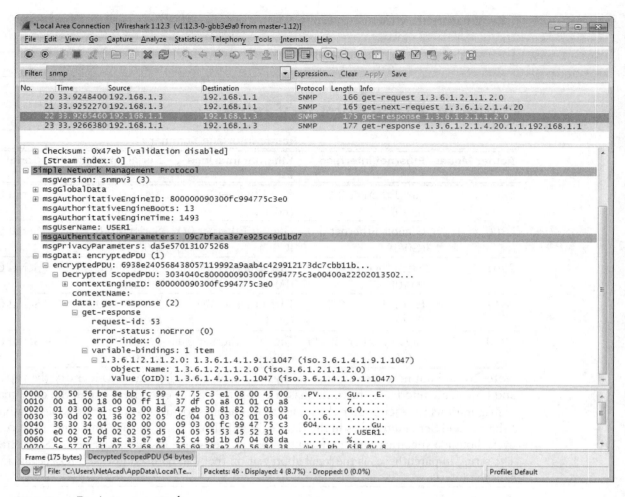

Step 4.   Review your results.

What are the IP addresses configured on R1 in the SNMPv3 results?

_____

Compare the Wireshark decrypted SNMP packets and MIB Browser results. Record your observations.

_____

_____

Reflection

1.   What are some of the potential benefits of monitoring a network with SNMP?

_____

_____

2.   Why is it preferable to solely use read-only access when working with SNMPv2?

_____

_____

3. What are the benefits of using SNMPv3 over SNMPv2?

_____

_____

Router Interface Summary Table

Router Interface Summary				
Router Model	Ethernet Interface #1	Ethernet Interface #2	Serial Interface #1	Serial Interface #2
1800	Fast Ethernet 0/0 (F0/0)	Fast Ethernet 0/1 (F0/1)	Serial 0/0/0 (S0/0/0)	Serial 0/0/1 (S0/0/1)
1900	Gigabit Ethernet 0/0 (G0/0)	Gigabit Ethernet 0/1 (G0/1)	Serial 0/0/0 (S0/0/0)	Serial 0/0/1 (S0/0/1)
2801	Fast Ethernet 0/0 (F0/0)	Fast Ethernet 0/1 (F0/1)	Serial 0/1/0 (S0/1/0)	Serial 0/1/1 (S0/1/1)
2811	Fast Ethernet 0/0 (F0/0)	Fast Ethernet 0/1 (F0/1)	Serial 0/0/0 (S0/0/0)	Serial 0/0/1 (S0/0/1)
2900	Gigabit Ethernet 0/0 (G0/0)	Gigabit Ethernet 0/1 (G0/1)	Serial 0/0/0 (S0/0/0)	Serial 0/0/1 (S0/0/1)

Note: To find out how the router is configured, look at the interfaces to identify the type of router and how many interfaces the router has. There is no way to effectively list all the combinations of configurations for each router class. This table includes identifiers for the possible combinations of Ethernet and Serial interfaces in the device. The table does not include any other type of interface, even though a specific router may contain one. An example of this might be an ISDN BRI interface. The string in parentheses is the legal abbreviation that can be used in Cisco IOS commands to represent the interface.

5.3.2.3 Lab–Implement Local SPAN

Topology

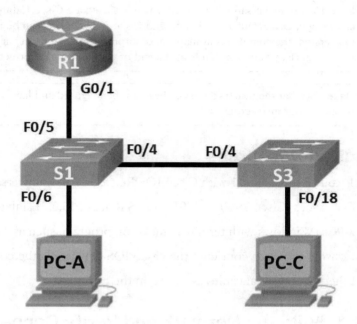

Addressing Table

Device	Interface	IP Address	Subnet Mask	Default Gateway
R1	G0/1	192.168.1.1	255.255.255.0	N/A
S1	VLAN 1	192.168.1.2	255.255.255.0	192.168.1.1
S3	VLAN 1	192.168.1.3	255.255.255.0	192.168.1.1
PC-A	NIC	192.168.1.254	255.255.255.0	192.168.1.1
PC-C	NIC	192.168.1.10	255.255.255.0	192.168.1.1

Objectives

Part 1: Build the Network and Verify Connectivity

Part 2: Configure Local SPAN and Capture Copied Traffic with Wireshark

Background/Scenario

As the network administrator you want to analyze traffic entering and exiting the local network. To do this, you will set up port mirroring on the switch port connected to the router and mirror all traffic to another switch port. The goal is to send all mirrored traffic to an intrusion detection system (IDS) for analysis. In this initial implementation, you will send all mirrored traffic to a PC that will capture the traffic for analysis using a port sniffing program. To set up port mirroring you will use the Switched Port Analyzer (SPAN) feature on the Cisco switch. SPAN is a type of port mirroring that sends copies of a frame entering a port, out another port on the same switch. It is common to find a device running a packet sniffer or Intrusion Detection System (IDS) connected to the mirrored port.

Note: The routers used with CCNA hands-on labs are Cisco 1941 Integrated Services Routers (ISRs) with Cisco IOS Release 15.4(3) (universalk9 image). The switches used are Cisco Catalyst 2960s with Cisco IOS Release 15.0(2) (lanbasek9 image). Other routers, switches, and Cisco IOS versions can be used. Depending on the model and Cisco IOS version, the commands available and output produced might vary from what is shown in the labs. Refer to the Router Interface Summary Table at the end of this lab for the correct interface identifiers.

Note: Make sure that the routers and switches have been erased and have no startup configurations. If you are unsure, contact your instructor.

Required Resources

- 1 Router (Cisco 1941 with Cisco IOS Release 15.4(3) universal image or comparable)
- 2 Switches (Cisco 2960 with Cisco IOS Release 15.0(2) lanbasek9 image or comparable)
- 2 PCs (Windows with terminal emulation program, such as Tera Term)
- Console cables to configure the Cisco IOS devices via the console ports
- Ethernet and serial cables as shown in the topology

Part 1: Build the Network and Verify Connectivity

In Part 1, you will set up the network topology and configure basic settings, such as the interface IP addresses, static routing, device access, and passwords.

Step 1. Cable the network as shown in the topology.

Attach the devices as shown in the topology diagram, and cable as necessary.

Step 2. Configure PC hosts.

Step 3. Initialize and reload the routers and switches as necessary.

Step 4. Configure basic settings for the router.

    a. Disable DNS lookup.

    b. Configure the device name as shown in the topology.

    c. Configure an IP address for the router as listed in the Addressing Table.

    d. Assign **class** as the encrypted privileged EXEC mode password.

    e. Assign **cisco** for the console and vty password, enable login.

    f. Set the vty lines to **transport input telnet**.

    g. Configure **logging synchronous** to prevent console messages from interrupting command entry.

    h. Copy the running configuration to the startup configuration.

Step 5. Configure basic settings for each switch.

    a. Disable DNS lookup.

    b. Configure the device name as shown in the topology.

    c. Assign **class** as the encrypted privileged EXEC mode password.

    d. Configure IP addresses for the switches as listed in the Addressing Table.

    e. Configure the default gateway on each switch.

    f. Assign **cisco** for the console and vty password and enable login.

    g. Configure **logging synchronous** to prevent console messages from interrupting command entry.

    h. Copy the running configuration to the startup configuration.

Step 6. Verify connectivity.

    a. From PC-A, you should be able to ping the interface on R1, S1, S3, and PC-C. Were all pings successful? _____

    If the pings are not successful, troubleshoot the basic device configurations before continuing.

    b. From PC-C, you should be able to ping the interface on R1, S1, S3, and PC-A. Were all pings successful? _____

    If the pings are not successful, troubleshoot the basic device configurations before continuing.

Part 2: Configure Local SPAN and Capture Copied Traffic with Wireshark

To configure Local SPAN you need to configure one or more source ports called monitored ports and a single destination port also called a monitored port for copied or mirrored traffic to be sent out of. SPAN source ports can be configured to monitor traffic in either ingress or egress, or both directions (default).

The SPAN source port will need to be configured on the port that connects to the router on S1 switch port F0/5. This way all traffic entering or exiting the LAN will be monitored. The SPAN destination port will be configured on S1 switch port F0/6 which is connected to PC-A running Wireshark.

Step 1. Configure SPAN on S1.

    a. Console into S1 and configure the source and destination monitor ports on S1. Now all traffic entering or leaving F0/5 will be copied and forwarded out of F0/6

```
S1(config)# monitor session 1 source interface f0/5
S1(config)# monitor session 1 destination interface f0/6
```

Step 2. Start a Wireshark Capture on PC-A.

    a. Open Wireshark on PC-A, set the capture interface to the Local Area Connection and click **Start**.

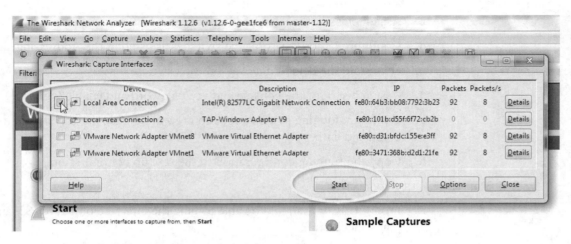

Step 3. Telnet into R1 and create ICMP traffic on the LAN.

a. Telnet from S1 to R1.

```
S1# Telnet 192.168.1.1
Trying 192.168.1.1 . . . Open

User Access Verification

Password:
R1>
```

b. From privileged mode, ping PC-C, S1 and S3.

```
R1> enable
Password:
R1# ping 192.168.1.10
Type escape sequence to abort.
Sending 5, 100-byte ICMP Echos to 192.168.1.10, timeout is 2 seconds:
!!!!!
Success rate is 100 percent (5/5), round-trip min/avg/max = 1/1/4 ms
R1# ping 192.168.1.2
<Output omitted>
R1# ping 192.168.1.3
<Output omitted>
```

Step 4. Stop the Wireshark Capture on PC-A and Filter for ICMP.

a. Return to PC-A and stop the running Wireshark capture on PC-A.

b.   Filter the Wireshark capture for ICMP packets.

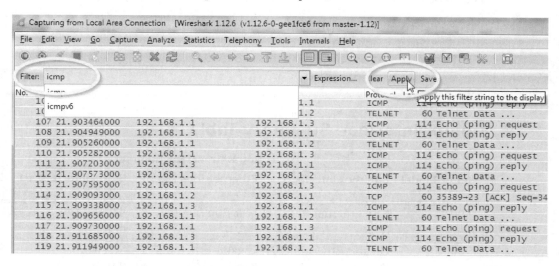

c.   Examine the Wireshark capture filtered for ICMP packets.

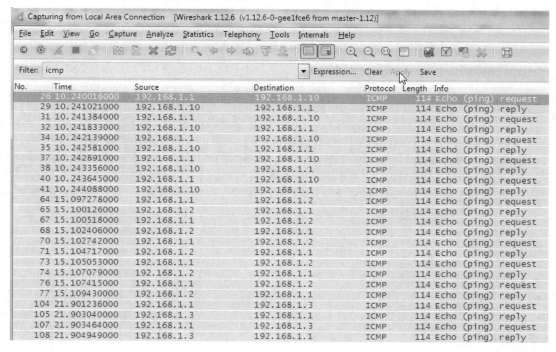

d.   Were the pings from R1 to PC-C, S1, and S3 successfully copied and forwarded out f0/6 to PC-A? _____

e.   Was the traffic monitored and copied in both directions? _____

Reflection

In this scenario, instead of using PC-A, and a packet sniffer, would an IDS or an IPS be more appropriate?

_____

_____

Router Interface Summary Table

Router Interface Summary				
Router Model	Ethernet Interface #1	Ethernet Interface #2	Serial Interface #1	Serial Interface #2
1800	Fast Ethernet 0/0 (F0/0)	Fast Ethernet 0/1 (F0/1)	Serial 0/0/0 (S0/0/0)	Serial 0/0/1 (S0/0/1)
1900	Gigabit Ethernet 0/0 (G0/0)	Gigabit Ethernet 0/1 (G0/1)	Serial 0/0/0 (S0/0/0)	Serial 0/0/1 (S0/0/1)
2801	Fast Ethernet 0/0 (F0/0)	Fast Ethernet 0/1 (F0/1)	Serial 0/1/0 (S0/1/0)	Serial 0/1/1 (S0/1/1)
2811	Fast Ethernet 0/0 (F0/0)	Fast Ethernet 0/1 (F0/1)	Serial 0/0/0 (S0/0/0)	Serial 0/0/1 (S0/0/1)
2900	Gigabit Ethernet 0/0 (G0/0)	Gigabit Ethernet 0/1 (G0/1)	Serial 0/0/0 (S0/0/0)	Serial 0/0/1 (S0/0/1)

Note: To find out how the router is configured, look at the interfaces to identify the type of router and how many interfaces the router has. There is no way to effectively list all the combinations of configurations for each router class. This table includes identifiers for the possible combinations of Ethernet and Serial interfaces in the device. The table does not include any other type of interface, even though a specific router may contain one. An example of this might be an ISDN BRI interface. The string in parentheses is the legal abbreviation that can be used in Cisco IOS commands to represent the interface.

5.3.3.2 Lab–Troubleshoot LAN Traffic Using SPAN

Topology

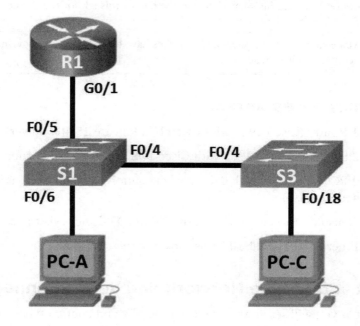

Addressing Table

Device	Interface	IP Address	Subnet Mask	Default Gateway
R1	G0/1	192.168.1.1	255.255.255.0	N/A
S1	VLAN 1	192.168.1.2	255.255.255.0	192.168.1.1
S3	VLAN 1	192.168.1.3	255.255.255.0	192.168.1.1
PC-A	NIC	192.168.1.254	255.255.255.0	192.168.1.1
PC-C	NIC	192.168.1.10	255.255.255.0	192.168.1.1

Objectives

Part 1: Build the Network and Verify Connectivity

Part 2: Configure Local SPAN and Capture Copied Traffic with Wireshark

Background/Scenario

As the network administrator you decide to analyze the internal local area network for suspicious network traffic and possible DoS or reconnaissance attacks. To do this, you will set up port mirroring on all active switch ports and mirror/copy all traffic to a designated switch port where a PC running Wireshark can analyze the captured traffic. The goal is to identify the source of suspicious traffic. To set up port mirroring you will use the Switched Port Analyzer (SPAN) feature on the Cisco switch. It is common to find a device running a packet sniffer or Intrusion Detection System (IDS) connected to the mirrored port.

Note: The routers used with CCNA hands-on labs are Cisco 1941 Integrated Services Routers (ISRs) with Cisco IOS Release 15.4(3) (universalk9 image). The switches used are Cisco Catalyst 2960s with Cisco IOS Release 15.0(2) (lanbasek9 image). Other routers, switches, and Cisco IOS versions can be used. Depending on the model and Cisco IOS version, the commands available and output produced might vary from what is shown in the labs. Refer to the Router Interface Summary Table at the end of this lab for the correct interface identifiers.

Note: Make sure that the routers and switches have been erased and have no startup configurations. If you are unsure, contact your instructor.

Required Resources

- 1 Router (Cisco 1941 with Cisco IOS Release 15.4(3) universal image or comparable)
- 2 Switches (Cisco 2960 with Cisco IOS Release 15.0(2) lanbasek9 image or comparable)
- 2 PCs (Windows with a terminal emulation program, such as Tera Term or PuTTY, Wireshark, and Zenmap)
- Console cables to configure the Cisco IOS devices via the console ports
- Ethernet and serial cables as shown in the topology

Part 1: Build the Network and Verify Connectivity

In Part 1, you will set up the network topology and configure basic settings, such as the interface IP addresses, static routing, device access, and passwords.

Step 1.   Cable the network as shown in the topology.

Attach the devices as shown in the topology diagram, and cable as necessary.

Step 2.   Configure PC hosts.

Step 3.   Initialize and reload the routers and switches as necessary.

Step 4.   Configure basic settings for the router.

    a.   Disable DNS lookup.

    b.   Configure the device name as shown in the topology.

    c.   Configure an IP address for the router as listed in the Addressing Table.

    d.   Assign **class** as the encrypted privileged EXEC mode password.

    e.   Assign **cisco** for the console and vty password, enable login.

    f.   Set the vty lines to **transport input telnet**

    g.   Configure **logging synchronous** to prevent console messages from interrupting command entry.

    h.   Copy the running configuration to the startup configuration.

Step 5.   Configure basic settings for each switch.

    a.   Disable DNS lookup.

    b.   Configure the device name as shown in the topology.

    c.   Assign **class** as the encrypted privileged EXEC mode password.

d. Configure IP addresses for the switches as listed in the Addressing Table.

e. Configure the default gateway on each switch.

f. Assign **cisco** for the console and vty password and enable login.

g. Configure **logging synchronous** to prevent console messages from interrupting command entry.

h. Copy the running configuration to the startup configuration.

Step 6. Verify connectivity.

a. From PC-A, you should be able to ping the interface on R1, S1, S3, and PC-C. Were all pings successful? _____

If the pings are not successful, troubleshoot the basic device configurations before continuing.

b. From PC-C, you should be able to ping the interface on R1, S1, S3, and PC-A. Were all pings successful? _____

If the pings are not successful, troubleshoot the basic device configurations before continuing.

Part 2: Configure Local SPAN and Capture Copied Traffic with Wireshark

To configure Local SPAN, you need to configure one or more source ports called monitored ports, and a single destination port, also called a monitored port, for copied or mirrored traffic to be sent out of. SPAN source ports can be configured to monitor traffic in either ingress, or egress, or both directions (default).

Step 1. Configure SPAN on S1.

a. Locate the switch ports that are up on S1.

```
S1# show ip interface brief
```

Which switch ports are physically up and logically up? _____

b. On S1, F0/6 connects to PC-A, which will be used for analyzing traffic with Wireshark. F0/6 will be the SPAN destination monitor port for duplicated packets. F0/4 and F0/5 will be the source monitor ports for intercepted packets. You can configure multiple source monitor ports but only one destination monitor port.

```
S1(config)# monitor session 1 source interface f0/4 - 5
S1(config)# monitor session 1 destination interface f0/6
```

Step 2. Start a Wireshark capture on PC-A.

a. Open Wireshark on PC-A, set the capture interface to the Local Area Connection and click **Start**.

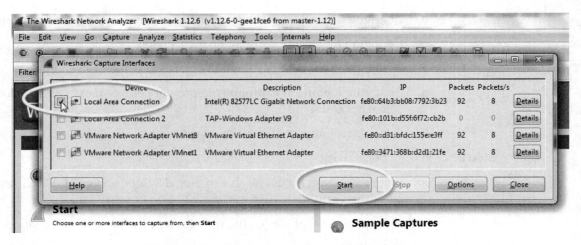

Step 3.   From PC-C, Use NMAP to generate suspicious traffic.

a.   If necessary, navigate to **NMAP.org** to download Zenmap. Scroll down the page to find the latest stable release for PC-C. Then follow the on-screen instructions to install Zenmap with default settings.

b.   Open Zenmap on PC-C and run a UDP ping scan to scan for available hosts (*nmap –sn –PU 192.168.1-6*). The scan result identifies three hosts on the network R1, S1, and S2 at 192.168.1.1, 192.168.1.2 and 192.168.1.3. Notice that Zenmap has also identified the MAC addresses of the three hosts as Cisco Systems interfaces. If this were a real network reconnaissance attack the scan might involve the entire range of network hosts as well as ports and OS fingerprinting.

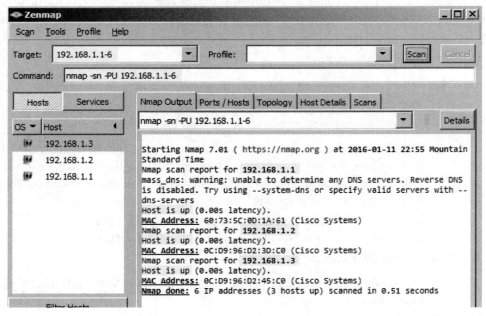

c.   The hypothetical attacker can now issue an intense scan on R1 at 192.168.1.1 (nmap –T4 –A –v 192.168.1.1). The scan result identifies an open port 23/Telnet.

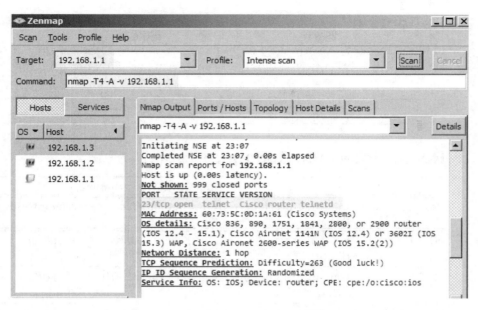

Step 4.   From PC-A stop the Wireshark capture and examine the captured SPAN packets.

   a.   Return to PC-A, and stop the Wireshark capture. Notice the non-standard traffic patterns between PC-C at 192.168.1.10 and R1 at 192.168.1.1. It is filled with Out-Of-Order segments and Connection resets (RST). This packet capture identifies PC-C as sending suspicious traffic to router R1.

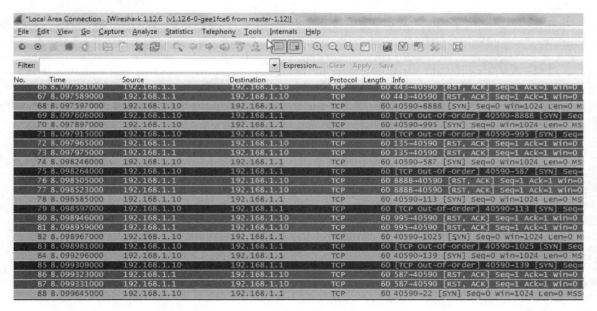

   b.   The attacker on PC-C knowing that the router has an open port on 23 could attempt an additional brute force attack or DoS style attack, like a LAND attack. A LAND attack is a TCP SYN packet with the same source and destination IP address and port number. Using Zenmap, the command **nmap –sS 192.168.1.1 –S 192.168.1.1 –p23 –g23 –e eth0** is an example. Notice how the LAND attack sets both the source and destination IP addresses to 192.168.1.1 and both the source and destination port numbers to the open port at 23. Although R1 with IOS15 is not vulnerable to this older type of DoS attack, many older systems and servers are still vulnerable. This attack will crash vulnerable systems, by setting them into an infinite loop.

Reflection

In this scenario, SPAN was used to troubleshoot and identify the source of suspicious activity on the network. What other troubleshooting scenarios might SPAN be useful for?

_____

_____

Router Interface Summary Table

Router Interface Summary				
Router Model	Ethernet Interface #1	Ethernet Interface #2	Serial Interface #1	Serial Interface #2
1800	Fast Ethernet 0/0 (F0/0)	Fast Ethernet 0/1 (F0/1)	Serial 0/0/0 (S0/0/0)	Serial 0/0/1 (S0/0/1)
1900	Gigabit Ethernet 0/0 (G0/0)	Gigabit Ethernet 0/1 (G0/1)	Serial 0/0/0 (S0/0/0)	Serial 0/0/1 (S0/0/1)
2801	Fast Ethernet 0/0 (F0/0)	Fast Ethernet 0/1 (F0/1)	Serial 0/1/0 (S0/1/0)	Serial 0/1/1 (S0/1/1)
2811	Fast Ethernet 0/0 (F0/0)	Fast Ethernet 0/1 (F0/1)	Serial 0/0/0 (S0/0/0)	Serial 0/0/1 (S0/0/1)
2900	Gigabit Ethernet 0/0 (G0/0)	Gigabit Ethernet 0/1 (G0/1)	Serial 0/0/0 (S0/0/0)	Serial 0/0/1 (S0/0/1)

Note: To find out how the router is configured, look at the interfaces to identify the type of router and how many interfaces the router has. There is no way to effectively list all the combinations of configurations for each router class. This table includes identifiers for the possible combinations of Ethernet and Serial interfaces in the device. The table does not include any other type of interface, even though a specific router may contain one. An example of this might be an ISDN BRI interface. The string in parentheses is the legal abbreviation that can be used in Cisco IOS commands to represent the interface.

CHAPTER 6

Quality of Service

In today's networks, users expect content to be immediately available. But if the traffic exceeds the bandwidth of the links between the source of the content and the user, how do network administrators ensure a quality experience? Quality of Service (QoS) tools can be designed into the network to guarantee that certain traffic types, such as voice and video, are prioritized over traffic that is not as time-sensitive, such as email and web browsing.

This chapter reviews QoS concepts, models, and implementation techniques.

QoS Overview

As users continue to increase their usage of voice and video applications on the network, QoS becomes increasingly important. Network administrators must be able to identify traffic sensitive to delays and choose queuing algorithms to fit the needs of the end users.

Network Transmission Quality Terminology

Match the definition on the left with the term on the right. This is a one-to-one matching exercise.

Definition

a. The number of bits that can be transmitted in a single second.

b. Creates higher expectations for quality delivery.

c. De-jitters a stream of packets out the interface.

d. This happens when congestion occurs.

e. The variable amount of time it takes for the frame to traverse the links between the source and destination.

f. Caused by variations in delay of received packets.

g. The fixed amount of time it takes to compress data at the source before transmitting to the first internetworking device.

h. When the demand for bandwidth exceeds the amount available.

i. The time it takes to encapsulate data with all the necessary header information.

j. Holds packets in memory until resources become available to transmit them.

k. Used to classify voice traffic for zero packet loss.

l. Interpolates what the audio should be for a missing packet.

m. The fixed amount of time it takes to transmit a frame from the NIC to the wire.

n. The time it takes to buffer a flow of packets and then send them out in evenly spaced intervals.

Terms

___ Serialization delay

___ Queue

___ Congestion

___ Packetization delay

___ Bandwidth

___ De-jitter delay

___ Digital signal processor

___ Packet loss

___ Propagation delay

___ QoS mechanisms

___ Voice and video traffic

___ Code delay

___ Jitter

___ Playout delay buffer

Traffic Characteristics

In Table 6-1, select the type of traffic described by each characteristic.

Table 6-1   Identify Traffic Characteristics

Traffic Characteristic	Voice	Video	Data
Traffic can be predictable and smooth.			
Cisco uses RTP ports 16384 - 32767 to prioritize this traffic.			
Traffic can be unpredictable, inconsistent, and bursty.			
Some TCP applications can be very greedy consuming a large portion of network capacity.			
Very sensitive to delays and dropped packets.			
Packet size varies every 33 ms.			
If packets are lost in transit, they will be resent.			
Without QoS and a significant amount of extra bandwidth capacity, this traffic typically degrades.			
Cannot be retransmitted if lost.			
Includes RSTP UDP packets on port 554.			
Must receive a higher UDP priority.			
Does not consume a lot of network resources.			
Requires at least 384 Kbs of bandwidth.			
Traffic can be smooth or bursty.			

Queuing Algorithms

The four queuing algorithms discussed in this chapter include:

- First In First Out (FIFO)

- Weighted Fair Queuing (WFQ)

- Class-Based Weighted Fair Queuing (CBWFQ)

- Low Latency Queuing (LLQ)

What is the queuing algorithm shown in Figure 6-1?

Figure 6-1   Queuing Algorithm #1

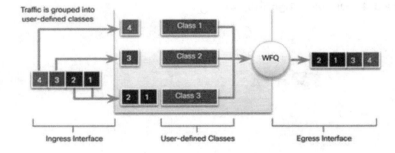

What is the queuing algorithm shown in Figure 6-2?

Figure 6-2   Queuing Algorithm #2

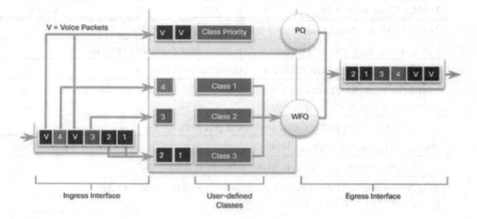

What is the queuing algorithm shown in Figure 6-3?

Figure 6-3   Queuing Algorithm #3

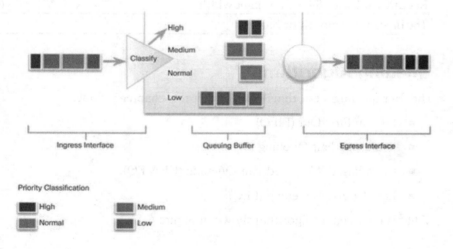

What is the queuing algorithm shown in Figure 6-4?

Figure 6-4   Queuing Algorithm #4

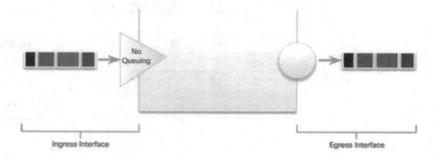

Queuing Algorithm Characteristics

In Table 6-2, select the queuing algorithm described by each characteristic.

Table 6-2   Identify the Queuing Algorithm Characteristics

Queuing Algorithm Characteristic	FIFO	WFQ	CBWFQ	LLQ
Important or time-sensitive traffic can be dropped when congestion occurs on the interface.				
Classifies traffic into different flows based on packet header addressing.				
Schedules interactive traffic to the front of a queue to reduce response time.				
Also known as first-come, first-served.				
Poses problems for voice traffic that is largely intolerant of delay, especially variation in delay.				
Cannot support links that use tunneling and encryption.				
The bandwidth assigned to the packets of a class determines the order in which packets are sent.				
Applies priority, or weights, to identify traffic and classify it into conversations or flows.				
Provides support for user-defined traffic classes.				
Effective for large links that have little delay and minimal congestion.				
Allows delay-sensitive data such as voice to be sent before packets in other queues.				
Used by default in all interfaces except some serial interfaces.				
Adds a strict priority queue for delay-sensitive traffics such as voice to be sent before packets in other queues.				
Access control lists (ACLs) are used to match criteria for each class.				
A FIFO queue is reserved for each class, and traffic belonging to a class is directed to the queue for that class.				
Fastest method of queuing.				
Packets satisfying the match criteria for a class constitute the traffic for that class.				
An automated scheduling method that provides fair bandwidth allocation to all network traffic.				

QoS Mechanisms

Each interface from source to destination can be configured with its own queuing algorithm. However, network administrators normally decide what QoS policy will be used throughout the network and then use a variety of tools to implement the policy.

QoS Models

In Table 6-3, select the QoS model described by each characteristic.

Table 6-3   Identify the QoS Model Characteristic

QoS Model Characteristic	Best Effort	Integrated Services	Differentiated Services
Per-request policy admission control.			
Scalability is only limited by bandwidth limits, in which case all traffic is equally affected.			
Uses a "soft QoS" approach where QoS mechanisms are applied on a hop-by-hop basis.			
Signaling of dynamic port numbers such as H.323.			
No special QoS mechanisms are required.			
Uses RSVP to signal QoS needs to all devices in the end-to-end path.			
Requires a set of complex mechanisms to work in concert throughout the network.			
There are no guarantees of delivery.			
No absolute guarantee of service quality.			
Explicit end-to-end resource admission control.			
No packets have preferential treatment.			
Resource intensive due to the stateful architecture requirement for continuous signaling.			
Flow-based approach not scalable to large implementations such as the Internet.			
Provides many different levels of quality.			
Highly scalable.			

QoS Implementation Techniques

QoS includes three categories of QoS tools including:

- Classification and marking tools
- Congestion avoidance tools
- Congestion management tools

As packets enter the interface, they are classified and marked according to the QoS policy established by the network administrator. As the packet queue fills up on an interface, congestion is avoided by using policing and shaping tools to selectively drop lower priority traffic.

Traffic Marking Tools

For each QoS tool shown in Table 6-4, fill in the Layer (2 or 3) field that is marked and the number of bits. Because there are two QoS tools for IPv4 and IPv6, the first one is filled in for you.

Table 6-4   QoS Tools for Traffic Marking

QoS Tool	Layer	Marking Field	Bits
Ethernet (802.1Q, 802.1p)			
Wi-Fi (802.11)			
MPLS			
IPv4 and IPv6	3	IP Precedence (IPP)	3
IPv4 and IPv6			

Marking at Layer 2

The 802.1Q standard for VLAN tagging includes a 3-bit field for identifying the Class of Service (CoS). This allows for eight different Layer 2 QoS markings. In Table 6-5, complete the description column to indicate the meaning for each CoS values 0–5.

Table 6-5   Description of the CoS Values

CoS Value	CoS Binary Value	Description
0	000	
1	001	
2	010	
3	011	
4	100	
5	101	
6	110	Reserved
7	111	Reserved

Marking at Layer 3

IPv4 and IPv6 specify an 8-bit field in their packet headers to mark packets. Called Type of Service (ToS) in IPv4 and Traffic Class in IPv6, these fields are used to carry the packet marking as assigned by the QoS classification tools. In Figure 6-5, label fields for each of the RFCs.

Figure 6-5   Type of Service and Traffic Class Fields

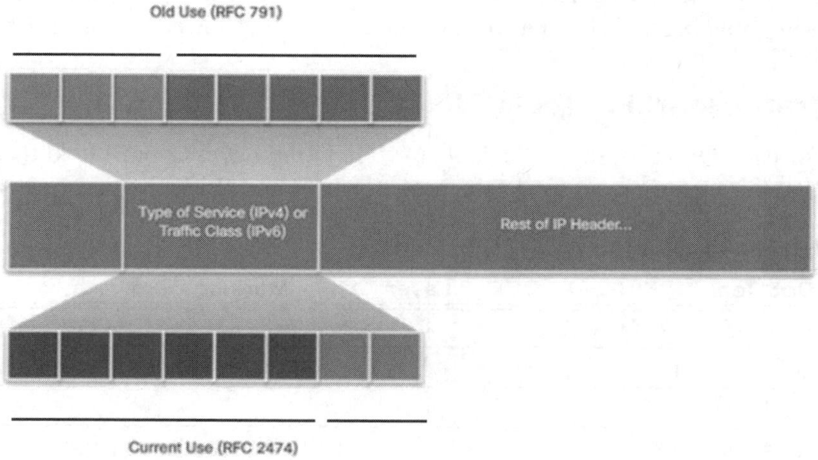

Old Use (RFC 791)

Type of Service (IPv4) or Traffic Class (IPv6)   Rest of IP Header...

Current Use (RFC 2474)

The 6-bit DSCP field allows for 64 values, which are organized into three categories:

- Best-Effort (BE)—Uses DSCP value 0

- Expedited Forwarding (EF)—Uses DSCP value 46

- Assured Forwarding (AF)—First 3 most significant bits define the class (class 1–4) and the next, the 4th and 5th bits, define the drop preference (low, medium, and high). The 6th bit is set to zero.

In Table 6-6, fill in the decimal and binary values, class, and drop preference for each AF value. A few of the rows are already filled in for you.

Table 6-6   Assured Forwarding Values

AF Value	Decimal	Binary	Class	Drop Preference
AF41				
AF31	26	011010	3	Low
AF21				
AF11				
AF42				
AF32	28	011100	3	Medium
AF22				
AF12				
AF43				
AF33				
AF23	22	010110	2	High
AF13				

QoS Mechanism Terminology

Match the definition on the left with the term on the right. This is a one-to-one matching exercise.

Definition	Term
a. Used to inform downstream routers that there is congestion in the packet flow.	___ Traffic shaping
b. Provides buffer management and allows TCP traffic to throttle back before buffers are exhausted.	___ Best-Effort (BE)
c. Queuing and scheduling methods where excess traffic is buffered while it waits to be sent on an egress interface.	___ NBAR
d. Adding a value to the packet header.	___ 802.1Q
e. Adds a 3-bit field to identify the Class of Service (CoS) markings.	___ Expedited Forwarding (EF)
f. Only QoS option available for switches that are not "IP aware."	___ ECN bits
g. Retains excess packets in a queue and then schedules the excess for later transmission over increments of time.	___ Marking
h. Mechanism for classifying traffic at Layers 4 to 7.	___ Assured Forwarding (AF)
i. Uses the 5 most significant bits to indicate class and drop preference.	___ Congestion avoidance
j. When the traffic rate reaches the configured maximum rate, excess traffic is dropped.	___ Layer 2 marking
k. Carries the QoS information from end-to-end.	___ WRED algorithm
l. An IEEE specification for implementing VLANs in Layer 2 switched networks.	___ Layer 3 marking
m. Has a DSCP value of 0.	___ Traffic policing
n. The first 3 bits in this DSCP category map directly to CoS value 5 for voice traffic.	___ 802.1p
o. Determines what class of traffic packets or frames belong to.	___ Classification

Labs and Activities

There are no Labs or Packet Tracer Activities in this chapter.

CHAPTER 7

Network Evolution

Major trends in network evolution include the Internet of Things (IoT), cloud computing and virtualization, and software-defined networking (SDN). This chapter reviews these emerging trends in today's networks.

Internet of Things

The IoT will continue to experience tremendous growth as we connect more traditionally unconnected devices. Dissimilar networks such as data, telephone, power, video, and other network systems will continue to converge to share the same infrastructure. The challenge for IoT is that this infrastructure must include comprehensive security, analytics, and management capabilities.

The Cisco IoT System is designed to address these challenges. It uses the concept of pillars to identify foundation elements. Match the definition on the left with the IoT pillar on the right. This is a one-to-one matching exercise.

Definition

a. Includes management tools such as the Cisco IoT Field Network Director

b. Enables end devices to connect to a local integrated computing, networking, and storage system

c. Identifies devices that can be used to provide IoT connectivity to various industries

d. Enables an organization to quickly and effectively discover, contain, and remediate an attack to minimize damage

e. Provides the infrastructure for application hosting and application mobility between cloud and fog computing

f. Consists of distributed network infrastructure components and IoT-specific, application-specific interfaces

IoT Pillar

___ Fog compting

___ Application enablement platform

___ Network connectivity

___ Management and automation

___ Security

___ Data analytics

Cloud and Virtualization

Cloud computing involves large numbers of computers connected through a network that can be physically located anywhere. Providers rely heavily on virtualization to deliver their cloud computing services. Some of the benefits of cloud computing include:

- Access to your data anywhere

- Pay for only needed services

- Reduce equipment and maintenance costs

- Respond quickly to change data volume requirements

Cloud computing and virtualization allow organizations to treat computing and storage expenses more as a utility rather than investing in infrastructure.

Cloud Computing Terminology

Match the definition on the left with the term on the right. This is a one-to-one matching exercise.

Definition

a. Two or more clouds where each part remains a distinctive object, but both are connected using a single architecture.

b. Access to the development tools and services used to deliver the applications.

c. Applications and services are intended for a specific organization or entity, such as the government.

d. Clouds built to meet the needs of a specific industry, such as healthcare or media.

e. Access to the network equipment, virtualized network services, and supporting network infrastructure.

f. Applications and services are made available to the general population.

g. Large numbers of computers connected through a network that can be physically located anywhere.

h. Access to services, such as email, communication, and Office 365 that are delivered over the Internet.

i. Defines three main cloud computing services.

j. Cloud service extended to provide support for other cloud services.

k. A facility that provides the infrastructure for offering cloud services.

Term

___ Public cloud

___ Private cloud

___ Custom cloud

___ SaaS

___ Data center

___ PaaS

___ IaaS

___ Cloud

___ ITaaS

___ Hybrid cloud

___ NIST SP 800-145

Virtualization Terminology

Match the definition on the left with the term on the right. This is a one-to-one matching exercise.

Definition

a. Takes advantage of idle resources and consolidates the number of required servers.

b. When all of a server's RAM, processing power, and hard drive space are devoted to the service provided.

c. Separates the application from the hardware.

d. Known as bare metal hypervisor with examples like KVM, VMware ESXi, Xen, and others.

e. Known as a hosted hypervisor with examples like Virtualbox, VMware Workstation, Parallels, and others.

f. The computer on which a hypervisor is supporting one or more VMs.

g. Services, OS, Firmware, and Hardware.

h. Protection from a single point of failure.

i. Separates the OS from the hardware.

j. A program, firmware, or hardware that adds an abstraction layer on top of the real physical hardware.

Term

___ Layers of abstraction

___ Type 1

___ Server virtualization

___ Dedicated server

___ Virtualization

___ Type 2

___ Redundancy

___ Host machine

___ Cloud computing

___ Hypervisor

Network Programming

Network programming includes the concepts of virtualization and SDN. The control plane for a collection of routers and switches can be centralized in one place so the network administrators can take advantage of programmatic tools to configure and maintain the network. Each device can focus all its resources on the forwarding traffic in the data plane.

Control and Data Plane

In Table 7-1, select the plane that is described by each characteristic.

Table 7-1   Identify the Control Plane and Data Plane Characteristic

Characteristic	Control Plane	Data Plane
Information sent here is processed by the CPU.		
Typically, the switch fabric connecting the various network ports on a device.		
Uses a digital signal process (DSP).		
In virtualized networks, this plane is removed from the device and centralized in another location.		

Characteristic	Control Plane	Data Plane
CEF uses an FIB in this plane.		
The brains of a device.		
Contains Layer 2 forwarding tables.		
Also called the forwarding plane.		
Makes forwarding decisions.		
Contains routing protocol neighbor tables and topology tables.		
Information in this plane is typically processed by a special processor.		
Contains IPv4 and IPv6 routing tables.		
Used to forward traffic flows.		

Types of SDN Controllers

In Table 7-2, select the SDN controller best described by the characteristic.

Table 7-2   Identify the SDN Controller Characteristic

Characteristic	Device-Based	Controller-Based	Policy-Based
OnePK is an example of this type.			
It uses built-in applications that automate advanced configuration tasks via a guided workflow and user-friendly GUI with no programming skills required.			
Cisco APIC-EM is an example of this type.			
Similar to Policy-based SDN but without the additional Policy layer.			
Devices are programmable by applications running on the device itself or on a server in the network.			
OpenDaylight is an example of this type.			
Does not contain an SDN controller.			
Enables programmers to build applications using C, and Java with Python, to integrate and interact with Cisco devices.			

APIC-EM Features and Terminology

Cisco's Application Centric Infrastructure (ACI) is a purpose-built hardware SDN solution for integrating cloud computing and data center management. The Cisco Application Policy Infrastructure Controller - Enterprise Module (APIC-EM) extends ACI to include enterprise and campus deployments. One of the most important features of the APIC-EM controller is the ability to manage policies across the entire network.

Briefly describe each of the following APIC-EM features:

- Discovery: _____
- Device Inventory: _____

- Host Inventory: _____
- Topology: _____

  _____

- Policy: _____
- ACL Analysis: _____
- ACL Path Trace: _____

  _____

Labs and Activities

This chapter has no Labs or Packet Tracer Activities.

CHAPTER 8

Network Troubleshooting

In an ideal world, networks would never fail. But mechanical failures happen. Users of the network do unexpected things. So, issues will arise that require a network administrator's effective troubleshooting skills—one of the most sought after skills in IT. This chapter reviews network documentation, general troubleshooting methods, and tools.

Troubleshooting Methodology

Documentation is the starting point and is a crucial factor in the success of any troubleshooting effort. With documentation in hand, a network administrator can choose a troubleshooting method, isolate the problem, and implement a solution.

Network Documentation

List three types of documentation a network administrator should have to effectively troubleshoot issues.

_____

_____

_____

List at least four pieces of information that could be included in a network device's configuration documentation.

_____

_____

_____

_____

_____

_____

List at least four pieces of information that could be included in an end system's configuration documentation.

_____

_____

_____

_____

_____

_____

In Table 8-1, indicate whether the feature is part of a physical topology document or logical topology document.

Table 8-1   Physical and Logical Topology Features

Feature	Physical Topology	Logical Topology
WAN technologies used		
Interface identifiers		
Connector type		
Device identifiers or names		
Cable specification		
Operating system version		
Cabling endpoints		
Device type		
Data link protocols		
DLCI for virtual circuits		
Site-to-site VPNs		
Static routes		
Cable type and identifier		
Routing protocols		
Connection type		
IP address and prefix lengths		
Model and manufacturer		

As you learned in Chapter 5, "Network Security and Monitoring," the purpose of network monitoring is to watch network performance in comparison to a predetermined baseline.

What is the minimum duration for capturing data to establish a baseline?

_____

When is the best time to establish a baseline of network performance?

_____

In Table 8-2, indicate which statements describe benefits of establishing a network baseline.

Table 8-2   Benefits of Establishing a Network Baseline

Statements	Benefit	Not a Benefit
Enable fast transport services between campuses		
Investigate if the network can meet the identified policies and use requirements		
Combine two hierarchical design layers		
Locate areas of the network that are most heavily used		
Identify the parts of the network that are least used		
Identify where the most errors occur		
Establish the traffic patterns and loads for a normal or average day		

When documenting the network, it is often necessary to gather information directly from routers and switches using a variety of **show** commands. Match the information gathered on the left with the **show** command on the right.

Information Gathered	Command

Information Gathered

a. Contents of the address resolution table

b. Uptime and information about device software and hardware

c. Detailed settings and status for device interfaces

d. Summary of the NetFlow accounting statistics

e. Contents of the routing table

f. Summarized table of the up/down status of all device interfaces

g. Summary of VLANs and access ports on a switch

h. Current configuration of the device

Command

___ show ip route

___ show arp

___ show vlan

___ show ip interface brief

___ show running-config

___ show version

___ show interface

___ show ip cache flow

Troubleshooting Process

All troubleshooting methodologies have four stages they share in common: three stages to find and solve the problem and a final important stage after the problem is resolved. In Figure 8-1, label the four major stages in the troubleshooting process.

Figure 8-1   Major Troubleshooting Stages

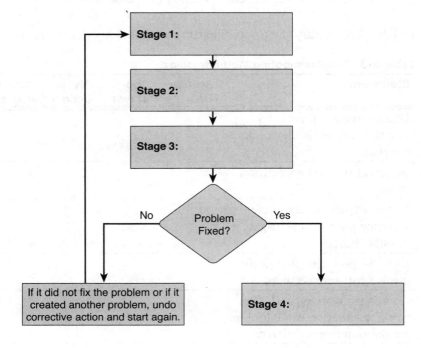

Note: The Academy curriculum does not label the last stage as Stage 4. However, that is most likely an oversight. Stage 4 is indeed the final and arguably most important stage.

The gathering symptoms stage can be broken into five steps:

Step 1. Gather information.

Step 2. Determine ownership.

Step 3. Narrow the scope.

Step 4. Gather symptoms from suspect devices.

Step 5. Document symptoms.

In Step 1, you will most likely use a variety of commands to progress through the process of gathering symptoms. In the following activity, match the information gathered with the testing command.

Information Gathered	Testing Command
a. Displays a summary status of all the IP version 6 interfaces on a device	___ show running-config
b. Shows the path a packet takes through the networks	___ debug ?
c. Displays the IP version 6 routing table	___ traceroute
d. Connects remotely to a device by IP address or URL	___ show ipv6 interface brief
e. Offers a list of options for real-time diagnostics	___ show protocols
f. Shows global and interface specific status of Layer 3 protocols	___ show ipv6 route
g. Sends an echo request to an address and waits for a reply	___ ping
h. Shows the current configuration of the device	___ telnet

In Table 8-3, identify the troubleshooting methodology described by each statement.

Table 8-3   Troubleshooting Methodologies

Statements	Bottom Up	Top Down	Divide Conquer	Educated Guess	Spot the Difference	Substitution
Disadvantage is it requires you to check every device and interface.						
Begins at the OSI application layer.						
Use an experienced troubleshooting guess to investigate a possible cause.						
Used for problems that likely involve software settings.						
Compare a working and non-working situation while looking for the significant differences.						

Statements	Bottom Up	Top Down	Divide Conquer	Educated Guess	Spot the Difference	Substitution
Use when suspected problem is cabling or device failure.						
Begins at the OSI physical layer.						
Swap the problematic device with a known-working device.						
Start with an informed guess for which OSI layer to begin troubleshooting.						
Disadvantage is it requires you to check every network application.						

Troubleshooting Scenarios

Effective troubleshooting requires good tools and systematic approaches. This section reviews some of the tools used in today's networks and some specific troubleshooting symptoms at various OSI layers.

Using IP SLA

A useful tool for proactively and continually monitoring and testing the network is the Cisco IOS IP Service Level Agreement (SLA). IP SLAs use generated traffic to measure network performance between two networking devices, multiple network locations, or across multiple network paths.

IP SLA Benefits

In addition to providing reliable measures that immediately identify problems, what are some additional benefits for using IP SLAs?

_____

_____

_____

_____

_____

_____

IP SLA Configuration

Before configuring an IP SLA, verify that the IOS supports IP SLAs by using the following command:

_____

Record the commands and router prompts to configure an IP SLA number 10 on router RTA that will send a ping to 10.10.10.1 every 90 seconds. Schedule the IP SLA to start immediately and to run until manually stopped.

_____

_____

_____

_____

_____

_____

_____

_____

Record the command and router prompt to cancel the scheduled IP SLA.

_____

Record the command that will display all the IP SLA configuration values including all the defaults.

_____

Record the command that will display the monitoring statistics that result from the IP SLA operation.

_____

Troubleshooting Tools

A wide variety of software and hardware tools is available to make troubleshooting easier. You can use these tools to gather and analyze symptoms of network problems. Match the description on the left with the tool on the right.

Description

a. Online repositories of experience-based information

b. Discovers VLAN configuration, average and peak bandwidth utilization using a portable device

c. Tools that document tasks, draw network diagrams, and establish network performance statistics

d. Measures electrical values of voltage, current, and resistance

e. Tests data communication cabling for broken wires, crossed wiring, and shorted connections

f. Powerful troubleshooting and tracing tool that provides traffic tracking as it flows through a router

g. Provides a graphical representation of traffic from local and remote switches and routers

h. Analyzes network traffic, specifically source and destination frames

i. Includes device-level monitoring, configuration, and fault management

j. Tests and certifies copper and fiber cables for different services and standards via a handheld device

Software and Hardware Tools

___ Host-based protocol analyzer

___ Cable tester

___ Portable network analyzer

___ Baseline establishment tool

___ Cable analyzer

___ Network Management System Tool

___ Cisco IOS Embedded Packet Capture

___ Knowledge Base

___ Network Analysis Module

___ Digital multimeter

Network Troubleshooting and IP Connectivity

A network administrator should be able to quickly isolate the OSI layer where an issue is most likely located. In Table 8-4, indicate the most likely layer associated with each issue.

Table 8-4   Isolating the OSI Layer Where an Issue Resides

Network Problems and Issues	OSI Layers				
	1	2	3	4	5, 6, and 7
A computer is configured with the wrong default gateway.					
The DNS server is not configured with the correct A records.					
Traffic is congested on a low capacity link and frames are lost.					
STP loops and route flapping are generating a broadcast storm.					
A cable was damaged during a recent equipment install.					

Network Problems and Issues	OSI Layers				
	1	2	3	4	5, 6, and 7
ACLs are misconfigured and blocking all web traffic.					
SSH error messages display unknown/untrusted certificates.					
The **show processes cpu** command displays usage way beyond the baseline.					
A VPN connection is not working correctly across a NAT boundary.					
A static route is sending packets to the wrong router.					
The routing table is missing routes and has unknown networks listed.					
On a PPP link, one side is using the default Cisco encapsulation.					
SNMP messages are unable to traverse NAT.					

Knowing which command to use to gather the necessary information for troubleshooting is crucial to effectively and efficiently resolve problems. All the commands you have mastered over the course of your CCNA studies are part of your troubleshooting toolkit. This next exercise only highlights a few.

Match the command output on the left with the command on the right.

Command Output

a. Displays all known destinations on a Windows PC

b. Displays all known IPv6 destinations on a router

c. Can be used to verify the transport layer

d. Clears the MAC to IP address table on a PC

e. Displays the MAC to IP address table for other IPv6 devices

f. Displays the known MAC addresses on a switch

g. Displays input and output queue drops

h. Displays the IP addressing information on a Windows PC

Command

___ **show ipv6 neighbors**

___ **ipconfig**

___ **show ipv6 route**

___ **telnet**

___ **show mac address-table**

___ **arp -d**

___ **route print**

___ **show interfaces**

Note: No book or study guide will effectively teach you how to troubleshoot networks. To get proficient at it, you must practice troubleshooting on lab equipment and simulators. This practice works best with a partner or a team because (1) you can collaborate together to resolve issues and (2) you can swap roles, taking turns breaking the network while the other person or team resolves the issue. For those readers with access to the Academy curriculum, the Packet Tracer activities in this chapter are great resources for just such practice sessions with your team. But you also know enough now that you can create your own troubleshooting scenarios to try out on each other. There is no doubt that you will be asked to troubleshoot several issues on the CCNA exam. So, practice as much as you can now in preparation for the test. You might be surprised how fun and rewarding it can be.

Labs and Activities

Command Reference

In Table 8-5, record the command, including the correct router or switch prompt, which fits the description. Fill in any blanks with the appropriate missing information.

Table 8-5   Commands for Chapter 8, Network Troubleshooting

Command	Description
	Verify that router BB1 can support IP SLAs.
	Enter the command to start an IP SLA configuration with number 25.
	Enter the command to send pings to 172.16.1.1.
	Enter the command to send pings every minute.
	Enter the command to schedule IP SLA 25 to start immediately and run until manually stopped.
	Enter the command to stop IP SLA 25.
	Enter the command to verify all the aspects of the IP SLA configuration.
	Enter the command to display all the information gathered by the IP SLA.

8.0.1.2 Class Activity–Network Breakdown

Objective

Troubleshoot IP connectivity using basic commands.

Scenario

You have just moved in to your new office, and your network is very small. After a long weekend of setting up the new network, you discover that it is not working correctly.

Some of the devices cannot access each other and some cannot access the router that connects to the ISP.

It is your responsibility to troubleshoot and fix the problems. You decide to start with basic commands to identify possible troubleshooting areas.

Resources

- Packet Tracer software

Directions

Step 1.   Create a simple network topology using Packet Tracer software, including:

    a.   Two connected 1941 series routers

    b.   Two Cisco 2960 switches, one switch connected to each router to form two LANs

    c.   Six end-user devices

        1)   A printer and three PCs or laptops on LAN1

        2)   Two servers on LAN2

Step 2.   Configure the network and user devices and verify that everything is working correctly. Make an error or two in the configurations. Be sure to **turn off** the Options, Preferences, and the Show Link Lights setting available on the Packet Tracer software.

Step 3.   Share your saved Packet Tracer file with another group—have them find and fix the problems using the following commands only:

- `ping`

- `traceroute`

- `telnet`

- `show interface`

- `show IP interface brief` or `show IPv6 interface brief`

- `show IP route` or `show IPv6 route`

- `show running-config`

- `show protocols`

- `show vlan`

Step 4.   Share the results of the activity with the class or your instructor. How did the groups fix the problems?

8.1.1.8 Packet Tracer–Troubleshooting Challenge–Documenting the Network

Topology

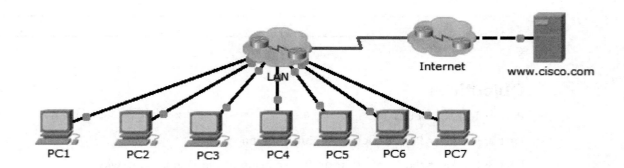

Addressing Table

Device	Interface	IP Address	Subnet Mask	Default Gateway
PC1	NIC			
PC2	NIC			
PC3	NIC			
PC4	NIC			
PC5	NIC			
PC6	NIC			
PC7	NIC			

Device	Interface	IP Address	Subnet Mask	Default Gateway

Objectives

Part 1: Test Connectivity

Part 2: Discover PC Configuration Information

Part 3: Discover the Configuration Information of the Default Gateway

Part 4: Discover Routes and Neighbors in the Network

Part 5: Draw the Network Topology

Background/Scenario

This activity covers the steps to take to discover a network using primarily the Telnet, **show cdp neighbors detail**, and **show ip route** commands. This is Part I of a two-part activity. Part II is **Packet Tracer—Troubleshooting Challenge—Using Documentation to Solve Issues.**

The topology you see when you open the Packet Tracer activity does not reveal all of the details of the network. The details have been hidden using the cluster function of Packet Tracer. The network infrastructure has been collapsed, and the topology in the file shows only the end devices. Your task is to use your knowledge of networking and discovery commands to learn about the full network topology and document it.

Part 1: Test Connectivity

Packet Tracer needs a little time to converge the network. Ping between the PCs and the www.cisco.com server to verify convergence and to test the network. All PCs should be able to ping one another as well as the server. Remember it may take a few pings before they are successful.

Part 2: Discover PC Configuration Information

Step 1. Access the PC1 command prompt.

Click **PC1**, the **Desktop** tab, and then **Command Prompt**.

Step 2. Determine the addressing information for PC1.

To determine the current IP addressing configuration, enter the **ipconfig /all** command.

Note: In Packet Tracer, you must enter a space between **ipconfig** and **/all**.

Step 3.   Document the information for PC1 in the Addressing Table.

_____

_____

_____

_____

_____

_____

_____

_____

_____

Step 4.   Repeat Steps 1 to 3 for PCs 2 to 7.

Part 3: Discover the Configuration Information of the Default Gateway

Step 1.   Test connectivity between PC1 and its default gateway.

From PC1, ping the default gateway to ensure that you have connectivity.

Step 2.   Telnet to the default gateway.

Use the **telnet** *ip-address* command. The IP address is that of the default gateway. When prompted for the password, type **cisco**.

Step 3.   View current interface configurations.

a.   Use both the **show ip interface brief** and **show protocols** command to determine the current interface configurations.

b.   Document the subnet mask information from the **show protocols** command.

Step 4.   Document the hostname and interface configuration of the PC1 gateway router in the Addressing Table.

Part 4: Discover Routes and Neighbors in the Network

Step 1.   On the gateway router for PC1, display the routing table.

a.   Display the routing table with the **show ip route** command. You should see five connected routes and six routes learned through EIGRIP, one of which is a default route.

b.   In addition to the routes, record any other useful information that the routing table provides to help you further discover and document the network.

c.   Determine if there are more IP addresses you can Telnet to continue discovering the network.

Step 2.   Discover directly connected Cisco devices.

On the gateway router for PC1, use the **show cdp neighbors detail** command to discover other directly connected Cisco devices.

Step 3.   Document the neighbor information and test connectivity.

The **show cdp neighbors detail** command lists information for one neighbor, including its IP address. Document the hostname and IP address of the neighbor, and then ping the IP address to test connectivity. The first two or three pings fail while ARP resolves the MAC address.

Step 4.   Telnet to the neighbor and discover directly connected Cisco devices.

    a.   Telnet to the neighbor and use the **show cdp neighbors detail** command to discover other directly connected Cisco devices.

    b.   You should see three devices listed this time. The PC1 gateway router may be listed for each subinterface.

Note: Use the **show interfaces** command on the switches to determine the subnet mask information.

Step 5.   Document the hostnames and IP addresses of the neighbors and test connectivity.

Document and ping the new neighbors you have discovered. Remember, the first two or three pings fail while ARP resolves MAC addresses.

Step 6.   Telnet to each neighbor and check for additional Cisco devices.

Telnet to each of the new neighbors you have discovered, and use the **show cdp neighbors detail** command to check for any additional Cisco devices. The access password is **cisco**.

Step 7.   Continue discovering and documenting the network.

Exit the Telnet sessions to return to the default gateway router for PC1. From this router, Telnet to other devices in the network to continue discovering and documenting the network. Remember to use the **show ip route** and **show cdp neighbors** commands to discover IP addresses you can use for Telnet.

Note: Use the **show interfaces** command on the switches to determine the subnet mask information.

Step 8.   Repeat Steps 1 to 7 as necessary to discover the entire network topology.

Part 5: Draw the Network Topology

Step 1.   Draw a topology.

Now that you have discovered all the network devices and documented their addresses, use the Addressing Table information to draw a topology.

Hint: There is a Frame Relay cloud in the middle of the network.

Step 2.   Keep this documentation.

    a.   Show your topology diagram and Addressing Table to the instructor for verification.

    b.   Your topology diagram and Addressing Table are needed for Part II of this activity.

Suggested Scoring Rubric

Activity Section	Question Location	Possible Points	Earned Points
Part 5: Draw the Network Topology	Step 2-a	100	
	Part 5 Total	100	
	Packet Tracer Score	0	
	Total Score	100	

8.2.1.5 Lab–Configure IP SLA ICMP Echo

Topology

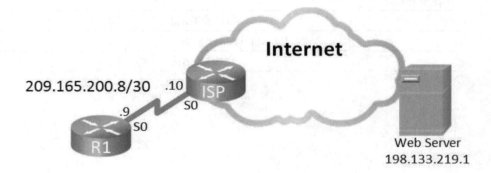

Addressing Table

Device	Interface	IP Address	Subnet Mask	Default Gateway
R1	S0/0/0	209.165.200.9	255.255.255.252	N/A
ISP	S0/0/0	209.165.200.10	255.255.255.252	N/A
	Lo0	198.133.219.1	255.255.255.255	N/A

Objectives

Part 1: Build the Network and Verify Connectivity

Part 2: Configure IP SLA ICMP Echo on R1

Part 3: Test and Monitor the IP SLA Operation

Background/Scenario

An outside vendor has been contracted to provide web services for your company. As the network administrator, you have been asked to monitor the vendor's service. You decide to configure IP SLA to help with that task.

Note: The routers used with CCNA hands-on labs are Cisco 1941 Integrated Services Routers (ISRs) with Cisco IOS Release 15.2(4)M3 (universalk9 image). The switches used are Cisco Catalyst 2960s with Cisco IOS Release 15.0(2) (lanbasek9 image). Other routers, switches, and Cisco IOS versions can be used. Depending on the model and Cisco IOS version, the commands available and output produced might vary from what is shown in the labs. Refer to the Router Interface Summary Table at the end of this lab for the correct interface identifiers.

Note: Make sure that the routers and switches have been erased and have no startup configurations. If you are unsure, contact your instructor.

Required Resources

- 2 Routers (Cisco 1941 with Cisco IOS Release 15.2(4)M3 universal image or comparable)
- Console cables to configure the Cisco IOS devices via the console ports
- Serial cable as shown in the topology

Part 1: Build the Network and Verify Connectivity

In Part 1, you will set up the network topology and configure basic settings, such as the interface IP addresses, static routing, device access, and passwords.

Step 1. Cable the network as shown in the topology.

Attach the devices as shown in the topology diagram, and cable as necessary.

Step 2. Initialize and reload the routers as necessary.

Step 3. Configure basic settings for R1.

    a. Disable DNS lookup.

    b. Configure the device name as shown in the topology.

    c. Configure an IP address for the router as listed in the Addressing Table.

    d. Assign **class** as the encrypted privileged EXEC mode password.

    e. Assign **cisco** for the console and vty password, enable login.

    f. Configure **logging synchronous** to prevent console messages from interrupting command entry.

    g. Configure the default route for R1 to the ISP S0/0/0 IP address.

    h. Copy the running configuration to the startup configuration.

Step 4. Copy and paste the configuration to the ISP router.

The ISP router configuration is provided below. Copy and paste this configuration into the ISP router. Loopback 0 is being used to simulate the Web Server shown in the Topology.

```
hostname ISP
no ip domain lookup
interface Loopback0
 ip address 198.133.219.1 255.255.255.255
interface Serial0/0/0
 ip address 209.165.200.10 255.255.255.252
 no shut
end
```

Step 5. Verify connectivity.

    a. From R1, you should be able to ping the ISP Serial interface IP address. Were all pings successful? _____

If the pings are not successful, troubleshoot the basic device configurations before continuing.

b. From R1, you should be able to ping the Web Server IP address. Were all pings successful? _____

If the pings are not successful, troubleshoot the basic device configurations before continuing.

Part 2: Configure IP SLA ICMP Echo on R1

In Part 2, you configure an IP SLA ICMP Echo operation on R1. Use the following parameters for this operation:

- Operation-number: **22**
- ICMP Echo Destination Address: **198.133.219.1**
- Frequency: **20 seconds**
- Schedule Start: **Now**
- Schedule Life time: **Forever**

Step 1.   Create an IP SLA Operation.

_____

Step 2.   Configure the ICMP Echo Operation.

_____

Step 3.   Set the rate the IP SLA operation repeats.

_____

Step 4.   Schedule the IP SLA ICMP Echo operation.

_____

Step 5.   Use a show command to verify the IP SLA configuration.

Part 3: Test and Monitor the IP SLA Operation

In Part 3, you will simulate an outage of web services. This can be done by an administrative shutdown of the loopback 0 interface on the ISP router. You will then display the IP SLA operation statistics to monitor the effect of this test.

Step 1.   Shutdown the loopback 0 interface on the ISP router.

```
ISP(config)# interface Lo0
ISP(config-if)# shutdown
ISP(config-if)#
*Nov 28 14:00:52.823: %LINK-5-CHANGED: Interface Loopback0, changed state to
administratively down
*Nov 28 14:00:53.823: %LINEPROTO-5-UPDOWN: Line protocol on Interface Loopback0,
changed state to down
ISP(config-if)#
```

Note: Wait a few minutes before executing Step 2.

Step 2.   Activate the loopback 0 interface on the ISP router.

```
R2(config-if)# no shutdown
R2(config-if)#
*Nov 28 14:04:23.263: %LINK-3-UPDOWN: Interface Loopback0, changed state to up
*Nov 28 14:04:24.263: %LINEPROTO-5-UPDOWN: Line protocol on Interface Loopback0,
changed state to up
R2(config-if)#
```

Step 3.   Issue the command used to display the IP SLA operation statistics on R1.

```
R1# show ip sla statistics
IPSLAs Latest Operation Statistics

IPSLA operation id: 22
      Latest RTT: 1 milliseconds
Latest operation start time: 18:44:45 UTC Thu Jan 28 2016
Latest operation return code: OK
Number of successes: 103
Number of failures: 10
Operation time to live: Forever
```

Note: You should see a failure count greater than zero if you waited more than 20 seconds before re-activating the loopback 0 interface on the ISP router.

The IP SLA configured in Part 2 will run forever. How would you stop the IP SLA from running but still leave the IP SLA configured to use at a future time?

_____

Reflection

Using the lab's **show ip sla statistics** example, what does the failure count indicate about the Web Server?

_____

_____

_____

_____

_____

Router Interface Summary Table

Router Interface Summary				
Router Model	Ethernet Interface #1	Ethernet Interface #2	Serial Interface #1	Serial Interface #2
1800	Fast Ethernet 0/0 (F0/0)	Fast Ethernet 0/1 (F0/1)	Serial 0/0/0 (S0/0/0)	Serial 0/0/1 (S0/0/1)
1900	Gigabit Ethernet 0/0 (G0/0)	Gigabit Ethernet 0/1 (G0/1)	Serial 0/0/0 (S0/0/0)	Serial 0/0/1 (S0/0/1)
2801	Fast Ethernet 0/0 (F0/0)	Fast Ethernet 0/1 (F0/1)	Serial 0/1/0 (S0/1/0)	Serial 0/1/1 (S0/1/1)
2811	Fast Ethernet 0/0 (F0/0)	Fast Ethernet 0/1 (F0/1)	Serial 0/0/0 (S0/0/0)	Serial 0/0/1 (S0/0/1)
2900	Gigabit Ethernet 0/0 (G0/0)	Gigabit Ethernet 0/1 (G0/1)	Serial 0/0/0 (S0/0/0)	Serial 0/0/1 (S0/0/1)

Note: To find out how the router is configured, look at the interfaces to identify the type of router and how many interfaces the router has. There is no way to effectively list all the combinations of configurations for each router class. This table includes identifiers for the possible combinations of Ethernet and Serial interfaces in the device. The table does not include any other type of interface, even though a specific router may contain one. An example of this might be an ISDN BRI interface. The string in parentheses is the legal abbreviation that can be used in Cisco IOS commands to represent the interface.

8.2.4.12 Packet Tracer–Troubleshooting Enterprise Networks 1

Topology

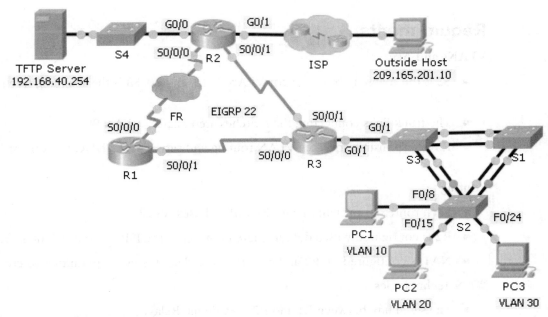

Addressing Table

Device	Interface	IP Address	Subnet Mask	Default Gateway
R1	S0/0/0	10.1.1.1	255.255.255.252	N/A
	S0/0/1	10.3.3.1	255.255.255.252	N/A
R2	G0/0	192.168.40.1	255.255.255.0	N/A
	G0/1	DHCP assigned	DHCP assigned	N/A
	S0/0/0	10.1.1.2	255.255.255.252	N/A
	S0/0/1	10.2.2.1	255.255.255.252	N/A
R3	G0/0.10	192.168.10.1	255.255.255.0	N/A
	G0/0.20	192.168.20.1	255.255.255.0	N/A
	G0/0.30	192.168.30.1	255.255.255.0	N/A
	G0/0.88	192.168.88.1	255.255.255.0	N/A
	S0/0/0	10.3.3.2	255.255.255.252	N/A
	S0/0/1	10.2.2.2	255.255.255.252	N/A
S1	VLAN 88	192.168.88.2	255.255.255.0	192.168.88.1
S2	VLAN 88	192.168.88.3	255.255.255.0	192.168.88.1
S3	VLAN 88	192.168.88.4	255.255.255.0	192.168.88.1
PC1	NIC	DHCP assigned	DHCP assigned	DHCP assigned
PC2	NIC	DHCP assigned	DHCP assigned	DHCP assigned
PC3	NIC	DHCP assigned	DHCP assigned	DHCP assigned
TFTP Server	NIC	192.168.40.254	255.255.255.0	192.168.40.1

Background

This activity uses a variety of technologies you have encountered during your CCNA studies, including VLANs, STP, routing, inter-VLAN routing, DHCP, NAT, PPP, and Frame Relay. Your task is to review the requirements, isolate and resolve any issues, and then document the steps you took to verify the requirements.

Requirements

VLANs and Access

- S2 is the spanning-tree root for VLAN 1, 10, and 20. S3 is the spanning-tree root for VLAN 30 and 88.

- The trunk links connecting the switches are in native VLAN 99.

- R3 is responsible for inter-VLAN routing and serves as the DHCP server for VLANs 10, 20, and 30.

Routing

- Each router is configured with EIGRP and uses AS 22.

- R2 is configured with a default route pointing to the ISP and redistributes the default route.

- NAT is configured on R2 and no untranslated addresses are permitted to cross the Internet.

WAN Technologies

- The serial link between R1 and R2 uses Frame Relay.

- The serial link between R2 and R3 uses HDLC encapsulation.

- The serial link between R1 and R3 uses PPP with CHAP.

Connectivity

- Devices should be configured according to the Addressing Table.

- Every device should be able to ping every other device.

Troubleshooting Documentation

Device	Problem	Solution

Verification Documentation

Capture output from verification commands and provide documentation proving that each of the requirements has been satisfied.

Suggested Scoring Rubric

Packet Tracer scores 60 points. The troubleshooting documentation and instructor verification is worth 40 points.

8.2.4.13 Packet Tracer–Troubleshooting Enterprise Networks 2

Topology

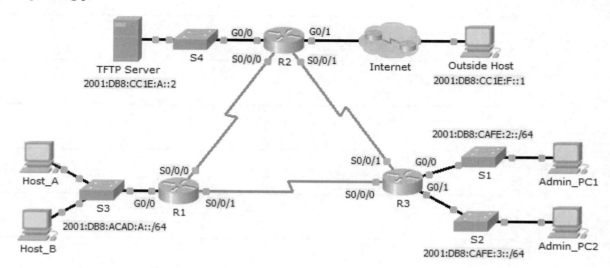

Addressing Table

Device	Interface	IPv6 Address/Prefix	Default Gateway
R1	G0/0	2001:DB8:ACAD:A::1/64	N/A
	S0/0/0	2001:DB8:ACAD:12::1/64	N/A
	S0/0/1	2001:DB8:ACAD:31::1/64	N/A
R2	G0/0	2001:DB8:CC1E:A::1/64	N/A
	G0/1	2001:DB8:ACAD:F::2/64	N/A
	S0/0/0	2001:DB8:ACAD:12::2/64	N/A
	S0/0/1	2001:DB8:ACAD:23::2/64	N/A
R3	G0/0	2001:DB8:CAFE:2::1/64	N/A
	G0/1	2001:DB8:CAFE:3::1/64	N/A
	S0/0/0	2001:DB8:ACAD:31::2/64	N/A
	S0/0/1	2001:DB8:ACAD:23::1/64	N/A
Admin_PC1	NIC	2001:DB8:CAFE:2::2/64	FE80::3
Admin_PC2	NIC	2001:DB8:CAFE:3::2/64	FE80::3
Host_A	NIC	DHCP Assigned	DHCP Assigned
Host_B	NIC	DHCP Assigned	DHCP Assigned
TFTP Server	NIC	2001:DB8:CC1E:A::2/64	FE80::2
Outside Host	NIC	2001:DB8:CC1E:F::1/64	FE80::4

Background

This activity uses IPv6 configurations that include DHCPv6, EIGRPv6, and IPv6 default routing. Your task is to review the requirements, isolate and resolve any issues, and then document the steps you took to verify the requirements.

Requirements

DHCPv6

- **Host_A** and **Host_B** are assigned through IPv6 DHCP configured on R1.

IPv6 Routing

- Each router is configured with IPv6 EIGRP and uses AS 100.

- **R3** is advertising a summary route to **R2** and **R1** for the two **R3** LANs.

- **R2** is configured with a fully specified default route pointing to the **ISP**.

Connectivity

- Devices should be configured according to the Addressing Table.

- Every device should be able to ping every other device.

Troubleshooting Documentation

Device	Error	Correction

Verification Documentation

Capture output from verification commands and provide documentation proving that each of the requirements has been satisfied.

Note: Some EIGRPv6 commands are not scored in Packet Tracer v6.0.1. Your instructor will verify that all requirements are met.

Suggested Scoring Rubric

Packet Tracer scores 50 points. The troubleshooting documentation and instructor verification is worth 50 points.

8.2.4.14 Packet Tracer–Troubleshooting Enterprise Networks 3

Topology

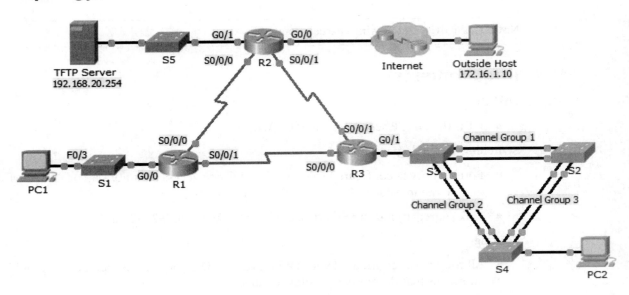

Addressing Table

Device	Interface	IP Address	Subnet Mask	Default Gateway
R1	G0/0	192.168.10.1	255.255.255.0	N/A
	S0/0/0	10.1.1.1	255.255.255.252	N/A
	S0/0/1	10.3.3.1	255.255.255.252	N/A
R2	G0/0	209.165.200.225	255.255.255.224	N/A
	G0/1	192.168.20.1	255.255.255.0	N/A
	S0/0/0	10.1.1.2	255.255.255.252	N/A
	S0/0/1	10.2.2.1	255.255.255.252	N/A
R3	G0/1	192.168.30.1	255.255.255.0	NN/A
	S0/0/0	10.3.3.2	255.255.255.252	N/A
	S0/0/1	10.2.2.2	255.255.255.252	N/A
S1	VLAN10	DHCP assigned	DHCP assigned	DHCP assigned
S2	VLAN11	192.168.11.2	255.255.255.0	N/A
S3	VLAN30	192.168.30.2	255.255.255.0	N/A
PC1	NIC	DHCP assigned	DHCP assigned	DHCP assigned
PC2	NIC	192.168.30.10	255.255.255.0	192.168.30.1
TFTP Server	NIC	192.168.20.254	255.255.255.0	192.168.20.1

Background

This activity uses a variety of technologies you have encountered during your CCNA studies, including routing, port security, EtherChannel, DHCP, NAT, PPP, and Frame Relay. Your task is to review the requirements, isolate and resolve any issues, and then document the steps you took to verify the requirements.

Note: This activity begins with a partial score.

Requirements

DHCP

- R1 is the DHCP server for the R1 LAN.

Switching Technologies

- Port security is configured to only allow **PC1** to access **S1's** F0/3 interface. All violations should disable the interface.
- Link aggregation using EtherChannel is configured on **S2, S3**, and **S4**.

Routing

- All routers are configured with OSPF process ID 1 and no routing updates should be sent across interfaces that do not have routers connected.
- R2 is configured with a default route pointing to the ISP and redistributes the default route.
- NAT is configured on R2 and no untranslated addresses are permitted to cross the Internet.

WAN Technologies

- The serial link between R1 and R2 uses Frame Relay.
- The serial link between R2 and R3 uses HDLC encapsulation.
- The serial link between R1 and R3 uses PPP with PAP.

Connectivity

- Devices should be configured according to the Addressing Table.
- Every device should be able to ping every other device.

Troubleshooting Documentation

Device	Error	Correction

Verification Documentation

Capture output from verification commands and provide documentation proving that each of the requirements has been satisfied.

Suggested Scoring Rubric

Packet Tracer scores 60 points. The troubleshooting documentation and instructor verification is worth 40 points.

Packet Tracer
☐ Activity

8.2.4.15 Packet Tracer–Troubleshooting Challenge–Using Documentation to Solve Issues

Topology

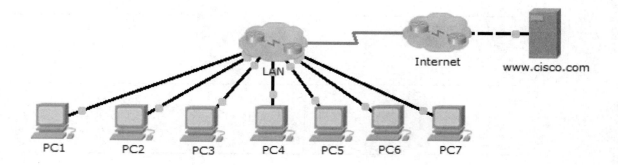

Addressing Table

Device	Interface	IP Address	Subnet Mask	Default Gateway
PC1	NIC			
PC2	NIC			
PC3	NIC			
PC4	NIC			
PC5	NIC			
PC6	NIC			
PC7	NIC			

Device	Interface	IP Address	Subnet Mask	Default Gateway

Objectives

Part 1: Gather Documentation

Part 2: Test Connectivity

Part 3: Gather Data and Implement Solutions

Part 4: Test Connectivity

Scenario

This is Part II of a two-part activity. Part I is **Packet Tracer—Troubleshooting Challenge—Documenting the Network**, which you should have completed earlier in the chapter. In Part II, you will use your troubleshooting skills and documentation from Part I to solve connectivity issues between PCs.

Part 1: Gather Documentation

Step 1.   Retrieve network documentation.

To successfully complete this activity, you will need your documentation for the **Packet Tracer—Troubleshooting Challenge—Documenting the Network** activity you completed previously in this chapter. Locate that documentation now.

Step 2.   Documentation requirements.

The documentation you completed in the previous activity should have an accurate topology and Addressing Table. If necessary, update your documentation to reflect an accurate representation of a correct answer from the **Packet Tracer—Troubleshooting Challenge—Documenting the Network** activity. You may need to consult with your instructor.

Part 2: Test Connectivity

Step 1.   Determine location of connectivity failure.

At the end of this activity, there should be full connectivity between PC to PC and PC to the www.cisco.pka server. However, right now you must determine where connectivity fails by pinging from:

- PCs to **www.cisco.pka** server

- PC to PC

- PC to default gateway

Step 2. What pings were successful?

Document both the successful and failed pings.

_____

_____

Part 3: Gather Data and Implement Solutions

Step 1. Choose a PC to begin gathering data.

Choose any PC and begin gathering data by testing connectivity to the default gateway. You can also use **traceroute** to see where connectivity fails.

Step 2. Telnet to the default gateway and continue gathering data.

a. If the PC you chose does not have connectivity to its default gateway, choose another PC to approach the problem from a different direction.

b. After you have established connectivity through a default gateway, the login password is **cisco** and the privileged EXEC mode password is **class**.

Step 3. Use troubleshooting tools to verify the configuration.

At the default gateway router, use troubleshooting tools to verify the configuration with your own documentation. Remember to check switches in addition to the routers. Be sure to verify the following:

- Addressing information
- Interface activation
- Encapsulation
- Routing
- VLAN configuration
- Duplex or speed mismatches

Step 4. Document network symptoms and possible solutions.

As you discover symptoms of the PC connectivity issue, add them to your documentation.

Step 5. Make changes based on your solutions from the previous step.

Part 4: Test Connectivity

Step 1. Test PC connectivity.

a. All PCs should now be able to ping each other and the **www.cisco.pka** server. If you changed any IP configurations, create new pings because the prior pings use the old IP address.

b. If there are still connectivity issues between PCs or PC to server, return to Part 3 and continue troubleshooting.

Step 2.   Check results.

Your Packet Tracer score should be 70/70. If not, return to Part 2 and continue to troubleshoot and implement your suggested solutions. You will not be able to click **Check Results** and see which required components are not yet completed.

Suggested Scoring Rubric

Activity Section	Question Location	Possible Points	Earned Points
Part 2: Test Connectivity	Step 2-a	15	
	Part 2 Total	15	
Part 3: Gather Data and Implement Solutions	Step 4-a	15	
	Part 3 Total	15	
	Packet Tracer Score	70	
	Total Score	100	

8.3.1.1 Class Activity–Documentation Development

Objective

Using a systematic approach, troubleshoot issues in a small- to medium-sized business network.

Scenario

As the network administrator for a small business, you want to implement a documentation system to use with troubleshooting network-based problems.

After much thought, you decide to compile simple network documentation information into a file to be used when network problems arise. You also know that if the company gets larger in the future, this file can be used to export the information to a computerized, network software system.

To start the network documentation process, you include:

- A physical diagram of your small business network.

- A logical diagram of your small business network.

- Network configuration information for major devices, including routers and switches.

Resources

- Packet Tracer software

- Word processing software

Step 1.   Create a Packet Tracer file to simulate a very small business network. Include these devices:

- One router with at least two Ethernet ports

- Two switches connected to the router (LAN1 and LAN2)

- Five user devices to include PCs, laptops, servers, and printers connected to either of the two LANs.

Step 2.   Create a word processing file in matrix format to record each of the following main network-documentation areas:

    a.   Physical topology and information

        1)   Type of device and model name

        2)   Network hostname

        3)   Location of the device

        4)   Cable connection types and ports

    b.   Logical topology information

        1)   IOS or OS image versions

        2)   IP addresses (IPv4, IPv6, or both)

        3)   Data link addresses (MAC)

        4)   VLAN addresses

    c. Network device configuration information

        1) Location of backup file (TFTP server, USB, text file)

        2) Text formatted configuration script per router and switch devices

Step 3. Share your Packet Tracer file and network documentation with a classmate, another group, the class, or your instructor according to the instructions provided. Discuss how this information could be useful to any network administrator.

8.3.1.2 Packet Tracer–CCNA Skills Integration Challenge

Topology

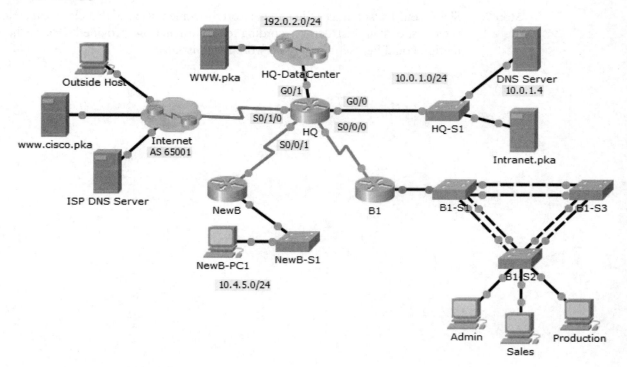

Addressing Table

Device	Interface	IP Address	Subnet Mask
HQ	G0/0	10.0.1.1	255.255.255.0
	G0/1	192.0.2.1	255.255.255.0
	S0/0/0	10.255.255.1	255.255.255.252
	S0/0/1	10.255.255.253	255.255.255.252
	S0/1/0	209.165.201.1	255.255.255.252
B1	G0/0.10	10.1.10.1	255.255.255.0
	G0/0.20	10.1.20.1	255.255.255.0
	G0/0.30	10.1.30.1	255.255.255.0
	G0/0.99	10.1.99.1	255.255.255.0
	S0/0/0	10.255.255.2	255.255.255.252
B1-S2	VLAN 99	10.1.99.22	255.255.255.0

VLAN Configurations and Port Mappings

VLAN Number	Network Address	VLAN Name	Port Mappings
10	10.1.10.0/24	Admin	F0/6
20	10.1.20.0/24	Sales	F0/11
30	10.1.30.0/24	Production	F0/16
99	10.1.99.0/24	Mgmt&Native	F0/1-4
999	N/A	BlackHole	Unused Ports

Scenario

In this comprehensive CCNA skills activity, the XYZ Corporation uses a combination of eBGP and PPP for WAN connections. Other technologies include NAT, DHCP, static and default routing, EIGRP for IPv4, inter-VLAN routing, and VLAN configurations. Security configurations include SSH, port security, switch security, and ACLs.

Note: Only **HQ**, **B1**, **B1-S2**, and the PCs are accessible. The user EXEC password is **cisco** and the privileged EXEC password is **class**.

Requirements

PPP

- Configure the WAN link from **HQ** to the Internet using PPP encapsulation and CHAP authentication.
    - Create a user **ISP** with the password of **cisco**.
- Configure the WAN link from **HQ** to **NewB** using PPP encapsulation and PAP authentication.
    - Create a user **NewB** with the password of **cisco**.

> **Note:** The **ppp pap sent-username** is not graded by Packet Tracer. However, it must be configured before the link will come up between **HQ** and **NewB**.

eBGP

- Configure eBGP between **HQ** and the **Internet**.
    - HQ belongs to AS 65000.
    - The IP address for the BGP router in the Internet cloud is 209.165.201.2.
    - Advertise the 192.0.2.0/24 network to the Internet.

NAT

- Configure dynamic NAT on HQ
    - Allow all addresses for the 10.0.0.0/8 address space to be translated using a standard access list named **NAT**.

- XYZ Corporation owns the 209.165.200.240/29 address space. The pool, **HQ**, uses addresses .241 to .245 with a /29 mask. Bind the **NAT** ACL to the pool **HQ**. Configure PAT.

- The connections to the **Internet** and **HQ-DataCenter** are outside XYZ Corporation.

Inter-VLAN Routing

- Configure **B1** for inter-VLAN routing.

  - Using the Addressing Table for branch routers, configure and activate the LAN interface for inter-VLAN routing. VLAN 99 is the native VLAN.

Static and Default Routing

- Configure **HQ** with a static route to the **NewB** LAN. Use the exit interface as an argument.

- Configure **B1** with a default route to **HQ**. Use the next-hop IP address as an argument.

EIGRP Routing

- Configure and optimize **HQ** and **B1** with EIGRP routing.

  - Use autonomous system 100.

  - Disable EIGRP updates on appropriate interfaces.

VLANs and Trunking Configurations

Note: Logging to the console is turned off on **B1-S2** so that the Native VLAN mismatch messages will not interrupt your configurations. If you would prefer to view console messages, enter the global configuration command **logging console**.

- Configure trunking and VLANs on **B1-S2**.

  - Create and name the VLANs listed in the **VLAN Configuration and Port Mappings** table on **B1-S2** only.

  - Configure the VLAN 99 interface and default gateway.

  - Set trunking mode to on for F0/1 - F0/4.

  - Assign VLANs to the appropriate access ports.

  - Disable all unused ports and assign the **BlackHole** VLAN.

Port Security

- Use the following policy to establish port security on the **B1-S2** access ports:

  - Allow two MAC addresses to be learned on the port.

  - Configure the learned MAC addresses to be added to the configuration.

  - Set the port to send a message if there is a security violation. Traffic is still allowed from the first two MAC addresses learned.

SSH

- Configure **HQ** to use SSH for remote access.

    - Set the modulus to **2048**. The domain name is **CCNASkills.com**.

    - The username is **admin** and the password is **adminonly**.

    - Only SSH should be allowed on VTY lines.

    - Modify the SSH defaults: version 2; 60-second timeout; two retries.

DHCP

- On **B1**, configure a DHCP pool for the Sales VLAN 20 using the following requirements:

    - Exclude the first 10 IP addresses in the range.

    - The case-sensitive pool name is **VLAN20**.

    - Include the DNS server attached to the **HQ** LAN as part of the DHCP configuration.

- Configure the **Sales** PC to use DHCP.

Access List Policy

- Because HQ is connected to the Internet, configure and apply a named ACL called **HQINBOUND** in the following order:

    - Allow inbound BGP updates (TCP port 179) for any source to any destination.

    - Allow inbound HTTP requests from any source to the **HQ-DataCenter** network.

    - Allow only established TCP sessions from the Internet.

    - Allow only inbound ping replies from the Internet.

    - Explicitly block all other inbound access from the Internet.

Connectivity

- Verify full connectivity from each PC to **www.pka** and **www.cisco.pka.**

- The Outside Host should be able to access the webpage at www.pka.

- All the test in Scenario 0 should be successful.